# AN AMERICAN EMMAUS

# AN AMERICAN EMMAUS

## Faith and Sacrament in the American Culture

*by*

REGIS A. DUFFY, O.F.M.

Crossroad • New York

1995
The Crossroad Publishing Company
370 Lexington Avenue, New York, NY 10017

Printed in the United States of America

*Library of Congress Cataloging-in-Publication Data*

Duffy, Regis A.
  An American Emmaus : faith and sacrament in the American culture /
Regis A. Duffy
    p.    cm.
  Includes bibliographical references.
  ISBN 0-8245-1540-4
  1. Catholic Church—United States.   2. Christianity and culture.
3. Catholic Church—United States—Liturgy.   4. Sacraments—Catholic
Church.   5. Catholic Church—United States—Doctrines.   6. United
States—Church history—20th century.   I. Title.
BX1406.2.D84   1995
282'.73—dc20                                        95-18593
                                                       CIP

# Contents

# Acknowledgments

Nearly eight years have passed since I first began the research for this book. In the interim the book has been completely rewritten once and gone through two major revisions after that. As a result of this long journey, I owe a number of people a debt of gratitude for their willingness to read the whole or a part of the manuscript in its various stages. Among these friends I must thank, in particular, T. O'Meara, J. Dolan, F. Oveis, N. Mitchell, J. M. West., and F. Fiorenza. Some of the ideas developed in this book were originally broached in journals whose editors graciously gave permission for their use in this book: for three articles in the *New Theology Review:* "The American Contribution to Liturgy" (1988), "Only the Dance? Ritual in a Technological World" (1989), "Post-Conciliar Liturgy in the United States: Received or Implemented?" (1990); and for "God's Time and American Time" (1988) in *Worship.* I must also thank Andrew Greeley, without whose work this book would have been difficult to write and Anne Carr, whose perceptive and challenging question at one of my public lectures made me think again. None of the persons cited, however, should be held responsible for the final direction and form this book has taken.

I dedicate this book to my former students and colleagues at the University of Notre Dame and to the Franciscan Friars of Holy Name Province.

# Introduction

Emmaus is not only the name of a town in the Gospel of Luke; it is also a state of mind. Luke, in his post-Easter accounts, tells of two troubled disciples who are walking from Jerusalem to Emmaus (Luke 24:13-25). The two disciples discuss the puzzle of Calvary with a sympathetic stranger, the as-yet-unrecognized Christ. As they struggle with the meaning of the death of Jesus, their questions reflect the problems of early Christian communities in confronting the scandal of the cross. But, as Christ unfolds God's answer, "their hearts burn within them" and they "recognize" (in Greek "know again") the Lord in his characteristic actions of blessing the bread at table.

Emmaus, then, also refers to the ongoing conversion of people who already thought of themselves as disciples of Christ. Luke's narrative provides a model by which all Christian communities must be measured: an explanation of Good Friday and Easter Sunday as God's radical answer to the problem of sin and to our inability, if left to ourselves, to praise and thank God. The early Christian communities learned the meaning of Christ's death on the cross by celebrating the Eucharist with its description of the crucified Lord as someone "on account of us."

Thus, the walk to Emmaus is part of the experience of each Christian community in every age. How a believing community interprets the cross cannot be separated from the way it celebrates the death of Jesus in liturgy and sacrament nor from the specific sociocultural world in which it finds itself. The American Emmaus refers to the ongoing conversion walk of twentieth-century Christians who attempt to recognize the crucified and risen Lord within the complex and pluralistic cultures of these United States.[1]

The difficulty of such a task should not be underestimated. J. Anthony Lukas, in his compelling account of the busing crisis in Boston in the late

1960s provides a contemporary American example of that difficulty. As told in his *Common Ground: A Turbulent Decade in the Lives of Three American Families,* three cultural groups—blacks, Irish Catholics, and liberal Yankee Protestants—are depicted as they confront the problem of racism and an attempted solution, school busing. Lukas carefully traces the complex and pervasive role of the pre- and postconciliar Roman Catholic church of Boston in the lives of the Catholics of Charlestown. When their priests attempt to introduce the gospel teaching on social justice into the emotional issues of housing and school busing, these Catholics are both confused and outraged by the apparent betrayal of their church.

Lukas uncovers the deeper roots of this confrontation between a traditionally American Catholic culture and a post–Vatican II church. Social justice in the preconciliar Irish church of Boston was a question of caring for the poor through personal almsgiving, participation in the St. Vincent de Paul Society and the support of Catholic Charities.

> [C]harity wasn't a lever for change, but a balm to make the Catholic worker more content with his meager lot on earth. . . . the parishioners of St. Mary's, St. Catherine's, and St. Francis de Sales' looked to their churches not for reform but for solace. As one Townie put it: "When I saw Christ bleeding on his cross, I knew he was there suffering for my sins. That was good enough for me. I didn't expect him to climb down and start lobbying for a minimum wage, urban renewal, and peace in Vietnam."[2]

This man and his neighbors in South Boston were good people with an inadequate theology of the cross. Their poignant and doubtlessly honest reaction to understanding "the word from the cross" in the sociocultural context of Boston in the 1960s illustrates why the local church must stay on the road to Emmaus. The preconciliar heritage of well-intentioned preaching and sacramental participation in the case of this South Boston Catholic seems to be this: the word from the cross may have personal and eternal consequences but no cultural and temporal implications.

On the other hand, it is too easy with hindsight to berate these Charlestown Catholics and to forget the difficult choices they had to make. As in the Corinthian situation that concerns Paul in his first letter to that community, the cultural as well as the religious implications of the cross are always more far-reaching and demanding for each Christian community than that community originally perceived. Paul criticizes the lack of connection between the Corinthians' Eucharist and their attitudes to the poor among them, but he quickly puts his finger on the underlying problem of this community: *not their liturgy but the concept of church that motivates their liturgy.* This is why the Emmaus walk must still be taken by honest but perplexed disciples.

My principal concern in this book is with the local ecclesial community, that is, a group of Christians united with their bishop, whose communal identity and efforts are shaped by a growing awareness of their mission to others in their historical and sociocultural situation as well as by their liturgical praise and thanksgiving. Vatican II spoke of such "particular churches" as "endowed with the cultural riches of their own nation," whose witness should serve as a sign of God's presence in the world.[3] But within the same local church there are sometimes neighboring parishes that are widely separated from one another in their operational ecclesiology and liturgy (that is, their way of actually being a church community and the real motivation of their worship in practice). Their rituals may be the same, but their intentions in being gathered and worshiping may be quite different.

In choosing this ecclesial focus, I am not minimizing the importance of other dimensions of a gathered church. Both the institutional and the personal dimensions of being a church are important and have received ample treatment elsewhere, especially in their connection with worship and sacrament, and they are also part of the discussion of this book. But Vatican II's Constitution entitled *The Church in the Modern World* and the 1971 Synod of Bishops' *Justice in the World,* among other official statements, have also emphasized the importance of a servant church proclaiming the peace and justice of God's kingdom. If we are concerned with the praying church in a particular culture, then we must also discern whatever aids or hinders that peace and justice.

I find Richard McBrien's definition of church, then, to be particularly comprehensive: "The Church is the whole body, or congregation, of persons who are called by God the Father to acknowledge the Lordship of Jesus, the Son, in word, in sacrament, in witness, and in service, and, through the power of the Holy Spirit, to collaborate with Jesus' historic mission for the sake of the Kingdom of God."[4] Since the reign of God, already touching us, is always present in a privileged way in any liturgical celebration, the mission to witness to that reign is particularly insistent in the liturgical community. Worship gives new sight to those who are sent to evangelize their own culture.

American Roman Catholics come to their worship and work with a highly dense and extended experience of their world. American cultural experience includes the verbal and nonverbal ways in which our society encodes its beliefs and values in our conscious and subconscious experience. Because culture seems as natural to us as the air we breathe, we seldom examine our cultural assumptions and heritage without some specific reason. In the Corinthians' case, Paul challenges some of the cultural assumptions about the moral values encoded in the way the Corinthians eat together, which they have uncritically transferred to the Christian love feast and eucharistic celebration. In our era, the American bishops have challenged some of our cultural assumptions about nuclear war and the economy. In both cases, the message is the same: the gospel must be heard and lived within the challenges and potential of our own culture.

"Culture" can be an elusive reality to describe. People, for example, will say: "That's as American as apple pie or the Fourth of July." The description attempts to catch what is distinctive about our American culture by certain images or symbols. Throughout this book I suggest that culture, in a general sense, is the vision and values that our society provides us with—a lens through which to view and understand our particular reality. Paul VI and John Paul II have emphasized the importance of culture for hearing and responding to the gospel invitation to conversion. Our culture provides the "ears" with which we hear the gospel message, the language to understand it, and also the situation in which the challenges of conversion must be lived out.

> "Inculturation" is the word commonly used to refer to efforts on the Church's part to immerse the Word of God in the lives of a particular people. Inculturation is a process of learning to "speak the language" of the people in the broadest sense. . . . And the people are encouraged to allow their culture's rich forms of expression to permeate their responses to the gospel.[5]

The interaction between American culture and the Roman Catholic church in this country is a complex one. Examining liturgy and its underlying notion of church in this culture is fraught with even more difficulties.[6] A number of evaluations and surveys of the American church have resulted in mixed and sometimes apparently conflicting data. Frequent charges of cultural individualism and privatism as characteristic of the American church have been countered by the work of other researchers, notably, Andrew Greeley. This debate has spilled over into the discussions of liturgy in the postconciliar American church with persistent questions about whether our Sunday celebrations are but another way of preserving our American individualism. Certainly, the white middle-class church can sometimes appear to be more tempted in this regard than Hispanic and African American Catholics. Monika Hellwig has noted with some justification that the history of the American Catholic church has not always prepared it to be countercultural or, at best, to be selectively countercultural.[7] As an immigrant church, Catholics sometimes tried to be more American than their contemporaries. This tendency has not always made for a prophetic church. And yet authentic worship, by its very nature, always challenges some assumed cultural values.[8]

This book, therefore, centers on the connections between being Catholic and American nearly three decades after the Vatican II council. It asks if the American church is in need of another Emmaus walk. The six chapters of this book examine the connections of being Catholic and American in view of the Christian emphasis on being gathered together as a particular or local church and as a liturgical church. The basic question of these chapters is, To what extent does our post-technological American culture help or hinder us as we gather to praise and thank God? In turn, what impact have the worship and witness of the American church had on the culture of this country?

The first chapter, "The Times and Places of the New Creation," reviews the Christian heritage on the subject of creation and the "new creation" in Christ as the proper basis for discussing questions of culture. In turn, Paul VI, in his teaching on evangelization poses some penetrating questions about the connections between culture and gospel. One such question is a major concern of this book: "Does the church or does she not find herself better equipped to proclaim the gospel and to put it into people's hearts with conviction, freedom of spirit, and effectiveness?"[9] The second chapter, "The Postconciliar Liturgy in the American Church," focuses on two quite different periods in the history of the American church in terms of an operational theology of local church and a pastoral approach to liturgy and devotions—the colonial era and the nineteenth century. John Carroll, our first bishop, emerged initially as a strong proponent of the local church and an inculturated liturgy. The nineteenth century's immigrant tides presented a totally different challenge to the church. The bishops' pastoral response of that era included a creative use of liturgy and devotions but also some possible loss of the sense of being local church. The postconciliar American church appears at times strangely dichotomized, with an often-relevant and persuasive sense of social justice that seems derived not from its worship but from its formal teaching.

The third chapter, "A Test of Liturgy: The Gathered American Community," benefits from the fairly large body of sociological analysis of the U.S. church (Andrew Greeley's outstanding contributions, the Gallup study, the Notre Dame Study of Catholic Parish Life, and others). These studies point to the remarkable profile of many American Catholics as well educated, affluent, and upwardly mobile. They crowd their churches on Sundays; they support a remarkable educational system; and their religious education system is one of the best in the Catholic world. From any viewpoint, these particular American endowments prepare some American Catholics for the tasks that God gives them. There are, however, other constituencies among American Catholics that are not as favored, for example, Hispanic and African American Catholics, immigrants from Asian countries, and others. These groups do not necessarily feel at home in a middle-class Anglo church.[10] Moreover, many American Catholic women feel that their gifts are not fully recognized by their church; yet women constitute a major part of the ministerial task force of the American church.

Therefore, the question must be asked: Has the American church fruitfully "received" (i.e., spiritually appropriated) the teaching and liturgical reform of Vatican II in such a way that all these groups are renewed? (I confess that my own answer was initially negative, but a question of Anne Carr and a second study of the work of Andrew Greeley made me radically reexamine the way in which I was dealing with the question. Readers can judge for themselves how the influence of Carr and Greeley changed my position.)

The fourth chapter, "American Time and God's Time," tests the validity of the first three chapters by examining how the mystery of Christ's dying and rising that we celebrate liturgically challenges our cultural sense of time. To put it another way, our use of time is the best test of how penetrating and ongoing our conversion is. Once again, our American sense of time is one of our most pervasive and influential cultural heritages: "Time is money" and "Thank God it's Friday" are but two examples. In contrast, worship celebrates God's purposes in giving us time: to begin to build God's peaceable reign before the end of time. But it is possible for an American community to worship and yet retain its cultural sense of time unchallenged. The celebration of a liturgical year, after all, has little value if the problems of our civil year have been ignored. One of the most practical pastoral tests of how deeply the liturgy is taking hold, I would argue, is our challenged sense of our culturally assimilated American time.

The final two chapters ("In the New Wilderness" and "American Sacramental Praxis") bring us back to gifts and problems of the American church in being a credible gospel community. One question in particular, as mentioned above must be faced: Is the American Roman Catholic church infected with the same individualism and privatism for which Robert Bellah and his colleagues have indicted the American churches in general? The prevalent position is that the American church is highly individualistic. (Although I was originally persuaded by this view, I have adopted a somewhat more nuanced position.) Finally, is liturgical participation authentic enough to question profoundly the intentions with which we celebrate as a church and individually? One practical and classical test is the willingness to bring the gospel message into the marketplace. A sense of mission is inextricably tied to that of communion, as John Paul II has reminded us.[11]

Although this book deals with the Roman Catholic community, the central question about the connection between church and worship in our American culture is a gospel concern for all the Christian communities. In this postconciliar and more ecumenical period, a number of the other Christian communities have renewed their own liturgies. But with liturgical renewal there is all the more reason to reexamine the connections between the worship and the sense of mission and witness of a gathered Christian community in its own culture and subcultures. My hope is that my work might be of some help for those churches who are examining similar questions.

Throughout this book, I employ the words "liturgy" and "sacrament" frequently. In general, liturgy is the larger term, encompassing the prayer and worship of the church. For a definition, I can do no better than cite the one that David Power gives: "The liturgy is an action wherein the testimony of God is heard and appropriated, the experience of the community is transformed, and a godly presence disclosed."[12] The narrower term is always sacrament and has a sevenfold expression in the Roman Catholic communion.

This book does not presume to be a theology of culture[13] nor a theology of liturgical inculturation: Anscar J. Chupungco, O.S.B., and others have already given us some distinguished work on the subject.[14] Michael Aune has also contributed some penetrating insights on dealing with the question of liturgy in a cultural context.[15] My own efforts are confined to the connections between church and liturgy in the American culture. Behind these efforts are two theological convictions. The first is that God is always doing much more in our midst than we might care to believe. In other words, no matter what the pastoral and personal constraints of our situation might be, God empowers the gathered church[16] to give adequate witness to the gospel message. The second conviction is that liturgy continues to connect the pastoral tasks of the local church and its understanding of theology.[17] Although pastoral meetings and strategic planning have their place, it is in its worship, above all, that the church once again takes the Emmaus walk and learns the practical local corollaries as well as the theology of a crucified and risen Lord.

I agree with Ronald Grimes's observation, cited above, that liturgy is "one of the hardest cultural forms to evaluate."[18] The approach I have used in this book is but one way to attempt such a task. I can only hope that it will prompt my colleagues to continue their own work in this area.

# CHAPTER ONE

# The Times and Places of the New Creation

"America the Beautiful" is both a hymn and a patriotic song. The text of the song describes some of the wonderful vistas of creation that are found on this continent and also asks God's blessing on this land. When one stands on the rim of the Grand Canyon or watches the grandeur of Niagara Falls, it is not difficult to be caught up in the spirit of that song. But in the burnt-out sections of the Bronx or Los Angeles, it may be more difficult to sing "America the Beautiful" with a great deal of conviction. In such situations, we realize that we always see God's creation through the eyes of our culture and our times, with all the limitations and blessings that implies.

In a more profound way, worship praises the God who creates and redeems us. Worship provides us with a new vision so that we can appreciate what God has done and continues to do among us. We do not praise God for abstract reasons but rather for the actions that happen in specific times and places of our lives. But once again, there are no perfect times or places from which to praise God this side of the reign of God. Imperfect situations, however, do not excuse us from praising God. Paul takes this very visibility of God's work in creation as an argument against those who claim to be agnostic or atheist: "So they are without excuse; for though they knew God, they did not honor him as God or give thanks to him" (Rom. 1:20–21).

A contemporary theology of worship must not only remind us of the universal reasons we have to thank and praise God (e.g., God's care for us) but must turn our attention to the very specific ways in which God acts in our time and particular culture. The black spiritual, for example, which implored God's deliverance from slavery in nineteenth-century America, took its inspiration from the psalms that deal with Israel's liberation from Egypt.[1] But the spiritual's message remains unique because it transposes Israel's need for freedom to the American situation. Our own praise must also be rooted in what God does in our culture and time to set us free.

This book is a reflection on the worship of the Roman Catholic church within the American culture. Such a reflection assumes that the contemporary religious experience as well as the liturgical celebrations of American Catholics are affected by the specific cultural setting and the historical situations in which the local church currently finds itself engaged. Before Vatican II Catholics knew that they would find the same Latin liturgy in a church in Paris, Chicago, or Bombay. But today American Catholics not only find the postconciliar liturgy in the vernacular but also are conscious that these celebrations are taking place within the American situation and culture with all the advantages and liabilities that might imply. The very notion of liturgical participation is premised on the knowing, active, and fruitful celebrations of individuals and groups richly endowed by their culture.

Early Christian prayer and worship were influenced by the Jewish predilection for blessing God the Creator, followed by thanksgiving to God the Redeemer. The Christian innovation was to reverse this order by thanking God for Christ our Redeemer and then blessing God for the new creation in Christ. But in the late twentieth century, as we face some of the far-reaching results of human irresponsibility for creation and its environment (e.g., the "greenhouse effect" and the pollution of air and water), we must ask how such situations affect our ideas of thanking and blessing God for creation and new creation. Does our post-technological American society and culture help or hinder us as we gather to praise the God of all reality?

This chapter prepares us to discuss this post–Vatican II situation by examining some underlying ideas. Since we experience creation as filtered through a particular cultural lens, our first concern is to clarify the connections between American culture and our Christian perspective. The Christian viewpoint on worship and on culture is, in turn, influenced by the notions of creation and of the "new creation" in Christ. The death and resurrection of Christ are the foundation of our hope of salvation. At the same time, this hope transforms our perspective on everything created. Our next task, then, is to review these ideas about creation and new creation and how they are expressed in the liturgy of the world and of the church.

We cannot disown our own cultural background as we try to understand the purposes of creation and welcome God's transforming and graced recreation in our midst. These same ideas have shaped the Christian notion of culture and grounded the church's long history of dealing with different cultures. When Vatican II began its discussions on living the faith within specific cultures, it had an extended experience of many centuries to reexamine. The reader may be surprised to discover just how challenging the church's position on the relation of faith, worship, and culture is. The final sections of this chapter must then reassess the position of the American Catholic church within the American culture.

## American Culture and Our Perspectives

Culture provides us with a perspective for understanding created reality and enables us, by means of symbolic language, to communicate to others the values and meanings we derive from that reality. Because culture is so much an unexamined part of ourselves, it is difficult sometimes even to discern how influential our culture and its assumptions are in our lives. Clifford Geertz has offered a more thorough definition of culture as "an historically transmitted pattern of meanings embodied in symbols, a system of inherited conceptions expressed in symbolic forms by means of which people communicate, perpetuate and develop their knowledge about and attitudes toward life."[2]

What is particularly important in Geertz's definition is that meanings are communicated by symbols. Meanings generally refer to whatever gives direction and value to our lives. In this sense, meanings are never really private, because, by their very nature, they affect other people as well as ourselves. In a much-cited line, Geertz reminds us that culture is public because meaning is.[3]

There are very close connections between religion and culture. Since religion, by definition, is concerned with meaning and values, culture cannot ignore religion. On the other hand, as Paul Tillich reminded us, culture is the form of religion. (Religion, for example, must use language, which is a cultural creation.)[4] Even more important is how the church and culture are under the same judgment because they are so closely connected. Tillich strongly criticized the Roman Catholic church because it seemed to think that it could judge a culture without being judged by it.[5]

Only a few years later, Vatican II insisted that the church profits "from the riches hidden in various cultures," and Paul VI acknowledged that the church must interact with the cultures it evangelizes.[6] For example, the American bishops, when speaking of the Hispanic presence in this country, cited Vatican II's teaching on culture and its intimate link with faith and then applied it: "As with many nationalities with a strong Catholic tradition, religion, and culture, faith and life are inseparable for Hispanics. Hispanic Catholicism is an outstanding example of how the Gospel can permeate a culture to its very roots."[7] For some African American Catholics, it may be a question of regaining their black experience, after rejecting certain elements of the white culture. To the extent that they have appropriated their own rich and creative heritage, they can transcend it in collaborating with other white and Hispanic cultures and creating indigenous liturgical expression.[8]

When Geertz, as an anthropologist, gives his working definition of religion, he adds the more elusive elements to the notion of symbol and meaning: "a system of symbols which acts to establish powerful, pervasive, and long-lasting moods and motivations in men by formulating conceptions of a general order of existence and clothing these conceptions with such an aura of factuality that the moods and motivations seem uniquely realistic."[9] "Moods and motivations" might be called the "unwritten" parts of religion within a culture. Thus, the American church shares the symbols and meanings with other local churches in the Roman Catholic community throughout the world, but it is precisely in its moods and motivations that the American church shows its distinct appropriation of the gospel as well as its cultural heritage.

When American religion is discussed, terms such as individualistic and privatistic are often used. Starting with the perceptive observations of Alexis de Tocqueville, two statements are usually made about the American way of "having religion." First, Americans are highly individualistic not only in dealing with their rough-and-ready frontier situation but also in their religion. Self-fulfillment and self-realization can become goals in this individualistic religious climate. Second, Americans uniquely combine a love of liberty with a commitment to religion. This concern with religion remains a pervasive part of our culture. Confronted with the fragmented contemporary systems of meaning and value, Americans still search for a religion that assures a commitment to transcendent values and a sense of the sacred in their lives.

In other mainline American churches that have never emphasized the communal (or ecclesial) dimension of religion, the charge of individualism might be accurate. Stephen Hart, for example, has suggested a number of factors that would explain the privatization that he sees in American churches: the "electronic" or television religion, church conceived as a voluntary association, individual responsibility and subjectivism, religion understood as a mainly private affair.[10] Are these categories applicable to American Roman Catholics?

The Roman Catholic church, after all, has always emphasized the importance of communal or ecclesial participation, at least in theory. Can the

American Roman Catholic church be accurately called individualistic? Robert Bellah and his colleagues have suggested that this is the case, and the Notre Dame Study of Catholic Parish Life would seem to agree.[11] Andrew Greeley, while acknowledging "powerful strains of individualism," has directly challenged this viewpoint.[12] For the moment it suffices to mention the possibility. We will have to return to this charge in a later chapter.

## Creation and the New Creation

The weather report provides one of the few ways in which many late twentieth century Americans look at creation with any interest. Despite space probes and space walks, we tend to take the planet earth for granted and seldom have any reason to regard it in a more dynamic way. Even the threat of irreparably destroying the environment only begins to disturb many people when their drinking water becomes polluted by industrial wastes or when they see the victims of the Chernobyl accident.

Such attitudes are very different from the Judeo-Christian tradition, which sees the power and compassion of God in all creation. In the early years of Christianity the threefold Jewish form of blessing, thanks, and supplication was adapted for use in the prayer of some Christian communities.[13] The Jewish prayer, as already noted, blesses God for all creation, then thanks God for his redeeming love, and supplicates God for his mercy. The Christian transformation of this threefold prayer starts with thanksgiving to God for his "servant-son" (*pais,* the usual Greek term employed by early Christian texts, has both meanings) Jesus, then remembers the food and drink of creation, which recalls the nourishment that Christ gives us, and prays for the church.[14] In an insightful way, the prayer speaks of the creation of this world in light of the new creation that Christ has achieved in his gathered people, the church.

Another example that shows this linking of the work of creation and the work of Christ is found in the life of the thirteenth-century St. Francis of Assisi. The general acceptance of the saint across denominational lines seems to be based on an awareness that appreciation of God's creation is directly linked to the love of God. This love took a radically new expression when Christ died for us so that all people might become a "new creation" in Christ. When Francis calls on brother sun and sister moon to bless God, there is more than a poetic imagination at work. Creation and new creation, employed as an incentive to the praise of God, is a familiar theme in scripture. Francis models his prayer on this scriptural precedent.

Creation in the Christian perspective is only the beginning of the story.

Paul argues that with the coming of Christ a radically "new creation" now exists (cf. 2 Cor. 5:17). What God accomplished in the genesis of this cosmos has been surpassed by the totally new kind of life in Christ. This new creation is visible in the Christian who has benefited from Christ's self-gift on the cross and who now lives as a child of God. This new creation is also visible in the body of Christ, the church.

This central Pauline idea of a new creation, however, only retains its full force when the first "creation," the world, is a dynamic reality. For the contemporary person that is not as easy as it might sound. In the twentieth century the destructiveness of war, famine, and environmental irresponsibility seem to have dulled our sense of wonder at God's creation. Furthermore, the specific cultural and historical situation in which people of today find themselves may seem to be an obstacle rather than a help in giving Christian witness. Surely the impact of Christ's death and resurrection spills over into the cultural fabric of our lives in this world, but this may not be immediately apparent.

## Liturgy in the World

As already noted, contemporary Christians appear to have difficulty with somewhat abstract notions of creation, but they are more likely to understand how salvation is worked out in the ordinary routines of daily living. Karl Rahner, a noted German theologian, suggested that the liturgy as such may also be considered some sort of "magical ritual" by contemporary people.[15] In response to this situation he urged theologians and those in pastoral ministry to help people first find their redemptive situations in God's world. Rahner coined the phrase "the liturgy of the world" to describe how God's first creation is the very place in which the "new creation" will be experienced. It is in the very act of living out the implications of the Christian way in this world that redemption is appropriated.

Once more Francis of Assisi provides a concrete example of someone who finds God in creation. His love of the crucified Christ paradoxically helps him to find the love and goodness of God in all of creation. Francis's response to this ongoing discovery of creation is constant praise. Furthermore, the poor man of Assisi finds this source of praise in the ordinary things of creation—the coolness of water and the singing of birds. In the sacramental tradition of the Christian church, Francis responds to the signs of God's mystery that are in creation.

Creation is, in fact, the training area in which we learn to welcome and respond to symbols of God's goodness that are etched in space and time.

In turn, liturgy in its constant and creative use of material reality encourages us to look at creation with deeper awareness and renewed gratitude. Our own symbolic capacity to communicate the more profound levels of our experience is rooted in the reality of creation. Rahner's insistence on our human capacity of being oriented toward the mystery of God is another way of reminding us of this symbolic capacity.[16]

God's self-communication continues to take place in creation. Our birth is a primary example of God's continuing creation. The parents of a newborn child are keenly aware not only of the mystery of life but of God's mystery, which is enfleshed in another living being. In fact, Vatican II insisted that as people provide for themselves and their families "in such a way as to be of service to the community as well, they can rightly look upon their work as a prolongation of the work of the creator."[17] As this child grows, her response to God will always take place within this world and in the specific times and places of a particular culture. Her salvation will not be worked out despite creation, but within it. It is this world as the locus of God's saving actions that is the primary liturgy in Rahner's sense of the term.

Why, then, is it so difficult to find God in the "liturgy of the world"? Rahner's answer is that evil also plays out its scripts in this same creation. When creation is experienced primarily as the scene of violence, greed, exploitation, and irresponsibility, it will be all the more difficult to find and praise the God of creation.[18] This is not to say that God's care and love are totally extinguished in these situations but to admit the difficulty of praise in some historical situations. To find reasons for the praise of God, for example, in the scared neighborhoods of Belfast or Brooklyn is the more difficult task of Christians who want to understand what "new creation" promises.

Although we are never obliged to be prisoners of our cultural worldview, it is sometimes quite difficult to transcend that initial cultural vantage point and to reassess critically the meanings and message of God's creation for us. On the positive side, our generation has been made vividly aware of the dynamic complexity of our universe by space exploration and medical research. These experiences have begun to reshape the boundaries of our imagination and the ways we symbolize. Vatican II, while distinguishing between earthly progress and the kingdom of God, noted that "such progress is of vital concern to the kingdom of God, insofar as it contributes to the better ordering of human society."[19]

Rahner's insight about the liturgy of the world, however, must be heard within our cultural situation. Otherwise, it is perceived as a theological theory rather than a reality that Rahner has expressed theologically. There are certain subtle cultural biases that can reduce the impact and application of this liturgy in the world. Despite the text of "America the Beautiful" with its references to God, our postindustrial culture treats creation as its own. Violence, poverty, and environmental irresponsibility, for example, are so common in our culture that their implicit and un-Christian message about creation as disposable is easily overlooked. Urban sprawl and blight are more destructive of the credibility of a liturgy in the world than any Manichean heresy ever was. American affluence, as an American subculture, can also be a more subtle cultural strategy against any liturgy in the world to the extent that it mutes our dependence on and incompleteness without God. Our use of time, as we shall see in chapter 4, is a crucial test of our theology of creation and of liturgy in the world. Above all, reverence for the human being as the apex of God's creation is as strong as its reverence for human life of the fetus, of the disabled, and of the poor. Yet the central Christian doctrine about our "new creation" in Christ rests on the notion of what creation is actually, not theoretically. In brief, reverence for creation and the possibility of liturgy in the world in our American situation cannot simply be assumed, as it too often is, by the liturgies or the pastoral ministries and leadership of the church.

## The Liturgy of the Church

Another reason for ignoring the presence of God in creation is that we somehow keep expecting to be redeemed outside of time and space, and despite other people. Rahner comments:

> When we say that we celebrate the death of the Lord until he returns, we are saying that we are giving space and time explicitly in our own life to the cross of Jesus. . . . This ecclesial worship is important and significant, not because something happens in it that does not happen elsewhere, but because there is present and explicit in it that which makes the world important. . . ."[20]

The salvation gained for us by Christ, which is the cause of our praise, gifts us with the freedom of choosing God. To choose God is also to make a decision about ourselves and our relation to others in the space and time that remain to us.[21]

The cross of Christ is not only the center point of the history of this world but the symbol of God's desire that all people be saved. Redemption is not a private enterprise, nor is it ever accomplished apart from others. The liturgy symbolizes the event of the cross and its transforming meaning for peoples' lives as lived out together in this creation. When a person is touched by God's new creation through the sacraments of initiation, that person through the death and resurrection of Christ becomes part of the people of God, the church. While there are many people who will only know God through the liturgy of the world, there is a special task given to those who form the body of Christ in this world. Christian communities in their lives together and in their worship show forth a unity of love and purpose: "not only are they to animate the world with the spirit of Christianity but they are to be witnesses of Christ in all circumstances and at the very heart of the community of mankind."[22] While sin always divides, salvation always introduces unity among divided peoples of this world.

That same liturgy can help contemporary people begin to see God's purposes and meaning for their own lives in the ongoing creation of the world. Thus, the liturgy of the world provides the context for the liturgy of the church, which helps us see all creation as God's. In turn, our new existence as Christians is lived out in a particular culture that frames and interprets our experience of time and place—and thus, of creation. As noted above, culture has also experienced the power of Christ's death for us. Although this new creation does not do away with evil in our world, it does offer new possibilities for receiving the gift of salvation.

But we must be careful here. Rahner insists on creation as the potential resource for widening our awareness of God's presence. The particular culture in which we live always provides the "eyes and ears" through which we appreciate creation, at least initially, and appropriate the liturgy of the church. But our particular culture or subculture may not help us to appreciate attitudes or practices foreign to that culture. An example might be taken from the African American sense of sacred song in Catholic worship. In contrast to the rather stolid singing of most white Catholics, African American Catholics have a rich musical heritage that includes improvisation and creativity:

> The African American assembly is not a passive, silent, nonparticipating assembly. It participates by responding with its own interjections and acclamations, with expressions of approval and encouragement. This congregational response becomes a part of the ritualized order of the celebration. The assembly has a sense of when and how to respond in ways that would no more disrupt the liturgy than applause would interrupt a politician's speech or laughter a comedian's monologue.[23]

A second problem may be that a subculture's influence in shaping its participants' view of creation may not be sufficiently taken into account. Two examples might help to focus this problem. There is much discussion of how our American youth are influenced by audiovisual culture, and even a cursory examination of young people's favorite rock videos demonstrates how a worldview with its own system of values and sense of time is consistently unfolded in these songs. A Sunday homily or even an ideal eucharistic prayer text does not supplant this pervasive subculture's influence so easily, especially when this influence is not even seriously acknowledged. (We will return to this problem in a later chapter.)

A second example would be the American subculture of senior citizens. Medical science continues to prolong life, but the subculture of the elderly shows that attitudes about the purposes of a prolonged life may be strikingly un-Christian in some of their most basic tenets. The sense of time and its purposes, for example, is both a cultural and a religious concern. In our culture there can exist a religious "piety" of the elderly that has little or nothing to do with the Christian view of why God gives us time. Pastoral care may collude with this cultural attitude by celebrating liturgy solely as comfort for the aging without any of the gospel questions about the purposes of a prolonged life. Vatican II spoke eloquently of how people should live together in social constituencies in such a way as "to dispose them to serve their fellow men. One is entitled to think that the future of humanity is in the hands of those men who are capable of providing the generations to come with reasons for life and optimism."[24]

A practical corollary of this discussion of creation is the recognition that a theology of liturgy must teach contemporary Christians to be aware of the "footprints of God" (to use St. Bonaventure's phrase) in this world. Vatican II, in urging Christians to discern the presence of God and his Spirit which fills the world, reminded them that "faith throws a new light on all things and makes known the full ideal which God has set for man, thus guiding the mind towards solutions that are fully human."[25] This new awareness also elicits our self-gift to God as a response.[26] One historical example is the church as a patron of the arts in the renaissance period. Music and painting were viewed as gifts from God and as a powerful means to turn people's hearts to God. A contemporary example might be the culture of instant communications in which we live. Such communications have culturally transformed our ability to be aware of others and to symbolize our presence to them. Young Americans, in particular, find meaning and expression for their lives in this cultural world of instant communication. If these Americans are to be evangelized, then the church will have to find new ways in which to be a patron of the arts. To continue this discussion of creation and new creation in the world we must now briefly examine some of the connections between our Christian faith and our culture.

## The Cultural Dimension of Christian Living

Roman Catholic concerns about culture are as old as the missionary endeavors of the church.[27] In general, the church's missionary policy on culture, in its better historical moments, could be summarized as a toleration of what was not against religion and morality and a limited and inconsistent use of cultural heritage in liturgical rituals. But there were always remarkable exceptions, such as the work of Sts. Cyril and Methodius in the ninth century in uniting the Slavic cultures (through written Slavonic) as they evangelized these people. Methodius eventually persuaded Pope John VII to permit the use of Slavonic language in the liturgy.[28] Another extraordinary example is the late sixteenth century Jesuit missionary to China, Matteo Ricci, who had a positive and dialogical attitude toward his host culture. This approach suggested that there was always something to be learned from the "foreign" culture that would facilitate the proclamation of the gospel among its people.[29] The pioneering efforts of the Jesuit missionaries to acculturate the Roman liturgy to its Chinese setting were eventually thwarted by fears that pagan elements would infiltrate Christian worship.

Vatican II returned to the early examples of evangelization by the missionary church to assess the contemporary connections between faith and culture. In the 1965 decree on the church's missionary activity (*Ad Gentes*), evangelization was described as purifying whatever good is already present in a culture, a thought already enunciated in the council's decree on the church.[30] An incarnational principle was then offered as a model of evangelization: as Christ completely committed himself to the social and cultural contexts of his contemporaries, so must the missionary. This principle entails a process of discernment to determine "the riches which a generous God has distributed among the nations."[31]

The decree on the church in the modern world (*Gaudium et spes*) completes this principle by providing connections between culture and gospel. Culture is defined in the broadest possible sense as all those elements which reveal the complexity of the human person and community and are summarized in its values.[32] The decree also acknowledges the profound cultural changes of our own day and new patterns of thinking, of acting, and of the use of leisure. These changes have been accompanied by a new humanism that takes responsibility for the direction of these cultural developments and a more dynamic view of our world.[33]

Not all of these changes are good, as even a cursory viewing of the evening news reminds us. Widespread famine and large-scale emigrations and displacements caused by political violence and social injustice, for example, threaten to overwhelm the fragile cultural fabric of nations as well as their political stability. The current interdependence and interchange among nations, while promising mutual enrichment, also shows that such disruptive events can jeopardize the delicate human situation in which people work out their salvation as they try to lead their lives. Since the social and cultural dimensions of our living are so intimately connected, the challenge of Vatican II seems all the more pressing today: "The social order requires constant improvement: it must be founded in truth, built on justice, and enlivened by love: it should grow in freedom toward a more humane equilibrium."[34] The Christian churches believe that the Holy Spirit has a crucial role to play in such a social order within the continuing purposes of God's creation.

In its long experience, the church has learned that culture can mediate the acceptance of the gospel and can give a specific expressive shape to liturgy. On the other hand, evangelization plays a transformative, purifying, and prophetic role in a culture: "It takes the spiritual qualities and endowments of every age and nation, and with supernatural riches it causes them to blossom, as it were, from within; it fortifies, completes and restores them in Christ."[35] To pursue their task of evangelization, local or "particular" churches must be rooted in their own cultures so as to benefit from the rich heritage of Christ to be found there.[36] The gospel life as lived by such communities must be enriched by the genius of their specific culture. The family is also a "domestic" church that transmits the Christian message in its cultural context. The American bishops specifically cited the Hispanic family, and Hispanic women in particular, as one of the historical reasons why the faith has survived and prospered in their midst: "Even at times when the institutional Church could not be present to them, their faith remained for their family-oriented tradition of faith provided a momentum and dynamism accounting for faith's preservation."[37]

Despite their generalized approach to the problems of Christian living within cultural contexts, these conciliar texts do make some classical connections between a theology of creation and that of our "new creation" in Christ. Another underlying assumption of the council was that the liturgy of the world and that of the church rely on particular cultures for their translation into lives of people in each time and place. A critical appreciation of the good as well as the flawed elements of culture is encouraged. There is some recognition of how pervasive cultural influence is in its sociological results. An incipient theology of local church is firmly situated within its own cultural setting, but these modest theoretical gains in the church's view of culture are not radical enough to confront the widening gap between culture and Christian living in our day. It was because of this gap that Paul VI wrote one of the more challenging papal documents of this century, *Evangelii Nuntiandi (On Evangelization)*.

## The Contemporary Cultural Challenge

When Pope Paul VI published his exhortation *On Evangelization (Evangelii Nuntiandi)* in 1975, its message had been prepared for by his actions and teaching, especially in regard to the churches of Africa. In his 1967 message to those churches, he cited specific values in their religious and cultural heritage: a spiritual view of life, an emphasis on human dignity, and a sense of family and community life. In his address at Kampala to the African churches in 1969, Paul VI not only allowed for a certain cultural pluralism in religious expression but specifically addressed the interaction of evangelization and culture. The African cultures were expected to contribute to the richness of gospel living and liturgical expression.[38]

Paul VI's 1975 exhortation *On Evangelization* contains two striking but classical proposals: (1) conversion and evangelization are grounded in a missioned community and (2) evangelization is always a radical process. Since ongoing conversion and evangelization are the necessary foundation for the liturgy of the world and of the church, these two proposals merit further attention. First, the notion of conversion, now resituated within the life of an evangelizing community, once again becomes a dynamic and demanding ecclesial as well as personal exerience: "The Church is an evangelizer, but she begins by being evangelized herself. She is the community of believers, the community of hope lived and communicated. . . . she needs to listen unceasingly to what she must believe. . . . she always needs to be called together afresh by him and reunited."[39] The liturgy of such a church is, in a sense, an extension of the ongoing process of conversion. Its praise and thanks are constantly nourished by gospel challenge and its further appropriation. The importance of the connections between culture, gospel, and liturgy are more easily appreciated if we follow for a moment Paul VI's thought on conversion.

In sharp contrast to descriptions of conversion that isolate gospel change from gospel tasks, Paul VI takes his inspiration from the early Christian communities of shared conversion and mission. He sounds his leitmotif from the book of Revelation: "See, I make all things new" (Rev. 21:5). This "newness" begins with an evangelization that is welcomed and continues with "new persons renewed by baptism and by lives lived according to the Gospel."[40] "Newness" was a catchword of early Christian communities caught up in the enthusiasm for the Good News they had received. As already noted, Paul describes the Christian as "a new creation" (2 Cor. 5:17), the result of a life transformed in Christ.

Paul employs the Greek adjective *kainos* for "new" because it conveys the sense of a reality so radically different that its like has never been seen before.[41] Furthermore, this "newness" already reflects and promises the reign of God coming toward us. The gospel, in turn, is described as "Good News" because of the radical surprise of those who welcome this new way of living. These ideas are beautifully summarized in the words of the celebrant to catechumens entering the process of evangelization and the eventual reception of the initiation sacraments: "You have followed God's light and the way of the Gospel now lies open before you. Set your feet firmly on that path and acknowledge the living God, who truly speaks to everyone."[42]

Second, Paul VI does not ignore the personal and communal difficulties in the gospel's call for radical change. On the contrary, he points to one of the major obstacles to welcoming the Christian message: the cultural context in which the personal and communal conscience must make decisions. "What matters is to evangelize man's culture and cultures (not in a purely decorative way as it were by applying a thin veneer, but in a vital way, in depth and right to their very roots)."[43] John Paul II, in speaking about the vocation and mission of Christians in the world today, reiterated some of Paul VI's key thoughts about evangelization. The pope then calls for a reevangelization of countries and cultures that were once Christian: "Without doubt a mending of the Christian fabric of society is urgently needed in all parts of the world. But for this to come about what is needed is to *first remake the Christian fabric of the ecclesial community itself* present in these countries and nations."[44] To phrase that thought within our concerns, what renewal of the American ecclesial community is needed so that our message to our world might be more credible?

Scripture scholars have recently been preoccupied with early Christianity's efforts to evangelize the cultures of its time. Wayne Meeks, in describing what the term "social world of early Christianity" means for scholars, echoes Paul VI's careful balance of gospel and culture: "It has a double meaning, referring not only to the environment of the early Christian groups but also to the world as they perceived it. . . . One is the world they shared with other people who lived in the Roman Empire; the other, the world they constructed."[45]

Robert Schreiter has noted that in the postconciliar church a new kind of Christian identity and theology began to emerge as the church once again took its sociocultural situation more seriously. This identity developed because the church was aware of three important areas: context, procedure, and history.[46] Because his model concretizes some of our discussion on culture and creation, a brief summary of these areas and an example of their application might be profitable. Context deals with the social, political, and economic dimensions of the cultural world of a particular local church. Procedure refers to the ways in which meaning is constructed communally in some religious communities that reflect the cultural construction of meaning. Finally, the histories of a local church also reflect the cultural contexts of that church (e.g., the ways in which our American sociocultural situation has unequally treated women and the reflection of this in the American church).[47]

One example that illustrates all three areas might be the process that the American bishops used in preparing their pastoral letters on the nuclear disarmament and on the economy. A process of consultation with different publics (both technical experts and interest groups) who had views on the topic was employed. The bishops' committee responsible for preparing the draft had the opportunity to hear positions on the topics that were sometimes in strong disagreement with one another and to question the presenters of those positions. These positions on the economy and nuclear disarmament, in a sense, were a microcosm of the American culture and its values. The procedure entailed a communal reexamination of how the gospel was to be lived in this particular sociocultural situation. Although the American bishops had an enviable history of addressing some relevant social issues, there were other "histories" of not dealing with unpopular issues.[48] But this process of consultation represented both an ecclesial and a theological process of a local church in an effort to make the gospel life and witness credible within a specific culture. My point in selecting this nonliturgical example is to emphasize how closely the ecclesial and liturgical dimensions of a particular church are. To the extent that the gospel issues and values raised in these letters were appropriated by American Catholics, communally and individually, the "liturgy of the world" had indeed enriched the "liturgy of the church."

In the real world, religion and culture are so interwoven that it is easy to confuse the two. (Some examples that illustrate this connection in the American context are the inscription "In God we trust" on our coins, or public prayer at the beginning of congressional sessions.) A delicate balance must be maintained here: some cultural elements are necessary for realizing the reign of God and yet the gospel's meanings, values, and vision transcend a specific culture. Paul VI contends that the gospel can permeate a culture without becoming subject to it.[49] To accomplish this, however, the gospel must challenge and transform our acculturated way of thinking and valuing. Such a profound change in our thinking and living can only be accomplished within the cultural context that first framed these aspirations and hopes. But how realistic are such expectations in the actual American cultures of our time?

### The Mrs. Ciardis of This World

The theory of how the gospel message should permeate our culture is clear enough. In practice, however, effective evangelization of a culture is a daunting task. John Ciardi has succinctly stated the difficulty in commenting on the probable pagan origin of St. Valentine's Day and the process of mingling pagan and Christian memories: "My own mother was essentially an Italian mountain pagan who had acquired a Catholic vocabulary in which to express *her essentially unchanged pagan views and emotions.*"[50]

Ciardi's judgment captures the problem of effective evangelization within a specific culture: Do the gospel proclamation and the eventual liturgical worship that it evokes profoundly transform our views and emotions about the values and vision of our cultural world? After all, it is not too difficult to find historical and contemporary examples of so-called Christian cultures whose basic pagan persuasion have been uncovered at crucial moments in its history. Paul VI specifically mentioned two groups needing evangelization because they confuse conversion and culture: "baptized people who do not practice, or people who live as nominal Christians but according to principles that are in no way Christian."[51] Worshiping communities who do not continually put themselves under the scrutiny of God's word are in real danger of celebrating the symbols of conversion without being converted.[52]

John Paul II has continued these same themes but with a somewhat different emphasis. Aylward Shorter has pointed out that the pope in his frequent pastoral journeys throughout the world has been adept in using the external signs of the particular culture in which he finds himself (e.g., walking a "dreamtime trail" with Australian aborigines) but he has tended to stress the universal magisterium in order to promote unity.[53] He has shown a keen interest in the question of culture and faith, as demonstrated in his founding of the Pontifical Council for Culture in 1982. John Paul has also spoken forcefully on the synthesis of faith and culture: "A faith which does not become culture is a faith which has not been fully received, not thoroughly thought through, not fully lived out."[54] He has also continued his predecessor's insistence on the link between gospel and culture and has drawn a liturgical corollary: liturgical prayer should benefit from the host culture for its signs, gestures, and words to convey adoration and celebration. Even more important, the ecclesial community, which is rooted in the Eucharist, must also profit from the particular culture in which it witnesses.[55]

To what, then, should we attribute Mrs. Ciardi's "Catholic vocabulary" with its superficial appropriation of Christianity that disguises an unexamined or unreformed performance we call living? Often enough, it is not a question of bad will but of ineffective evangelization which hinders a more authentic appropriation of the meaning of worship. Effective evangelization and honest worship must provide a vantage point for both the community and the individual to assess critically their relations with their world. As one writer has perceptively pointed out, liturgy not only retells the story of a people but also transposes the worshiper into the story as an actor who may confront his or her position in a particular world: "prayer and the act of praying engage the participant in public and private statements about their relationship to the community, and the community's place in the world."[56]

Nor should we forget that the Christian transformation of a culture takes time. The Mrs. Ciardis of this world may have made many changes in their lives because of the gospel. If these changes seem unimpressive, perhaps it is because they are being judged from another cultural position or from a theoretical theological position that does not deal with the messiness of reality. In a later chapter, when the connection between popular religion and worship is discussed, we will have occasion to return to this topic. Our immediate task is to take the challenging teaching of Vatican II, Paul VI, and John Paul II and to see how the American Roman Catholic church has implemented these ideals.

## The Postconciliar American Church

Several years ago a Lutheran bishop and a Roman Catholic pastoral theologian from Germany were my guests. One of the expressed purposes of their visit was to become familiar with the American church in all its diversity. On one particular Sunday, I brought them to an African American Catholic parish in Washington, D.C., that is noted for its lively liturgies and its excellent catechetical program. The following Sunday we participated in the Eucharist of a Georgetown parish where the beautifully celebrated classic liturgy and the thoughtful preaching drew people from great distances.

Two reactions stood out as my German colleagues compared these liturgical experiences to those of the German church. First, they were pleasantly surprised by the different kinds of informality of parishioners in both churches. These people were obviously "at home" in their parish celebrations. Second, the preaching in both communities was relevant and challenging. This was obvious from the quiet attention and occasional smiles or nods from the congregations. My friends' explanation for these differences was simple: "What else would we have expected from American Catholics!" In other words, the cultural dimension was seen as an important factor in explaining the differences between American and German Catholics using the same post–Vatican II rituals.

I had selected parishes, of course, that I thought would impress my German visitors. There were certainly other parishes in the same city that might not have elicited such positive evaluations. Yet even in such parishes my friends would have been struck by the crowds of people and the number of masses, in sharp contrast to Sunday participation in many European churches. In other words, the U.S. church is "successful" in ways that might be the envy of other local churches throughout the world. A high percentage of U.S. Catholics regularly go to Sunday Eucharist and financially support their parishes. In the more active parishes, there are surprising numbers of parishioners who are involved in the liturgical, educational, and charitable responsibilities of their community. The number of American Catholics who have received continuing education or academic certification in religious education is impressive.

These facts point to the vitality of the American church and to the generosity and commitment of many U.S. Catholics. A large number of Catholics appear to be satisfied with their own parish and the service it provides.[57] The earning power and advanced education of many Catholics have made them an important influence in U.S. culture and politics.[58] Finally, the U.S. church seems to have been particularly effective in implementing the liturgical reforms of Vatican II.[59] On the other hand, there sometimes seems to be a selective approach to social justice that is completely divorced from the liturgies celebrated. Hispanics and other minorities too often perceive the American church as middle-class in its pastoral interests and strategies.[60]

Although my German visitors could certainly recount the achievements of their own churches, they were struck by the characteristics that they considered particularly "American" and how these features had left their mark on the local church and its celebrations. Behind the "success" story of the U.S. church there is a much more complex group of local churches that reflect the cultural diversity of this country. The two parishes in Washington, D.C., that we visited, for example, though only fifteen minutes' distance from each other, are worlds apart in terms of their sociocultural makeup. In view of this cultural complexity, the overall positive pastoral achievement of the American church is all the more impressive.

Recent studies of the American Catholic church have generally reenforced these positive assessments. The recent Gallup poll study of the American church is consistently positive in its analysis of an extensive survey of U.S. Catholics.[61] The Notre Dame Study of Catholic Parish Life, which surveyed about a thousand parishes in this country, while being critical of certain aspects of church life still gives the American church high marks.[62] On the other hand, some researchers would suggest that there are a larger number of "cultural Catholics" (those who are Catholic by birth rather than choice) than we might care to believe.[63] But it is the ongoing sociological commentary of Andrew Greeley on the American church over more than two decades that represents the most in-depth study.

Extensive use of Greeley's work will be made throughout this book. For the moment, a statement of some of his salient positions on the American Roman Catholic church will suffice. A central thesis of his work continues to be that American Catholics have a sacramental or analogical imagination which encourages them to see God as present in this world, which, in turn, is revelatory. It is this type of imagination that lends importance to the ideas of community, ritual, the arts, a devotional life, and the use of sacramentals.[64]

Although many American Catholics appear to differ with the teaching church on issues such as birth control, they have no intention of leaving the church. American Catholics under twenty demonstrate a deeper religious sensibility, imagining God in more positive ways, and are more open to serving others.[65] Parishes are an important part of the American church because "they are the religious counterparts of neighborhoods."[66] Such parishes are a social and recreational center and contribute to the cultural and political life of the larger community.[67] Catholics have a sense of organic community in which "salvation comes to you in the storytelling community that has shaped your experience, provided you with the repertory of images to articulate those experiences and the story line with which to describe them, and is waiting for you to present yourself in order that you might tell your story."[68]

Greeley faults the current postconciliar liturgy for not encouraging religious sensibility and helping Catholics find God in this world. With the exception of one dramatic but temporary decline, it would appear that attendance at the Sunday Eucharist has remained constant.[69] The quality of preaching, as part of liturgy, is poor. It does not correlate with peoples' stories of faith or their struggles to be Christian. The poor quality of liturgical music and the lack of devotional practices have also contributed to dissatisfaction with postconciliar changes.[70] The extensive criticisms in Greeley's work are directed chiefly at the hierarchy, the clergy, and theologians. Although Greeley's optimism about the future of American Catholicism is founded on the resilient loyalty factor among U.S. Catholics, he contends that there is a great deal for the postconciliar church in this country to do, not only in terms of liturgy and preaching but also in regard to the quality and style of moral leadership.[71]

My initial evaluation of the American Catholic church, as I noted in the introduction, has been substantially changed by the work of Andrew Greeley. He does not ignore the negative aspects of that church but rightly insists that the positive aspects far outweigh them. As we shall see, his notion of the "sacramental imagination" is not only a valid but an insightful way of connecting the liturgical and the cultural dimensions of being an American Catholic. Greeley's examination of the "loyalty" factor among American Catholics also represents a major insight. This loyalty has permitted Catholics who dissent from certain moral or leadership directions of the church to remain active liturgical participants. This situation necessarily demands a new look at the classical axiom "the law of worship is the law of belief."

Although I do have some reservations about the ecclesial corollaries of his position, I believe that Greeley creatively poses the question of being Catholic in our culture and invites some careful rethinking about the future of the church in this country. Thus, we will return with some regularity to Greeley's findings and positions throughout this book.

## Initial Suggestions for Looking at Our Culture

God's creation remains an abstraction until we see it with the eyes of our own culture. God's new creation in Christ remains a pious corollary until we deal with the implications of that phrase in terms of our own culture. Culture, while always somewhat flawed, still provides us with a practical testing point for gospel living in the real world. The conciliar and papal teaching on the connections between gospel and culture suggest some initial guidelines for looking at the Roman Catholic church within the American context.

First, *the liturgical life and the moral witness of the local church should be expected to have some positive impact over a period of time on the host culture.* Liturgy's purposes can be unwittingly reduced to theological descriptions of the inner conversion of the individual and the external praise of God. In such a reductionist view, the liturgy of the church in the world and the mission of the church in the world are invariably separated, with little expectation that worship will have any impact beyond the walls of our churches.

A criterion for judging the "liturgy in the world" is to ask to what extent our honest praise of God has challenged our own country and its cultural assumptions. David Tracy reminds us, "Any major religious tradition does disclose in its symbols and in its reflections upon those symbols (i.e., theologies) some fundamental vision of the meaning of individual and communal existence providing disclosive and transformative possibilities."[72] Culture's best friend should be Christian celebrations that enable that culture to open up the vision and goals of its adherents. The current debates in our country about the environment, for example, should be clarified and sharpened by Christian communities who regularly praise the God of creation. (The scandal is that the church seems to have so little to say about this crucial subject.)

One current example of such prophetic impact might appear to be the American bishops' statements on nuclear disarmament and on the economy. These statements have had an unquestionable impact in the larger forum of American life. At first glance, these topics seem to represent current moral questions which have little or no connection with the liturgical life of the American church. But surely the primary place where God continues to teach the church the implications of the gospel is in the symbols of God's presence among us, the liturgy. The practical implications of Christian life in American culture, then, can hardly be divorced from the privileged process of ongoing Christian formation, the liturgy. On the other hand, it is possible to take a moral stand on a particular issue that derives no force or inspiration from the liturgy. Whether this is a desirable alternative is another question. (We will return to this topic in a later chapter.)

A second guideline expands the meaning of the first: *The liturgical life and the moral witness of the local church should be characterized by a sense of discernment and evaluation on cultural and religious values.* Liturgy involves symbolic participation, which, by definition, is always an educational and revelatory process. Symbols disclose the hidden meanings and values of God and of our own American cultural system. Cultures, on the other hand, can sometimes encourage short-range values that betray their users. The popular charge that our American culture is a consumer culture, for example, may also indict the Christian churches of this country who do not seem to have been able to present a convincing alternative to our fellow Americans. Some might argue, in fact, that the actual affluent status of many American Catholics and their churches may reduce or negate their witness on consumerism.

On the other hand, the American culture has continued to provide a complex and creative context in which to practice religion. A comparison of the European churches of the past century with those of the United States would certainly bear this out. In the case of the Roman Catholic church in this country, there are a number of specific characteristics that support this view. Some of the salient features of the post-Vatican II church in this country are the following: (a) the very high rate of liturgical participation[73] by American Catholics; (b) the active and generally successful implementation of the postconciliar reforms; (c) a highly developed religious education network with unusually well-trained religious and lay teachers; (d) an extensive educational system on all academic levels, which, even in its current reduced form, is still a unique achievement; (e) a critical but profound loyalty to the Roman Catholic tradition.[74]

Perhaps one of the most telling characteristics of American Catholics is in the delicate area of formation of conscience. As already noted, Greeley has documented the "loyalty" factor among American Catholics, that is, the willingness to disagree with the teaching church on certain issues and yet remain active participants in the church.[75] Quite understandably, he attributes this attitude to the "combination of symbol, ritual, and community (that) provides a partial 'identity'" to American Catholics.[76] In a similar vein, Patrick McNamara, in his study of young American Catholics of high school age (many of whom are highly critical of the church) has emphasized the often-unappreciated and positive role that liturgy and ritual play in the formation of individual conscience in this age group.[77] While some might view this "loyalty" characteristic of American Catholics as completely negative, there is the positive factor of the church being present, and sometimes prophetic, to otherwise alienated members.

Finally, *the liturgical life and moral witness of the local church should always evoke some transforming and liberating effect on the members of that group so that they will have a clearer sense of mission to the world.* Community is the achievement of common meaning that has been forged by shared decisions, values, and vision of the participants.[78] Any Christian community should be able to be tested by the values and sense of mission it celebrates. That same liturgy not only expresses God's meaning for us but reflects our flawed appropriation of that meaning. When, on the other hand, a particular ecclesial community's actions do not seem to be fully or constantly shaped by the values and vision of the kingdom of God, then we must question what this group's symbolic participation in worship is all about.

## Conclusions

It should surprise no one that any discussion of the contemporary American Roman Catholic church must begin with the perennial theology of creation and new creation. Rahner's insight about the connections between liturgy and creation is an important one because it grounds any praise and thanksgiving on our part in the continuing creative act of God. Furthermore, our symbolic response to God makes use of the created world around us to express our gratitude and wonder. The practical question is to what extent our own cultural world helps us to see or hinders us from seeing God's "footprints" in creation and enables us to symbolize our thanks. Problems of consumerism and individualism are always rooted in the deeper cultural problem—a subtle devaluation of creation and God's purposes for it.

In American culture it is easy, if we are not aware, to pay lip service to a theology of creation without taking seriously any of the practical corollaries of such a theology. How often does the liturgy proclaim, in one form or another, "God, you have created the world in a wonderful beauty and order." But there is a whole range of cultural realities from a damaged and polluted environment to a creation of "virtual reality" that can effectively mute any Canticle to Brother Sun and Sister Moon.[79] There is also much in our culture that still allows us to sing "America the Beautiful" with conviction. In both cases, liturgical creation texts should not be expected to carry the whole burden of restoring a sense of wonder and gratitude for ongoing creation.

Our particular cultural context is also the time and place for God's new creation in Christ. Only a heightened awareness of creation can help us to measure Paul's radical insistence on the total newness of life in Christ. In turn, all liturgy fleshes out this Christian newness and its powerful assurance that the reign of God has already begun. The cultural overflow from this awareness is probably most easily seen in the church music of Bach or Palestrina, which mirrors Bach's German Lutheran culture and Palestrina's Italian Counter-Reformation culture. But such cultural resonance is to be found everywhere. Within our own culture, some of the better characteristics of the American spirit certainly have their source in the Christian belief of new beginnings in Christ. Religious toleration, for example, emerged from the early colonial experience as a religious and cultural value that was to be protected from the vagaries of American political life. At Vatican II, one unique theological contribution that the American church made was the insertion of a conciliar statement that praised and appropriated such toleration.[80]

One scholar has summarized some of the Catholic church's experience of the American culture in these points: "The continuity of religious faith is not necessarily affected by profound cultural change. . . . The religious pluralism of the host society was a critical factor in the process. . . . A gradual transition was possible. . . . The great fear is that, in their adjustment to middle-class American society, Catholics have simply accepted the dominant values of American life."[81] In other words, both the strengths and the weaknesses of American culture have had their effects on the American church. But there is no better place to have a more precise view of these effects than in the worship of that church. This is because of the symbolic dimension. As David Power pointed out, "It is at the juncture of the symbolic that religion either fits into a culture or is at odds with it."[82] Liturgy, as symbolic action, uses cultural expression at the same time that it casts a prophetic and discerning glance on that culture.

But it is precisely this connection between being Christian and being American that provokes a more difficult question: To what extent does the worship of the American church shape its conduct outside as well as inside its walls? Are there real connections between the liturgical life and moral witness of the American church, or, rather, are worship and moral witness two separate functions of Christian life that only occasionally and superficially refer to one another?

Such questions invite us to examine certain aspects of our ecclesial and liturgical heritage as the American Roman Catholic church. The colonial and the nineteenth-century immigrant American church present an interesting study in contrasts. Since we still live with some of the ecclesial and liturgical corollaries of the pastoral decisions of those historical periods, we should be aware of what actually went on. The guidelines we have just examined might provide a lens for seeing that history with new insight.

# CHAPTER TWO

# The Postconciliar Liturgy in the American Church

Liturgy is one of the major reasons why the American church is such a lively and varied community. Liturgy is always a meeting place for God's meanings and our own. On the other hand, the more liturgical a church is, the more closely it must scrutinize what it means when it worships. More than twenty years ago, the U.S. Bishops' Committee on the Liturgy characterized authentic worship as "when we mean the words and want to do what is done."[1] That advice has always been a classical part of the liturgical spirituality of individual Christians, but it also applies to the gathered community as such. Liturgy, as ritual, can offer escape from God's meaning or invite disclosure of that meaning for both individuals and for the whole community.

Liturgy forms and reforms a community because it celebrates the values and goals of the reign of God. Worship does not simply give glory to a generic God but rather offers thanks and praise to a God who saves us through the Son and in the power of the Spirit. The actions and words of the liturgy are forceful symbols that disclose the central meanings of our death and resurrection in Christ. Because these meanings are shared, they form a "gathering," a church community that is truly Christian. Because these meanings are rooted in a crucified Lord, these celebrating Christians are meant to form a prophetic community. Because these meanings are celebrated in a world not yet fully redeemed, these assembled Christians must be a credible community.

The world has a right to expect more than good singing and interesting worship services from such a community. Just as we accept the classical axiom, "The law of worship is the law of belief," might it not be equally true that the law of worship shapes the church's witness to the world about God's values and priorities? In other words, is it not legitimate to ask how the worship of the American church prophetically forms that church's conduct within and outside its walls? The moral law taught by the church deals with specific principles and problems faced by those who attempt to live God's law of love. But liturgy always makes present the very ground of that law, a redeeming Lord. The recurring classical question that ended the last chapter stems from this enabling presence of the Lord: *Are there real connections between the liturgical life and moral witness of the American church?*

No response to this question is possible without reviewing some of the important historical data, now available, on the American church. A few of the studies that deal with the Roman Catholic church in the United States in this postconciliar age have already been noted. Other important studies that have also examined various aspects of the U.S. church will be cited. The history of the preconciliar liturgical movement in this country also reveals the early connections between liturgy, culture, and social justice in the prophetic thinking of liturgical pioneers like Virgil Michel and Monsignor Martin Hellriegel. The purpose of this chapter, however, is not to attempt a summary of this large body of historical data but rather to highlight those findings and analyses that might help us to answer some of the questions already posed. The three guidelines for looking at our culture suggested toward the end of chapter 1 will provide an initial direction for examining the postconciliar liturgy in the American church.

### Cultural or Christian Impact?

As we saw in chapter 1, God redeems us within the context of our own culture and time. When we attempt to scrutinize our American situation, it is perhaps easier to ask what impact American culture has had on the church than to find out what influence the church has had on this culture. We begin with the easier questions: What is the influence of American culture on the Catholic church in this country? And is this influence discernible in the ways that liturgy and the sense of being church interact? Though the basic answer is that the American culture seems to have provided an excellent context in which to be a Catholic individual and community, this is more true of some historical and ethical groups than others. The colonial and the immigrant periods of American history offer two different historical and pastoral situations and responses that might afford some insight about our contemporary situation.

## One Colonial Example

In the early colonial period there were actually several local churches: the West and Southeast Spanish Franciscan mission to Native Americans,[2] the French Jesuit mission to Native Americans principally in Canada and the Great Lakes area, and the mainly English Jesuit ministry to Catholics in what eventually became the thirteen colonies. Each of these local churches was unique not only because of the cultural identity of its members but also because of the implicit concept of church that their missionaries followed and the distinct groups of Spanish, French, and English Catholics whose bishops initially had to deal with civil representatives of the European powers.

These secular powers also had a highly defined notion of the role of the local church in their colonization of the New World, which might run counter to that of the missionaries. Whatever problems this complex situation caused, it also allowed for a healthy pluralism in the conduct of the local church and for creative liturgical experimentation. What sort of impact native cultures had on European missionaries is still a debated historical question, but it is undeniable that the post-Reformation notion of church could not be so easily duplicated in this new cultural situation. The small groups of American Catholics within the thirteen colonies offer one example of this complex situation.

As far back as 1790, when John Carroll was ordained first bishop of the Roman Catholic church in the colonies, the American influence on the local church was already considerable, as reflected in the phrase "republican Catholicism."[3] David O'Brien has described this unique Catholicism as having "opened the door to distinctive national traditions, to an ecclesiology that allowed local churches to adapt to their unique circumstances, to define a relative independence of Rome and a vision of the universal church as a communion of local churches."[4] This context is important not only because it specifies the impact of the culture on the young American church but also because it casts a somewhat different light on somewhat ordinary worship of that church.

Carroll himself had fought for selection of bishops by the local church and had sought to maintain a relative autonomy for the colonial church and to encourage episcopal collegiality.[5] After a century of anti-Catholic bias and persecution, Catholics had achieved a certain acceptance among their fellow Americans and, in turn, had learned a respectful tolerance for other Christian traditions.[6] The laity had a more active role in parish life, and there was some initial interest in celebrating the liturgy in the vernacular, though this trend was reversed in Carroll's own lifetime.[7] Because of Carroll's insistence on the importance of Catholic education for the nurture of the young local church, he made major efforts to bring women religious to this country. Yet he considered the idea of women missionaries to be unprecedented.[8] In other matters, Carroll's attitudes toward women reflect both the limitations and openness of contemporary American culture.

Even in its struggles with trusteeism (lay control of a parish) and the rights of priests, Carroll and his fellow bishops learned to value some form of active lay participation in the parish.[9] In the case of the parish priests of St. Mary's in Philadelphia, who were in litigation with their trustees, the advice of Pennsylvania's supreme court judge William Tilgman is insightful:

> If those who govern the church exercise their power with great moderation, if they are not too forward in assuming the direction of temporal affairs, if they consult the reasonable desires of the laity, both in the appointment and removal of pastors, in all human probability, they may long retain their domination . . . [for] *it is scarcely possible that the Roman Catholics of the United States of America would not imbibe some of that spirit of religious freedom which is diffused throughout the country.*[10]

This statement is prophetic in view of the influence the American church was to have at Vatican II on the question of religious tolerance and freedom.

This colonial church, with its innovative ecclesiology, does not so much provide a paradigm for the contemporary American church as remind us of a heritage of being a local church and the formative role that worship has in this task. Carroll felt that the local church was in the best position to judge what was needed for the faith life of colonial Catholics. His initial call for some vernacular in the liturgy and for the local nomination of bishops should be appreciated within that context. There was less emphasis on a devotional piety than would be the case for the immigrant church, but Carroll did encourage meditation, spiritual reading, and retreats. (We will have occasion in later chapters to return to some specific aspects of liturgical and devotional life in the colonial church.) His pastoral approach to lay participation in parish life and to the liturgy reflected the situation of eighteenth-century East Coast America and the impact of colonial culture on the young church. Carroll and his fellow bishops rejoiced in the freedom and toleration that invigorated American Catholics and set them apart from the European church.[11] As the eighteenth century drew to a close, neither Carroll nor his fellow Catholics could have anticipated the sea change that was about to occur. The huge tides of nineteenth-century immigrants would challenge the American bishops to rethink the nature of their pastoral mission, with practical corollaries for the future shape of the local American church and its liturgical life.

## The Immigrant Church

In the nineteenth century, American culture seemed to evoke a counter-cultural response from the American church as it attempted to minister pastorally to the immigrant tides of culturally displaced Italian, Polish, German, and Irish Catholics. One of the more forceful spokesmen for this new pastoral policy was the archbishop of New York, John Hughes. Hughes argued from the American tradition of separation of church and state to the civil right of the Catholic church to maintain its unique identity. The traditional emphasis on the unifying role of authority, the communion of saints, the practice of charity, and the need for penance was to promote this Catholic identity.[12]

Hughes saw the liturgical calendar and the celebrations it called for as a response to the social distinctions and economic pressures of nineteenth-century America. Liturgy provided a pastoral antidote to the prevalent selfishness of industrial America. Joseph Chinnici has pointed out that Hughes actually baptized the economic culture of his time, even as he appeared to criticize it. Sundays as days of rest with their celebration of the mass as a sacrifice were redeeming acts of justice for the working week.[13] In what appeared to be a culture hostile to Catholic immigrants, the American church shaped a pastoral policy in which the local parish was both a cultural and a religious haven and educated priests were spokesmen and defenders of their immigrant flocks.

One of the practical ways in which the American hierarchy sought to off-set the alienating effects of the American culture on the newly arrived immigrants was to revert to a more European model of parish and liturgy. For the immigrant, the parish church was to become a home away from home. The American church adopted the successful European "parish mission" as a pastorally effective way of renewing sacramental life, giving doctrinal instruction, and bringing back lapsed Catholics.[14] This Catholic form of revivalism combined stern moral reminders, a fervent devotion-alism, and an emphasis on the "four last things" (death, judgment, heaven, hell). Although the Eucharist began each day of the mission, it was the number of confessions heard that was the test of a successful mission. These parish missions faithfully mirrored the prevalent pastoral view of liturgy: sacraments and devotions strengthened personal union with God and visible union with the church. Liturgy maintained the internal identity of Catholics and their church in an otherwise alien world.[15]

Catholic identity was further delineated by the specific character of devotionalism in the nineteenth-century American church.[16] In contrast to the Protestant devotion to reading the Bible, Catholic devotions to the

Blessed Sacrament, to Mary, and to the saints assumed new vitality in the
nineteenth-century American Catholic parish. Despite the opposition of a
minority to these developments, such devotions allowed for a more acces-
sible and affective participation than the incomprehensible Latin rites.
They also afforded a unifying praxis in the face of immigrant diversity in
the American church.[17]

But the inward-looking character of these devotions might seem to indicate that they would have little social or public application and that they
could reenforce any individualistic tendencies among the immigrants.
Even the splendor of the Roman liturgy, which served as a social and spiritual oasis in the otherwise bleak lives of the immigrants in the tenements
of New York or Chicago, underlined a highly personal spirituality and a
more narrow ecclesial understanding of the Eucharist.

Yet there was also a communal self in these nineteenth-century liturgies.
Timothy L. Smith has argued persuasively that with the migration to
America there was a redefinition of peoplehood, often in religious terms,
an intensification of religious belonging and commitment, and a revitalization of the ideas of human community. The clergy were often seen as
mediators of culture, ethnicity, and religion.[18] Smith sees migration as
"often a theologizing experience—just as it had been when Abraham left
the land of his fathers, when the people of the Exodus followed Moses into
the wilderness, and when Jeremiah urged the exiles who wept by the rivers
of Babylon to make the God of their past the hope of their future."[19]

In this new culture, each immigrant faced the challenge of dealing not
only with the new "host" culture but also with a number of competing
subcultures, all of which were readjusting to the materialism and the prag-
matism of the new era. As Smith argues, this new situation demanded of
the immigrants a conception of faith as a highly personal experience that
also bonded them to new communities of belief and action.[20] The parish
became the social and cultural center of "most immigrants" lives, something it had seldom been in Europe. (As we shall see in a later chapter, what
sometimes appeared to be devotionalism among immigrants had far-
reaching results in helping them to redefine their primary groups and, in
doing so, to give the church a new place in their lives.) Immigrant parishes,
often established as national parishes, empowered their members in both
religious and sociocultural ways to deal with a complicated and often
threatening situation. Educational as well as financial resources were
mobilized to help in this task. Liturgy and popular devotions were a
powerful underlying factor in this process. The sociocultural plight of the
immigrants spurred a different ecclesial and sacramental approach that in

some important ways is far from the reactionary impression it might at first suggest. There was a countercultural response and a new bonding with the local church which contextualized the liturgy in a new way for these immigrants. Contemporary American Catholics have continued to identify with their local parishes—an important cultural and ecclesial strength.[21]

The pastoral flexibility and creativity that generally characterized the care of nineteenth-century European immigrants was not generally employed, however, in dealing with the Hispanic population of the Southwest in the nineteenth century nor with the large Hispanic immigrations of the first half of the twentieth century.[22] This particular history recalls the lack of a pastoral strategy, which has sometimes resulted in the separation of church and liturgy for the Hispanic peoples.

## A Different Situation and Pastoral Response

New waves of Catholic immigrants in the latter part of the twentieth century have not always evoked the same creative pastoral response as that of the nineteenth century. One such group is the Hispanic church in the United States. The evaluation of the III Encuentro (1985), the gathering of representatives of the Hispanic church convoked by the American bishops, reflects a very different reaction to the pastoral ministry of the American church: "One perceives a 'cold' Church, without fraternal love or a communitarian dimension . . . without a missionary dimension, and that is why it is not reaching the poor, the marginalized, the alienated, those in jails, gang members and others."[23] This statement reflects a long history that can be alluded to only briefly.

This candid evaluation is in stark contrast to that of the American bishops in their pastoral letter *The Hispanic Presence, Challenge and Commitment* (1983); the letter calls the Hispanic community, in a much-quoted phrase, "a blessing from God." After alluding to the pastoral care of nineteenth-century immigrants by the American church with justifiable pride as "unmatched," the bishops admit that "the survival of faith among Hispanics seems little less than a miracle. Even at times when the institutional church could not be present to them, their faith remained, for their family-oriented tradition of faith provided a momentum and dynamism accounting for faith's preservation."[24] The letter mentions that a committee for the Spanish-speaking was established in the 1940s at the urging of Archbishop R. Lucey of San Antonio and similar diocesan offices in New York and Boston in the 1950s.

But the pastoral and liturgical history of how Hispanics have been cared for is more complicated than this. With the American annexation of the Southwest in 1848 there followed a century in which "Hispanic-American Catholicism suffered under official pro-Anglo policies that resulted in serious pastoral neglect, discrimination, declericalization, and efforts to eradicate Hispanic cultural patterns."[25] Unlike many of the nineteenth-century immigrants, few native priests accompanied the migrations of nineteenth- or twentieth-century Hispanics.[26] There was little provision made for the training of clergy who might minister to Hispanics, and the use of Spanish was actively discouraged.[27] Assimilation rather than pluralism was not only a civil but also an ecclesial goal.

Although the American church failed to support the initial attempts of Hispanics to protest inhuman working conditions and unjust pay scales, the Chicano and farm-worker movements of Cesar Chavez and others finally aroused the conscience of the church leadership to some extent.[28] After no representation on the hierarchy, twenty-three Hispanic priests were ordained bishops between 1970 and 1992, and the number of Hispanic priests and religious is on the rise.[29] The American hierarchy has taken a more active role in applying the social teaching of the church to the situation of Hispanics (e.g., in protesting violence against illegal Hispanic workers) and in elaborating a pastoral plan for Spanish-speaking Catholics that resulted in the first *Encuentro,* or encounter, between the bishops and Hispanics in 1972. The American church has made a major effort to prepare Catholics to open their hearts to these people, and some dioceses have ministered in exceptional ways to their Hispanic members (the New York Archdiocese, e.g., reports that 29 percent of all parishes have the Eucharist in Spanish every Sunday, usually with a priest who has been trained in both the language and the culture).[30]

But the current problems of immigration, education, economic disadvantage, and violence suffered by Hispanics continue to test the pastoral creativity of the American church for the foreseeable future.[31] Joseph Fitzpatrick has noted another problem that is often missed: "The Hispanics are among the poorest population of the United States, while the Church is largely middle class. . . . the Church finds itself in a situation not only where an American clergy must minister to Catholics of another culture, but as a middle-class clergy they must minister to Hispanics who are largely poor."[32] Any discussion of the liturgy must be contextualized within this complex historical situation.

Two general observations are regularly made about the nature of Hispanic religious practice: it expresses a "popular religiosity" and has been fostered in the family, which is a "domestic church."[33] Virgil Elizondo, in recalling Paul VI's plea to the Hispanic Catholics of the United States to retain their popular religiosity, insists that these are "concrete manifestations of the tradition of the Church . . . interiorized in the hearts of the faithful by the Spirit. . . . If you will listen to our prayer forms, take part in our processions, devotions, and liturgical fiestas . . . you will quickly discover that faith for us is not an abstract formula or merely a Sunday affair but the fundamental living reality of our lives."[34] In other words, the threads of liturgical and popular celebration are inextricably woven into the cultural fabric of the people.

In view of this rich cultural background, why has there been such an alarming rate of defection among Hispanics? Andrew Greeley has estimated that as many as sixty thousand Catholics of Hispanic origin are defecting to Protestant denominations.[35] In 1984 Rome began its own inquiry. The Secretariat for Promoting Christian Unity noted, in its summary of the results of its questionnaire, the need for community patterns more adapted to the life situation of people, more "basic ecclesial communities, more attention to the experiential dimension of discovering Christ, the rediscovery of the Word of God for community-building, a greater sense of communal celebration and inculturation, and preaching that presupposes the witness of the preacher's life."[36] Until recently, however, because of the lack of Spanish-speaking priests, the vernacular liturgy was not and still is not available to many Hispanics in this country. Language is a key cultural expression and the unavailability of liturgy in Spanish, often excused in the past as the need for assimilation, is pastorally crucial. With the establishment of the Mexican American Cultural Center in San Antonio, Texas, in 1972 and the Instituto de Liturgia Hispana in 1979, a new era of liturgical and popular research was inaugurated. One of the purposes of these institutions is to promote the liturgical life and its inculturation in Hispanic communities. The result has been a rich harvest of publications and liturgical translations and conferences.[37]

When we turn to the question of the impact of the liturgy on our culture, there are markedly different answers for the nineteenth-century American church, the preconciliar twentieth-century church, and the postconciliar church. The immigrant culture, as would be expected, reacted strongly to the American culture in both positive and negative ways. As already indicated, the liturgy of the immigrant church became a fortress against the alien non-Catholic world. Community was defined not only by what was shared in ritual and meaning but also by a marked separation from outsiders, who could not share in these same rituals. At the same time, the liturgy also helped to integrate the immigrants' symbolic migration experience into the beginnings of a cultural transformation.

Conversely, the impact of culture was to identify many immigrants with the church in new and more committed ways.

American Catholics, then, represented a distinct minority because of the strangeness of their rituals and the highly defined borders of ecclesial belonging. In the colonial period, Protestants were welcome in Catholic churches. (We still have John Adams's vivid description of a Catholic mass he attended in Philadelphia in 1774.[38]) But the immigrant church forbade any attendance at a Protestant service and punished the couple involved in a "mixed marriage" (i.e., a Catholic with a Protestant) by a minimal marriage ceremony. Liturgy reinforced faithfulness and distinguished Catholics from other Americans. While much of this may seem negative to our twentieth-century eyes, there was a high degree of integration between being a community and participating in worship and popular piety. National parishes, while often being a thorn in the episcopal side, were also sites of remarkable cultural and religious transformation.[39] There were important connections made between being American and being Catholic, between cultural and religious identity.

On the other hand, this ideal of assimilation, in which one relinquished language and other cultural heritage, worked havoc in the pastoral care of Mexican American Catholics in the nineteenth and early twentieth centuries.[40] (One example is the way in which Hispanic seminarians until fairly recently were forced into the Anglo mode, their cultural heritage being ignored.[41]) Today, the ideal of cultural pluralism seems to be replacing that of assimilation.[42] The American bishops have caught the pastoral potential of such pluralism: "In committing ourselves to work with Hispanics and not simply for them, we accept the responsibility of acknowledging, respecting, and valuing their presence as a gift."[43]

This overview of pastoral responses to European and Hispanic Catholics in the nineteenth and twentieth centuries should remind us how closely cultural and ecclesial-liturgical contexts are connected. The pastoral care of European immigrants was, on the whole, surprisingly innovative in a highly complex situation. Within the limitations of the pastoral theology and praxis of the time, a new and creative process of ecclesial bonding was employed within a complex sociocultural situation. Until recently, however, the pastoral care of Hispanics was not one of the proudest chapters of the American church. One of the major reasons for this failure was cultural rigidity on the part of the American church, the inability or unwillingness to recognize the riches of another culture's expression of gospel life and worship. Another theological reason was perhaps the Emmaus problem: a too narrow conception of what Good Friday and Easter Sunday mean in a particular context and how they were meant to be celebrated. On the other hand, the more recent willingness of American bishops to enter the *encuentro,* or encounter, process of dialogue and consensus building from parochial and basic communities to regional and national meetings of Hispanics demonstrates an alternative approach to renewing the sense of a gathered church by respecting its cultural gifts and ecclesial charisms. (We will discuss this process in a later chapter.)

## Transition to the Twentieth Century

In the transition from the nineteenth to the early twentieth century, some attention must be given to several issues that reflect the heritage of the largely immigrant church as it moved into a new social as well as historical period. (Our focus here is restricted to the influences that touched on the liturgical life of the church in this country.) Three areas that merit attention are the ethnic and racial attitudes of American Catholics, their impact on African American Catholics, and women's place in the American church.

The term "racial attitudes" is not necessarily pejorative; it can refer to the limited, but not necessarily permanent, cultural attitudes of a particular ethnic group about its own identity, which hinders it from sufficiently valuing other ethnic groups. Intermarriage, for example, often challenges and enlarges such attitudes of individuals and groups over a period of time. National parishes reflect the problem of racial and cultural attitudes within the church. National parishes in this country were the result not only of the desire of Irish, Poles, and Germans to preserve their cultural heritage but also of the American bishops to provide a transitional phase in which the reassurance of familiar parochial and liturgical life might help immigrants to adapt successfully to their new situation.

The relationship between religion and ethnicity is a complicated one, and its long-term effects are not always immediately visible. Recall Timothy L. Smith's thesis that in ethnic groups' migration to the United States, there was usually a redefinition in religious terms of the group's boundaries as well as an intensification of the psychic dimension of its commitment and revitalization of its notion of community.[44] These observations are certainly borne out in the history of national parishes in this country,[45] and they are concretized in remembering how ethnic Catholic parishes formed neighborhoods around them: "Unsurprisingly, oral histories often record parishioners describing the neighborhood as nearly all-Irish, Polish or Italian. . . . The significant point is that the parish itself, because of its size and community base, helped define what neighborhood would mean. For the parishioners, the neighborhood *was* all-Catholic, given the cultural ghetto constructed by the parish."[46]

Behind this social reality was the conviction that the Catholic faith and culture were closely connected. But a practical ecclesial awareness was also shaped within a parish, not only by its "official" teaching and liturgy but also by the cultural context in which all this transpired. The Catholic schools, for example, attached to national parishes, usually taught prayers, devotions, hymns, and sacramental preparation in the ethnic language of the group well into this century. Preaching was still done in German, Polish, or whatever the language of the group was. Banners of religious societies still carried wording in the "mother tongue." Since each language is a cultural creation that communicates much more than vocabulary, its dictionary meanings and grammar, the religious use of these languages brought with them not only memories but also the values of culture, including convictions about what "church" and "parish" meant. As these ethnic groups became assimilated into American culture, the religious use of "foreign" languages declined.[47] It is more difficult, however, to determine to what extent these culturally shaped religious ideas remained or disappeared.

In examining some early twentieth century parishes, it is sometimes difficult to separate the cultural and the religious in such events, when in the same parish ten thousand parishioners attended a parish roller-skating event and eighty-five hundred, Friday night novena services.[48] The blessing of church bells and pious societies' banners or Corpus Christi celebrations in the German-speaking parishes of Milwaukee in the late nineteenth century could attract the participation of several thousand people.[49] Inevitably, there was a transition from religious celebrations reminiscent of the mother country to those reflecting the adopted culture. Liturgical celebrations began to take note of civil holidays such as the centennial of the signing of the Declaration of Independence and Thanksgiving Day.[50] One test of such church communities would be their willingness gradually to transcend the limitations of their original cultural identity in order to be able to welcome other Americans of different cultural backgrounds. This test would also apply to the treatment of African American[51] and women Catholics in church.


## African American Catholics

Although there had been problems between ethnic Catholic groups within the same diocese or the same parish since the nineteenth century, the reception of African Americans—Catholics and non-Catholics—would provide another testing point in the twentieth century of how the notions of "church" and "sacrament" were understood in typical Catholic parishes across this country. To contextualize this problem, John McGreevy has used the insight of sociologist Robert Park that social relations are frequently tied to spatial relations, that is, to the question of neighborhood and home ownership.[52]

Immigrants to this country usually associated the ownership of their own home with success in their adopted country.[53] Thus, even at the beginning of this century surprisingly large percentages of homeowners in some areas were foreign born.[54] Catholic immigrants shared this goal of homeownership and gathered into neighborhoods that centered around their parishes: "Catholics ascribed sacramental qualities to the neighborhood, with the cross on top of the church, the bells ringing each day before Mass, and the religious naming of the area serving as visual, aural, and verbal reminders of the sacred."[55] Intrusion by other ethnic groups could be a source of tension. In other words, the scene was the type of situation that Lukas's book *Common Ground* described in Boston in the 1960s but which began much earlier.

As African Americans, most of whom were non-Catholics, moved into white areas, this became a pastoral problem. There are certainly examples of pastors trying to teach their people a welcoming tolerance for the newcomers.[56] But for many other parishes the question was not toleration but preservation of the parish community and the devaluation of parishioners' property by the influx of African Americans. Some pastors actively promoted the exclusion of "outsiders" who might disturb parish structures.[57] In some cases, bishops viewed the problem as an economic problem (e.g., the devaluation of church property), not a moral one.[58] What is troubling in this history is the lack of connection between the ecclesial notion of oneness with its liturgical expression and the "practical" ways in which the problem was often pastorally handled.

When small groups of Catholic African Americans moved to the north from the Gulf states, they worshiped in their own parishes as other ethnic groups had done. The argument advanced for this situation was that African American Catholics preferred this separation, though there is evidence to the contrary.[59] There was also a strong reluctance to ordain black clergy or, in some cases, even to evangelize African Americans.[60] Despite the attempts of the Josephite Fathers and later of the Society of the Divine Word to educate a black clergy and the direct intervention of Rome at several points, there was little episcopal support for this project.[61]

An incident occurred in October 1955 that epitomizes this situation. A black priest, the Reverend Gerald Lewis of the Society of the Divine Word, was prevented from celebrating mass by the parishioners of a white parish outside New Orleans. Archbishop Joseph Rummel, after duly warning the parish, suspended the celebration of the Eucharist in that parish. As a seminarian in Washington, D.C., I heard Archbishop Rummel speak about the incident shortly after it occurred and vividly remember his lament that a parish could so regularly celebrate the Eucharist and yet nourish such un-Christian intolerance. He reminded us that the canonical suspension of sacramental celebration was classically considered a "medicinal" penance to effect a new and more faithful healing of unity in a Christian community.[62]

My purpose in citing these vignettes from the American church's dealings with African Americans is not to oversimplify this highly complex social and religious history. Once again, some of the colonial and early nineteenth century American church's positions on African American slaves, for example, do not make for edifying reading (e.g., the ownership of slaves by men's and women's religious communities).[63] But the religious orders of women and men in this country, for example, achieved notable success in educating and integrating African American Catholics with others. Archbishop Rummel's remarks summarize a classic Augustinian connection between church and sacrament: fruitful reception of a sacrament eventually reveals itself in the deepening unity of the local church community and is a prophetic symbol of the reign of God already begun among us. Corinthian situations in which frequency of liturgy is confused with appropriation of liturgy's meanings are also a reminder of the continual need for Christian communities to be honest in their celebrations.

## Women in the American Church

At the turn of the century a major pastoral effort focused on increased male participation in the liturgical and social life of the parish, since religion seems to have been considered a feminine pursuit by many Catholic men. Women were, in fact, the backbone of the typical parish. William Stang, in his influential *Pastoral Theology* (1897), reflects the negative interpretation of this situation: "Women . . . push themselves forward in church as if they owned it. . . . They often keep men away from the confessional by their bold manoevres."[64]

Catholic women, while exercising important roles in the average parish, had an officially subordinate role in the institutional church. The disgraceful and even un-Christian way in which religious women were regularly treated by some nineteenth-century American bishops makes for disturbing reading.[65] Leslie Tentler has suggested that "Catholic worship worked powerfully to legitimize those social arrangements where women enjoy a certain authority and status as long as they remain within an acceptably female sphere."[66] Nonsacramental devotions, which remained an important part of parish life until the Second World War, seem to have had a mainly female following. But even here the hierarchy of sex was in force: women were the main "celebrants" in Marian processions, while men assumed the principal roles in eucharistic processions.[67] (This is particularly ironic since historically women were often originators or promoters of such celebrations.)

There are a number of cultural and religious reasons that historians might give to explain this subordination. Anne Carr has probably touched one of the most fundamental causes—the divinization of male authority and power, which effectively does away with any lip service given to equality: "For symbolism is so deeply embedded in Christian theology, church structure, and liturgical practice that the Christian imagination unconsciously absorbs its destructive and exclusionary messages from childhood on."[68] (James Kenneally has tellingly documented how such attitudes played themselves out historically for American Catholic women.[69]) The question of the ordination of women, while being one of the most debated examples of such symbolism, is but one aspect of this larger problem. To what extent has the church colluded with culture in its view and treatment of women?[70]

Individual bishops and groups of bishops wrote pastoral letters on the role of women in the church in the 1970s and 1980s.[71] These letters span a number of approaches to the question. Maureen Aggeler, in her perceptive examination of these letters, suggests that there are three paradigms that sum up these various episcopal positions.[72] In the first paradigm, some letters accept the cultural situation of women but attempt to reaffirm their dignity by alluding to the complementarity of men and women in their respective roles. A second paradigm searches for new and more collaborative models within the existing structures. A third paradigm represents a radical departure because it views the system rather than women as the problem. On this level, the need for conversion is actively entertained.

Christian families image "church" on the local level because they are indeed a domestic church. Pope John Paul II was both eloquent and emphatic on this point.[73] In other words, not only culture but theology insists on the crucial nature of parenting images, for a variety of reasons.

From a theological viewpoint, contemporary culture has yet to catch up with the Pauline doctrine of radical equality ("neither slave nor free, neither male nor female for all are one . . ." [Gal. 3:28]).[74] From the cultural viewpoint, contemporary acculturated American ecclesial attitudes may also need to be reviewed. Once again, it is not the issue of ordained ministries that urges this question but the more basic and general issue of women's role in the American church. Recent research, for example, has emphasized "the influence a mother's lifestyle has on her daughter's ability to develop an identity and continue religious practices, an indication that the 'evangelization' that takes place in a family can be either positive or negative."[75] One may reasonably expect that this is but one of many such connections to be made. Laudatory theological statements about the valued role of women, while important, do little to correct operational cultural attitudes that are perpetuated in religious guises. But such corrections are crucial, for liturgy celebrates an eschatology in which Paul's teaching on equality will finally be fully implemented at God's table: neither accents nor genders will hinder community. Our history on this question in the American church should make us all the more eager to take the Emmaus walk.

In examining briefly the situation of African American Catholics and Catholic women, my purpose was neither to denigrate the pastoral accomplishments of the American church nor to propose solutions. The American church's approach to African Americans and women reminds us of the connections between being church (i.e., the people of God) and doing liturgy, which are always worked out within a cultural context. Official positions on equality, for example, if contradicted consistently in practice, not only shred the "seamless garment of Christ" (to use Cardinal J. Bernardin's image) but also ask what the church means when it worships. When Paul applies the famous judgment theme ("You are eating and drinking judgment to yourself in your Eucharist" [1 Cor. 11:29]), his concern is that the uncontested pagan cultural assumptions of the Corinthian community are seriously damaging the ecclesial fabric for which the Eucharist is the privileged symbol ("Because the bread is one, we though many . . ." [1 Cor. 10:17]). In doing this, Paul was calling into question not the validity of the Eucharist but the credibility of this community as the body of Christ.

## Some Corollaries

As the American church slowly emerged from its immigrant character in the early twentieth century, four salient features remained from this experience. First, the parish church was still the center of neighborhood identity, even if it was no longer a strictly ethnic neighborhood. But the cultural Catholicism of some parishes confused ethnic cohesiveness and mutual support with ecclesial and sacramental challenges to deeper unity and openness. Second, the importance of Catholic education was such that often enough the school was built before the church. The contribution of women is particularly striking here. They not only staffed parish and diocesan schools but founded schools for African Americans and Native Americans, despite actively hostile resistance.[76] This type of witness, by its very nature, enlarges what popularly is understood as "church." Third, attendance at Sunday mass and frequent confession were so effectively emphasized that by the 1950s the American church had enviable statistics to prove the faithfulness of large numbers of Catholics. Despite these impressive figures, liturgical reformer Virgil Michel's question remains: How can American Catholics participate in the liturgy and yet be so impervious to the individualism and consumerism of their culture? (But at times it seemed as if confessions were more frequently made than communions were received.) Fourth, the American church on occasion would take public and sometimes prophetic positions on certain questions of morality and the social teaching of the popes. Yet immigrant reticence remained, and American Catholics sometimes felt compelled to prove themselves more American than their contemporaries with a resulting split between liturgy and public praxis (e.g., on the question of the slave trade and the post–Civil War treatment of African American Catholics as well as of Hispanics.)

The answer to our opening question about the influence of American culture and the American church on each other must be as complex and nuanced as the American Catholic scene itself. At times, the American church has been prophetic and countercultural in its use of liturgy and devotional practices to anchor people more firmly in their church and their culture (e.g., the immigrant period). At other times, the church has colluded with some of the more negative aspects of our culture so that the "law of worship" did not seem to affect the public Catholicism of its members. From the outset the liturgical movement in this country attempted to challenge this dichotomy.

## The American Prophets

In the earlier decades of the twentieth century, the quiet emergence of the liturgical movement in this country helped to prepare the American church for Vatican II and a new self-awareness as a local church. William

Halsey has used the evocative term "innocence" to characterize U.S. Catholicism in the years 1920–1940. Innocence, in this historical sense, refers to the bedrock convictions and values of nineteenth-century America: belief in a rational world, in the moral structure undergirding reality, and in the unlimited possibilities of the American dream.[77] Halsey maintains that, unlike other Americans, Catholics after World War I held on to the ideals and optimism of the previous century. Although some Catholics of the 1890s were accused of being too individualistic and optimistic, the Catholics of the 1920s who harbored these same attitudes were not considered heretics: "The methodology and presuppositions of Scholastic and neo-Thomistic philosophy provided the intellectual means for Catholics to appropriate large areas of the American experience without threat of appearing radical."[78]

Equally important for understanding the transition from an immigrant to a post–Vatican II church in this country, is the rise of the American liturgical movement in the decades before World War II.[79] Like its European counterparts, the American liturgical movement emphasized the connections between community, lay participation, and worship but also insisted on the connection between worship and social justice. Although the pioneers of the U.S. liturgical movement in this century were inspired by the work of European liturgical centers (such as Maria Laach in Germany and Mont César in Belgium) and by European theologians and liturgists such as M. Scheeben, J. Franzelin, K. Adam, Dom Marmion, Dom Beauduin, and Pius Parsch, it was the insight of Martin Hellriegel on the pastoral level and of Dom Virgil Michel on a theological and public level that made the crucial link in this country between liturgy and social life.[80]

The wide-ranging achievements of Dom Virgil Michel in the areas of social and economic awareness, religious education, and philosophy as well as theology and liturgy have received detailed study and appreciation.[81] Michel was founder and first editor of *Orate Fratres* (now *Worship*), a key force in popularizing the liturgical movement in this country. Michel was a monk of St. John's Abbey (Collegeville, Minnesota), and these Benedictines deserve a place of honor with their confreres at the great Abbey centers of liturgical scholarship and reform in Europe. They have continued Michel's forward-looking thought and activism in liturgical reform. What is not so well known is that Michel founded the Institute of Social Study at St. John's Abbey to discuss social questions and the related papal encyclicals, cooperatives and credit unions, Christian culture, and socioliturgical activities.[82] He took part in the National Catholic Rural Conference's work and was an early champion of Dorothy Day's and Peter

Maurin's Catholic Worker movement as well as the work of Baroness Catherine de Hueck.

But these activities were motivated by Michel's close reading of the encyclicals on labor and social justice. Another great pioneer of the U.S. liturgical movement, Hans Ansgar Reinhold, sums up Michel's insight: "For Virgil Michel the labor encyclicals of Leo XIII and the liturgical reforms of Pius X did not just by accident happen within one generation, but were responses to the cries of the masses for Christ. . . . They belonged together."[83]

In a 1935 article entitled "The Liturgy, the Basis of Social Regeneration," Michel answers his own question about whether the liturgy can give jobs or raise wages. He builds his response on Pius XI's *Quadragesimo Anno*, as well as on the encyclicals of Leo XIII and Pius X to argue the basic connection between worship and the world. Michel saw that the underlying but unexplicated theological argument for these papal positions was the Mystical Body of Christ, a point to which we shall return later.[84] He then offers a summary and well-known syllogism: Pius X tells us that the liturgy is the indispensable source of the true Christian spirit; Pius XI says that the true Christian spirit is indispensable for social regeneration. Hence, the conclusion: "The liturgy is the indispensable basis of Christian social regeneration."[85]

A few months later, he returned to this question in "Frequent Communion and Social Regeneration," where he took up *Quadragesimo Anno*'s challenge to return to gospel values as an antidote to modern selfish individualism.[86] Michel then asks how people can receive the Eucharist and still persist in their lack of compassion, their snobbishness, and their racial prejudice. Ultimately, his radical belief in the totally transforming nature of honest liturgy always leads to the same conclusion: liturgy builds anew a Christian social order.[87] Mark Searle has noted that the liturgical movement for Michel "was to restore non-individualistic modes of participation which would expose the faithful to the divinely established pattern of social life and thus contribute to the restoration of a Christian social order."[88]

Although it is not evident at first glance, Michel has a somewhat different ecclesiology from that which Pius XII was to propose in *Mystici corporis* (1943) and *Mediator dei* (1947). Michel's link between liturgy and the social order was a pastoral strategy with an implicit practical ecclesiology. In contrast to Pius XII's inward-looking idea of church with its sharp distinctions between hierarchy and laity, Michel insisted on the mission of the church in the world.[89] Both Hellriegel and Michel saw the practical dynamic of an ecclesial community that honestly hears the Word and praises God for it as the pastoral antidote to selfish individualism.[90] Michel saw the church as a missioned community and the parish as a local church long before these ideas were current in theological circles in this country.[91] Michel and Gerald Ellard also wrote and spoke often about the complementary idea of the church as "the people of God" and drew out the implications of the priesthood of the faithful.[92]

The teaching of Vatican II, of course, emphasized and developed these ideas forty years later. But in *Gaudium et spes,* the cultural dimension of being a Christian community was also boldly sketched in a way highly reminiscent of Michel's writings. The document speaks of people everywhere who are becoming conscious of themselves as "artisans and authors of the culture of their community" with the duty to build a world "based upon truth and justice."[93] But Mary Collins has insightfully noted that the crucial focus of Michel's work—the connection between active liturgical participation and the social reform and transformation—did not find a place in the constitution on the liturgy, *Sacrosanctum concilium* (1963).[94] In fact, it would seem to some that this connection of liturgy and sociocultural transformation was lost with the death of Michel, despite the efforts of the Liturgical Conference in this area.

Neither Michel nor Ellard was content to theorize about church and liturgy. Hellriegel had already implemented his liturgical ideas on the pastoral level. Now both men translated their ideas into catechetical language. Michel collaborated on a series of catechetical texts for grammar and high school levels in the thirties and authored college level texts, *Our Life in Christ* (1934) and *The Christian in the World* (1937) whose themes of liturgy and the mission of the church were well ahead of their time. In addition to more than twenty-five articles on religious education, Michel regularly returned to this subject in his editorials in *Orate Fratres.*[95]

Gerald Ellard, S.J., usually described as the first academically trained American liturgist, also saw the need for contemporary texts that would educate and inspire young people about the connections between liturgy and life. His college texts remain an example of an integrated approach to education and liturgy at its best.[96] Finally, as already noted, Monsignor Martin Hellriegel's pastoral implementation of the best available theological and liturgical insights did much to quiet the charges of liturgical elitism and utopianism that were current before Vatican II at the same time that it provided a praxis model from which others could learn.[97]

Michel's ideas were also taken up and developed by Hans Ansgar Reinhold (known as H.A.R.), a priest whose expulsion from Nazi Germany deepened his appreciation of the need for a more vital connection between liturgy and life. His sometimes trenchant style underlined his urgently repeated question: "How can people who have seen and experienced the 'organism' feeling of a new living parish or its new family in Christ fail to grasp the idea of a new organic order of society?"[98] Reinhold continued to challenge the American church with such questions in his articles in *Orate Fratres,* but his influence was limited to a comparatively small group of interested readers.

When the Liturgical Conference began its annual meetings in 1940, these same concerns found a national forum. As early as 1946 the Liturgical Conference resolved not to hold its annual meeting within the confines of any diocese where the law of segregation was enforced (this excluded quite a few cities at that time).[99] In his history of the U.S. Liturgical Conference, L. Madden points out that "literally no Liturgical Week was ever held which did not attempt to integrate the Christian's active involvement in the worship of the church with a lively concern for the reconstruction of society along Christian lines."[100] As Madden systematically documents the individual talks at the annual gatherings of the conference over the years, there are consistent references to the connection between a liturgical participation grounded in the Body of Christ and questions of racial prejudice, rural life, unionism, collective bargaining, Catholic Action, the political order, and social reconstruction.[101]

In retrospect, these years were exciting and constructive for an American approach to the theory and praxis of liturgy. Virgil Michel intuitively made crucial connections between liturgy and life and gave an early analysis of American individualism that is still relevant in some respects today. Monsignor Hellriegel demonstrated how liturgy could renew a parish even in the sometimes stifling and suspicious atmosphere of the preconciliar days. Michel's and Ellard's textbooks were already influencing American high school and college students at a time when seminarians were still reduced to reading the little that manual theology had to say about the liturgy. If the postconciliar liturgical implementation in this country has generally been considered successful, then much credit must given to these amazing pioneers.

The second guideline offered in the last chapter asked what kind of discernment and evaluation on cultural and religious values the liturgical life and moral witness of the American church prompted. The answer is that small prophetic circles of the liturgical movement in this country did challenge the American church to connect worship and life. This practical pastoral approach suited the unique history and gifts of the American church and its people. Even those who dismissed the preconciliar liturgical movement in this country as elitist and perhaps even heretical had at least heard the questions long before Vatican II gave the answers.

## The Postconciliar Catholic

For anyone born after Vatican II it is difficult to appreciate how challenging the conciliar emphasis on "being church"—that is, on being the "people of God"—and on the communal dimension of all liturgy sounded even to those acquainted with the liturgical movement. The revision of liturgical rites was to include this rediscovered ecclesial dimension. The American church already had developed a particularly strong sense of parish, in great part due to a strong Catholic school system in each diocese and to a complementary religious education program for those attending the public school system. Even on the eve of the Vatican council, many Catholic churches, especially in large cities, were at the center of an ethnic neighborhood. People identified themselves (and many still do) not by their street but by their parish ("I'm from St. Agnes").

Andrew Greeley has cogently argued that these neighborhood parishes continue many of the functions of the immigrant parish of the last century. Effective parishes remain a social center for parishioners and provide opportunities for them to share recreation and to be challenged by the needs of the larger world.[102] They connect the values of God's visible world with those of the world to come: "a successful parish is one in which laity and pastoral leaders (especially the pastor) share a vision of its meaning, when the community works together to continue God's presence in its time and place."[103]

It should not be surprising that when Catholics discuss the purposes of a parish or describe their own pastoral involvement, there are a wide range of answers. In general, the parish is described as the people of God, the body of Christ, a community, or as a place for religious activity with charitable outreach, liturgical life, and personal religious growth.[104] When questioned about their participation in parish life, 48 percent of American Catholics mention social or recreational participation, liturgical ministries, and education (in that order) as preferred forms of activity in the parish. Fifty-two percent do not participate in any activity of their parish.[105] Participation in social action programs ranks near the bottom of the scale (4 percent) while 48 percent of parishes have no programs that minister to the needy. The importance attached to gathering, for example, after Sunday mass for coffee also reflects the attitudes of parishioners about the nature and purpose of their parish.[106] Only 5 percent mention the mass as one of the activities that their parish does best. Some commentators on the Notre Dame Study point to this last statistic as showing that while the pastor may think of "the parish as a center of worship, their parishioners are more likely to think of it in terms of communal life and education."[107]

Another way of testing how American Catholics view their parish is to ask them what problems they bring there. Religious education seems to be the most consistent problem for which Catholics look to their parish for help, followed by the need to have their faith supported or for premarital counseling.[108] (From a more objective viewpoint, if parishes are classified according to the cluster of activities they engage in, then parishes from moderately complex to very complex all engage in mass, religious education, ministry to the sick and youth ministry.[109]) These results from the Notre Dame Study contrast with Gallup surveys of American Catholics. In the latter studies, the need for more light shed on moral issues ranks equally with the need to deepen their relationship with Christ (both 32 percent).[110] A related issue is the desire of a large number of Catholics to have more frequent informal relationships with their priests. As lay Catholics assume more roles within the parish, the priest is seen as the hub of their activity.[111] In fact, Greeley's study of young Catholics demonstrates the powerful influence a parish priest can have: not only do four-fifths of young Catholics approve of their pastor's performance but one-half admit that sermons have positively affected their religious development.[112]

What initially emerges from these studies of the American Roman Catholic parish is the variety and complexity of such gatherings. Catholics have rather high expectations of their parishes in many different areas. While liturgy is one of the more visible activities of a parish, it does not always seem to be the highest priority in the minds of parishioners. Gallup notes that while American Catholics approve, in the vast majority, the postconciliar changes, they do not assign high ratings for the manner of their implementation (47 percent rate implementation "excellent" or "good"; 46 percent rate it "fair" or "poor").[113] Furthermore, the economic and educational level of responding Catholics does affect their criticism of the church. Affluent, white, middle-class Catholics tend to be more positive toward the church's performance than less privileged groups.[114]

When theologians write about ecclesiology—that is, the theology of the church—they are usually concerned with the way the church should be. But what we have described above are some of the ways in which the church in this country is actually perceived and experienced by its members. These perceptions presumably affect the ways in which they participate on deeper levels in liturgical and nonliturgical activities. We might call these reactions "operational ecclesiologies," that is, attitudes and perceptions of Catholics about the purpose and the performance of their own local church that influence their participation in it.

Furthermore, American Catholics do not use the jargon of theologians. They do not normally, for example, speak of the "mission" of their "local church" but can be quite eloquent on the "outreach" a Catholic parish should have and the specific forms it should take. And in liturgical matters, they probably will not discuss the "epicletic" awareness of their celebrating fellow Catholics but they can be very insightful about the devotion and conversion that occur in their midst. As South American theologians have learned from the basic Christian communities in which they live and work, the "nontheological" awareness of committed Christians can sometimes put to shame the categories of theologians.

Before we turn to American Catholics' perceptions about the liturgical praxis of their parishes, we should examine Andrew Greeley's model of sacramental imagination of the American Catholic, for it provides a potential frame of reference for reviewing American liturgical practice.

## Greeley's Sacramental Imagination

The most obvious difference between the Tridentine and Vatican II liturgies is that Catholics participate and minister more in the current liturgy. The majority of Catholics sing during the liturgy, and most receive the Eucharist. People lector and minister the Eucharist. They seem to welcome the kiss of peace and its ritual and most receive the Eucharist under both species when it is offered. But Andrew Greeley is quick to remind us that these "gains" in liturgical activity should be judged by a more demanding criterion: Have the religious imagination and sensibility of American Catholics been enlarged or restricted by the post–Vatican II approach to worship? This is an important question that deserves some response.

Greeley has creatively examined the question of religious imagination in much of his later writing. His starting point is the classical Catholic emphasis on the "sacramental" or analogical imagination which finds God in this world. The distinct Catholic insistence on community, sacrament and symbol, and devotions are reflections of this conviction about the revelatory nature of all that God has created.[115] His argument connects religious experience of American Catholics with the pictures and images of the person's and community's religious imagination. The ways in which the apostles dealt with the experience of the resurrection afford an excellent example. The already existing Jewish images of Moses, Adam, prophet, and messiah are transformed by the early church as they are used to retrieve the Easter experience: "Jesus was 'like' a new Adam, and yet there was more to be said because the 'Adam' story had been changed as a result of the Easter experience."[116]

Thus, the creative action of the preconscious summons up the vast repertory of intuitive personal knowledge to produce symbols which accurately reflect the experience.[117] The experience of Catholics is rooted in the deeply positive theology of God's creation, and this experience is radically broadened by their new creation in Christ. The imagery and story of their religious experience as used by the religious imagination "shape [our] sacramental encounters with others and have been shaped by prior sacramental encounters with others."[118]

Greeley constructed testing that inquired about the ways in which people image Jesus, Mary, and God as judge, mother, stern, warm, challenging, etc. Through statistical procedures he was then able to measure response patterns to religious imagination questions and to arrive eventually at scales in which "Jesus and Mary are pictured as 'warm,' God is 'mother/lover,' and heaven 'a paradise and action-filled like our own.' . . ."[119] Greeley notes that people who rate high on the religious imagination scale are "more likely to go to Mass every week, to receive communion every week, and to pray every day."[120]

Greeley's subsequent criticism of the postconciliar liturgy must be understood in terms of his insistence that the sacramentality of life experiences and their retrieval through the religious imagination must be connected with worship: "The Eucharistic liturgies of the post–Vatican II Church are not, in most instances, grace-filled moments that touch the religious imaginations of the congregation and help people see the links between what is being celebrated (however poorly) and their lives. In other words, correlation is not occurring in most liturgies."[121] In his most recent work, Greeley has expanded these ideas to suggest that these religious symbols are so intricately bound up with our total experience that they give meaning to any experience that touches on the ultimate questions of human living.[122]

The first beneficial result of Greeley's work is that it calls into question the ways in which theologians and liturgists discuss the appropriation of faith and sacrament in the United States. Some of our most cherished theories may be challenged by the contrary weight of evidence from sociological analysis. One of the most creative parts of Greeley's work, it seems to me, is his effort to uncover the connections for American Catholics between imagination and worship. The important corollary of these connections is the loyalty factor of American Catholics, that is, their basic love for the church and its liturgy even when disagreeing with its teaching. A second result of Greeley's work is the need to reexamine the studies of the American church for data that can be read in a more positive fashion. With these cautions in mind, we turn to the implementation of the postconciliar liturgical reforms of Vatican II by the American Roman Catholic church.

## American Liturgical Participation

Much has been made of the dramatic decline of the attendance of American Catholics at weekly mass in the 1960s. Greeley has argued that this decline was temporary and was due to Paul VI's position on birth control, not on dissatisfaction with the liturgical changes of Vatican II.[123] American Catholics approve of the council's reforms by a large majority (67 percent), and younger Catholics are even more in favor of these reforms.[124] In any case, eucharistic participation of Catholics has stabilized in this country.[125] In fact, Gallup points out that there has been an overall increase in religious activities among Catholics between 1977 and 1986.[126]

Among the purposes of the parish, Catholics rank liturgy fourth in terms of importance.[127] Involvement in liturgical ministries placed second in type of participation chosen by American Catholics.[128] The Notre Dame Study notes that differences in prioritizing participation in parish life is explained at least partially by the preconciliar or postconciliar ideas of church that parishioners have. A major finding of the Notre Dame Study (and much contested by Andrew Greeley) is that although American Catholics may have adopted the conciliar terminology and images of a communal Catholicism, there is a great deal of self-centered religiosity and individualism (a topic to which we will return).[129]

Not surprisingly, the relation between the liturgical celebrant and the community directly affected the performance of individual parts of the mass.[130] Priests who omitted opening remarks, for example, or a welcome to the congregation usually had a generally poor rapport with them, resulting in less community awareness and poor congregational participation.[131] Where homilies based on the readings of the day were given, there was a higher degree of engagement and devotion among the congregation, while homilies based on traditional doctrine "were more often accompanied by relatively low levels of popular participation in the Mass."[132] The congregation also seems to appreciate liturgical situations in which they are expected to sing a portion of, but not all of, the music at the liturgy.[133]

The Notre Dame Study emphasizes that parishioners' attitudes toward the liturgy are directly tied to their perception of the parish as a whole: liturgy is usually an accurate reflection of the life of the community.[134] Where homilies are perceived as relevant to their daily lives, where there is a wide pastoral concern for the particular problems of this community of parishioners, there is usually a lively participation in the liturgy. This seems to be borne out even by data that note that only 3 percent of parish-connected Catholics (11 percent in the suburbs) "shop around" for better liturgies.[135] Enjoyment in liturgical participation (28 percent), the need to be in contact with God (37 percent) or to receive the Eucharist (20 percent) or to hear the Word of God (19 percent) are the important motives for Catholics who celebrate.[136]

From this overview several impressions emerge. First, although the current levels of liturgical participation are fairly high, it is the potential for expanded participation that is most striking. Where parishioners discern a pastoral respect for their gifts and pastoral zeal for the relevancy of the Word of God, there will be deepened liturgical and social response on the part of parishioners. Second, the final assessment of liturgical practice should be done in relation to the larger pastoral concerns of the community. If religious education and care of the poor, and not liturgical matters, rank first in parishioners' minds, then it may indicate that the connections between liturgy and life are better recognized by Catholics than they are sometimes given credit for.

On the other hand, more radical critics of the American mainline churches would probably not agree with this last statement. The style of liturgy and the fairly comfortable content of the Sunday homily, they argue, only reenforce and prolong the smug righteousness and self-centered concerns of many Christians.[137] These criticisms should not be lightly dismissed. In the following chapters, we will return to this problem of what an authentic gospel church might look like in the pluralistic contexts of American society.

## Some Conclusions

Pluralism continues to be an important characteristic of our American culture and society. The American church of both the nineteenth and twentieth centuries reflects that pluralism in the complexity of its attitudes and practice. This complexity shows the potential for growth as a local church and also reaffirms the problems of liturgical ministry. As late twentieth century America continues to experience large waves of immigrants, reminiscent of nineteenth-century immigration and its pastoral challenges, the American church will be tested to the limit in its ability to facilitate the appropriate ecclesial and liturgical expressions of this diversity.

In response to the cultural and social problems that massive immigration stirred up in the nineteenth century for the American church, there was a radical and creative rethinking of pastoral and liturgical priorities. Not surprisingly, liturgy strengthened the Catholic and cultural identity of these immigrants. What initially might appear as a conservative move on the part of the American episcopacy was probably the best course of pastoral action that could have been taken. Further, Timothy Smith's general assertion also seems to be particularly true of these Catholic immigrants: "Migration and resettlement, then, altered the relationship between faith and ethnic identity by redefining the boundaries of peoplehood and by intensifying religious reflection and commitment."[138]

It is precisely this type of foundational experience that should make us reexamine the ecclesial and liturgical life of the American church in the nineteenth century and should also provide a possible criterion for looking at these same dimensions in the twentieth-century church. On the other hand, the examples of African American Catholics and Catholic women did not suggest a redefining of boundaries but rather an unprophetic and unreformed cultural position. How are the connections between church and liturgy affected in such situations?

A very different picture resulted from our overview of the Hispanic immigration and presence. For a variety of reasons, the initial response of the American church did not meet the sociocultural and ecclesial needs of Hispanics. As the American bishops noted, it was the "domestic church" of the Hispanic family and its popular religion that maintained some connections with the institutional church. This pastoral situation has gradually changed in the last four decades. There has been a mutual enrichment of the Anglo and Hispanic areas of the American church. In particular, the Hispanic notion of *encuentro* (the gathering of hierarchy and representatives of ecclesial communities and ministries), of ministries rooted in the domestic as well as the institutional community, and of the connection of popular and liturgical devotion has provided insight for the mission of the American church. We will examine the possibilities of this notion in future chapters.

The twentieth-century descendants of immigrants retained the loyalty and devotionalism of their forebears. What had changed was their social and educational position which in good part, it might be argued, owed something to the American church. The pioneering work of early twentieth century liturgical activists like Hellriegel, Michel, and Ellard reached out far more widely than the readers of *Orate Fratres* and the groups of the Catholic Worker and Grail movements: these liturgists had begun, in a distinctly American fashion, to connect liturgy and the sociocultural world of the United States. In response to the questions at the end of chapter 1, it should be noted that Michel and his liturgical colleagues were indeed attempting to make relevant connections between liturgical life and moral witness in the American church. Whether these initial attempts were continued will be discussed in the following chapters.

In the years immediately preceding and during Vatican II, the Liturgical Conference's annual meetings had swelled from a few hundred devoted souls to several thousand at the meeting in St. Louis in 1964. This interest reflected the profound conciliar changes that were anticipated (or dreaded) by many American Catholics.

The naïve optimism, as well as the exciting ferment of liturgical and ecclesial reform of those postconciliar days, has dissipated. Questions of liturgical change have given way to more difficult concerns about whether many contemporary parishes reflect the gospel qualities of authentic Christian community or have simply become centers for religious validation and comfort. Thus, it is time to reassess the American Catholic parish as a gathered community of witness and worship.

# CHAPTER THREE

# A Test of Liturgy:
# The Gathered American Community

When, as recounted in chapter 1, my guests from Germany had experienced the Sunday Eucharist in two Washington parishes, they immediately saw these experiences as typifying the American church. These liturgical experiences were understood from their German perspective as typical of a community of Catholics who live in the American culture. Just as perspective in painting invites the viewer to look at reality in a certain way, so a particular culture invites participants and onlookers to understand and live life from a certain viewpoint.

One of culture's most important perspectives is its understanding of what constitutes community, of how and why people are together. In the German language, for example, a clear distinction is made between *Gemeinschaft* (community) and *Gesellschaft* (business group). In English we distinguish a community from a club, a family from a corporation. Some charge that within our American culture what sometimes passes for community may, in fact, be a life-style enclave (sharing certain patterns of consumption or dress, for example, but not interdependent).[1] On a religious level, the New Testament offers certain identifying marks of a Christian community (e.g., belief in a crucified and risen Christ), but that community will also take on certain characteristics of a particular culture (e.g., the differences between the early Judeo-Christian communities and the Gentile Christian communities).

In chapter 1 we discussed one characteristic of any authentic Christian community, that of being a "new creation" that exemplified the transforming effects of gospel life within a created and cultural world. When we then described the worship of such a community, the general terms of "thanksgiving/blessing" had to be translated into the cultural experience and expressions of each community. Not only will the language be different, but often the whole system of symbols will be unique to each culture.

When Paul evangelizes the Gentiles, he not only speaks their language (Greek) but also employs aspects of their cultural life to illustrate his arguments (e.g., the sacrifices offered in pagan temples). The brief overview, in the first chapter, of how the Roman Catholic church has dealt with various cultures offered some historical examples.

In chapter 2 the past and the current history of the worship of the American church suggested other cultural examples. Democracy, for example, has cultural effects that appear in our language and in our religious perspectives on people and values. American Catholics of the colonial period valued religious toleration as part of their cultural heritage, a heritage that most European Catholics never knew. The American church, for the most part, dealt creatively with the sociocultural situation of immigrants through ecclesial and liturgical/devotional bonding. This same creativity was not so much in evidence in the case of the Hispanic and African American Catholics. Catholic women who have been the mainstay of the American church in good times and bad are still in dialogue with the bishops on a reexamination of their role in the ministries of the church. Recent studies of the American church show a postconciliar community of loyal if questioning faithful. Certainly Greeley's explanation of the "sacramental imagination" and loyalty factor of American Catholics has definite cultural traits. The current profile of the American church, as revealed in the different sociological studies, shows other examples of cultural influence.

This chapter continues these lines of discussion. From our initial look at the American church, what does it mean for American Catholics to be "gathered," that is, to be an ecclesial community with certain tasks and mission in a definite historical period and in a very specific culture? The Word of God not only gathers the church but also challenges the communal as well as the individual assumptions of the faithful. Is the local church more open to mission because of the liturgical celebrations of that Word? This kind of question suggests another: Has the American church "received" or only implemented the reforms of Vatican II? As a test case of "reception," how has the Word of God, as celebrated in the postconciliar reforms, benefited from the specific cultural strengths and values of the American church?

## Whose Church?

The pre–Vatican II church in the United States is sometimes better described by novelists than by ecclesiologists. American Catholic novelists such as Flannery O'Connor and Joseph Powers very accurately sketched the outlines of the modern American Catholic church. Although still very much the latecomer and immigrant, this church of the 1940s and 1950s was also becoming aware of its strengths: an enormous population of U.S. Catholics that crowded confessionals and Sunday masses, that filled downtown churches on weekdays that were holy days of obligation, that reluctantly but regularly ate fish, that generously supported large Catholic educational systems and parish "plants," that could be counted on to fill a stadium to overflowing on the annual Holy Name Sunday, whose image of the priest was Bing Crosby and Fulton J. Sheen.

The post-Vatican II church in the United States presents a transformed profile: actively lay rather than clerical, a local church rather than a branch office of a worldwide institution, part of a world church rather than a European church, a church that encouraged new social and political participation rather than almost exclusively ritual participation, a prophetic church rather than a museum of older cultural models of church.[2] This postconciliar church brought with it changes that were generally welcomed by American Catholics, once the initial shock wore off. Although liturgical changes were the most immediate points of contact with Vatican II's reforms, American Catholics began to understand that a more vibrant and demanding notion of "church" was also being encouraged not by words so much as by actions. Notions of parish council and lay lectors and ministers invited a wider participation in being church. The catechetical movement that was engendered by the "new" (actually classical) conciliar theology educated and implicated thousands of American Catholics in the teaching ministries of the church.

All these changes are rooted in the startling way in which Vatican II retrieved a theology of church that was classical in its inspiration. In the first major document issued by the council in 1963, the phrase "the wondrous *sacrament* of the whole church" is taken from one of the prayers of the preconciliar Holy Saturday liturgy.[3] Later, the council in several documents described the church as "in the nature of a *sacrament*," that is, a symbol of communion with God and union among people and a "universal sacrament of salvation."[4] The use of "sacrament" to describe the church suggests the saving and dynamic presence of God celebrated in God's world. Such descriptions of "being church" suggest how the mystery of God's salvation touches us and how that, in turn, affects the reasons and the way we are together in this world. Expressed differently, the council describes the actual practice (praxis) of being church as the powerful symbol of all that God intends for us. It is not surprising, then, that the council sought its practical descriptions of church in the actual liturgical gathering of Christians in God's world in the process of participating in the building of God's peaceable reign: "every liturgical celebration, because it is an action of Christ the Priest and of his Body, which is the Church, is a sacred action surpassing all others. No other action of the Church can equal its efficacy by the same title and to the same degree."[5]

This connection between the church and liturgy, conceived as a dynamic action, is a classical one.[6] Augustine, for example, as a bishop, had learned a practical ecclesiology that connected the process of salvation, the worship of the gathered church, and being living stones in the temple of God.[7] In his theological battle with the Donatists on the question of what constitutes valid sacraments, Augustine had to distinguish between "the communion of sacraments" and "the society of saints" (communio sacramentorum, societas sanctorum) or, as Yves Congar put it, between "the church which passes away . . . and the church which remains, the church, a mixture of the good and bad . . . and the church without spot or wrinkle, the church of signs, thus of servitude, and the church of Reality, thus of liberty."[8] For Augustine, the authenticity of being a church of "saints" was directly connected to the fruitfulness of sacraments celebrated. In other words, Augustine as both pastor and theologian, insisted that sacraments and worship were meant to be much more than outward and valid signs. In fact, they were crucial for the church to be both church and sacrament.

In contemporary theology, these connections have taken on new importance, especially because the notion of "action" and "communicative action" has been a source of new insight about God's message of salvation and the church's mission to evangelize.[9] Communicative actions are rooted in (though not limited to) language (which is itself a cultural creation) and might be described as enabling understanding and consensus.[10] Such symbolic actions invite productive interaction and consensus that are grounded in deeply held convictions. In this approach, there is great emphasis on dealing with all of lived reality ("the life-world") in a critical way. Although the model can be critiqued for trying to achieve too much, its concerns are certainly congenial to anyone asking what a missioned church community should be like.[11] Paul Lakeland has appropriately described the church as "a community of communicative action," that is, the faith community that enables individuals to appropriate God's message and the experience of redemption.[12] This is the ideal, but Lakeland warns that it is one thing to call the church the People of God and quite another to own the consequences of such action.[13]

A local church, for example, has to evangelize within a specific culture that includes both communicative actions and distorted communication. Historically, that church can become so identified with the culture that it no longer adequately distinguishes between the radical values of the gospel and accepted values of the culture. (The cases of certain minorities cited in chapter 2 might serve as examples of this problem.) Second, the church may have ceased to examine critically its actions precisely because they are acceptable within that culture. The result is a distortion of communication. One example might be the uncritical way in which the American church accepted the cultural stereotypes and prejudices about women. Distorted communication inevitably results and betrays itself in both language and action.[14] Another historical example would be the attitudes of the majority of American bishops toward the question of African American priests.[15] Such cultural blind spots distort the message and witness of the church; and, although they cannot touch the sacramental integrity of the church's worship, they certainly do not encourage the fruitfulness of its celebration.

To "be church" and to "celebrate the liturgy" are communicative actions of the most radical kind.[16] In celebrating the sacraments in public, the church defines its relation to the world as God's creation in which God's mystery of salvation is being realized. These sacramental actions, precisely because they are communicative actions, constantly "re-new" the church in what is most essential to her mission to the world: communication of God's mystery of salvation.[17] Sacraments are not defined by our cultural world but rather make visible God's definition of reality to that world. The sacraments are prophetic action words that make God's future promise already experienced in our present time. Within this perspective, sacraments are not simply to be performed but to accomplish God's intention—the salvation of the world.[18] ("Salvation of the world," however, must be translated into the cultural ways in which we perceive and experience that reality.) Although contemporary theology expresses these views in twentieth-century language, Augustine certainly understood this idea as the "fruitfulness" of sacraments within a church whose mission to the world was never separated from its liturgy.

One of the the best ways, then, to develop an adequate idea of "church" is to scrutinize a liturgical gathering of Christians. Both the Word of God and the sacraments conspire to teach these gathered Christians what it means to be "church." It is the Spirit of God who convokes Christians in a liturgical assembly just as that same Spirit had opened the way for each of these Christians to be baptized in the name of the Trinity. It is the Spirit of God who has anointed them to hear not simply words *about* God but the Word *of* God. The

Word of God as proclaimed and received is a radical (Latin *radix,* "root") and communicative action of the gathered community.


## Word or Words?

The Word of God forms the first part of any liturgical celebration because it always invites a specific group of Christians to a more profound communion, that is, a deeper unity. Jean-Marie Tillard has described the purpose of this communion:

> Christians receive from the Spirit the vocation to be together (cf. 2 Cor. 1:7; Phil. 1:5) in *communion* with Christ in his courageous and costly involvement for the coming of the Kingdom. What we call today the apostolic task of the community and its effort for the renewal of human society are not a Christian realm added over and above *communion.* They come . . . from its most profound root: communion with Christ himself.[19]

The practical corollary is that communion is the result of a constant *listening* to the Word, not only as individuals but also as a group gathered by the Spirit. The very unity of this gathering is rooted in the growing awareness of what the Word of God calls them to—common purposes and shared tasks. Whenever sacrament is celebrated, it can never be simply a repetition of a familiar ritual. The Word of God once again transforms the meaning of the Eucharist or baptism or anointing of the sick. The vocation of this group to be together as church is renewed and widened in sacramental celebration.

The liturgical reforms of Vatican II did more than give us English translations of the liturgy. These reforms restored the importance of the calling down of the Holy Spirit (the *epiclesis*) in the eucharistic prayers as well as in other sacramental celebrations. In the Eucharist the Spirit is called down over people as well as over the gifts to be transformed. In the power of the Spirit, this community prays to be the body of Christ. These ritual actions reflect the perennial conviction of the church that if the Holy Spirit is sincerely called down, then the Spirit is given. As Jesus was anointed by the Spirit for his mission, so are contemporary Christians.

Without such an assurance, listening to the Word of God would be a terrifying and frustrating experience. Like the stammering prophet, we would ask God to send someone else to do such work. Paul's argument in Romans 8, however, assures a liturgical gathering that the Spirit alone knows our redemptive needs and pleads accordingly for us. In the Pentecost description of the transformation of the terrified disciples into ardent proclaimers of God's Word, the bridging of the cultural boundaries of the ancient world is dramatically shown by listing Jews from all the races who hear one common language.

The Pentecost scene is still a paradigm for every local church. Once anointed by the Spirit, Peter and the others immediately begin to evangelize. But, as we saw in chapter 2, effective evangelization must take place within a specific culture in order to be heard. Culture's meanings and God's meanings must confront one another. This process continues each time a parish community hears the Word of God. The community brings to each listening the values and meanings of its culture. Honest listening uncovers the cultural strengths that will support gospel living at the same time that it may point to a conflict of meanings, for example, on the question of how money or leisure time should be used in that same culture. Honest listening may also challenge the sense of mission in a community. What type of outreach does the gospel inspire a group of Christians to make? What are the gifts in a community that have not yet been shared with the world around them? Again, Paul VI's criterion for an evangelized community is that they, in turn, evangelize others. In more practical language this means that the community begins to hear more of God's questions than before and that these questions have their full impact only within the cultural context of the listeners.

One of the reasons why this liturgical call to proclaim the Word that we have celebrated is so difficult to implement is that a local church must do this in a very specific historical time and in an already existing culture. Michael Warren has caught the nature of the problem in his cogent phrase "the materiality of discipleship."[20] Every time a local church has underestimated the difficulty of implementing the Word in its own cultural situation, there has been a problem. Church history warns us of local churches that have gone before us where the gospel was still read but no longer listened to or where culture's meanings had simply replaced the gospel's meanings. The late New Testament writings are not hesitant about narrating such problems. Inevitably, part of the problem is inadequate translation of the gospel values into the cultural terms of a community's situation. Timothy, for example, writes to an experienced Christian community struggling in the cosmopolitan situation of Ephesus, while Titus's listeners are addressed somewhat differently since their less complicated rural situation in Crete is appreciated. Although the basic gospel message is the same in these two pastoral letters, its implementation requires a cultural sensitivity.

The African American Catholic church offers one salient example of how the Word of God must be celebrated within a specific culture. Clarence Rivers catches the specific cultural heritage of black celebrations by making a distinction between the oral African tradition and the ocular Western tradition.[21] With this distinction he recalls the Western church's tendency to intellectualize religion as opposed to the African insistence on the connection between poetic insight and religious experience. Rivers notes that he never heard a black minister urging his people to attend a religious celebration without promising, "We're going to have a good time." and that "to have church" is synonymous with having a good time.[22]

The experience of slavery in this country, however, gave a sharp focus to such gifts, as African black Christians spoke the Word of God to one another, a tradition that the black spirituals have canonized: "Recalling the melodies of Mother Africa; using the hymnody of a new land; recalling the stories from the Bible; and using clapping, moaning, shouting, waving hands, and dance, this community sang songs of life and death, suffering and sorrow, love and judgment, grace and hope, justice and mercy. . . . And in singing these 'spirituals', they expressed all manner of things."[23] The powerful and poetic imagery of these spirituals captures what proclamation of the Word of God means and provides a model for interaction with that Word. Even when these spirituals are heard in a secular concert (and thus, out of context), they still retain a power to move an audience.

These African differences are summarized in one telling example. Rivers cites the preaching of Martin Luther King in which many of his classical references might seem over the heads of his listeners but were used to involve his audience not in intellectual but in poetic participation (e.g., "And I would see Plato, Aristotle, Socrates, Euripides and Aristophanes assemble around the Parthenon . . ."). Rivers concludes: "A people brought up in an oral culture are not only not literal-minded; their whole approach to life is different. They have a different way of knowing and relating to the surrounding world, a way that is based on the way in which the other senses perceive when not dominated and muted by the sense of sight."[24] His reflections suggest another example from an earlier Africa. How often does Augustine note the enthusiastic reaction of his congregation when in his preaching, for example, he has employed a particularly striking rhetorical expression or suggested an insight that has touched their experience: "You receive him hungrily, in feasting on him you praise him; *what's the meaning of your shouts, if no food has reached your minds?*"[25]

As we continue to examine the gathered Christians of the local church in the United States, we will see that the mission the Word of God gives to contemporary Christian communities is no less complex than in the first

Pentecost situation, where the peoples of many cultures were assembled. As Americans, we inevitably bring our cultural expectations to the building up of the local Christian community.

## An Inculturated Church?

At a recent religious education congress of my home diocese of Brooklyn, I was amazed to hear the number of languages that were used at the proclamation of the Gospel and the prayers of the faithful—Haitian French, Vietnamese, Philippine dialect, and so on. As a white, lower-middle-class Roman Catholic in Brooklyn in the 1930s and 1940s, with the exception of the languages spoken in a few ethnic parishes, I heard one spoken language—English. Among my parochial grammar school classmates, there were quite a few second-generation Italian Americans whose parents spoke English with a strong accent and whose grandparents spoke no English at all. Although their cultural heritage was still somewhat intact, my classmates were more American than Italian.

Today many dioceses are stretched to their pastoral limits in trying to minister to the more recent immigrant tides not only in terms of their languages but also in view of their cultures.[26] The Notre Dame Study of Catholic Parish Life, for example, acknowledges that Spanish-speaking parishes were not included since their unique cultural background would require a separate study.[27] In fact, the 1985 U.S. census gave the figure of 16.9 million Hispanics, which would constitute 40 percent of the possible Catholic population of this country and would represent at least six different Hispanic groups.[28] There are also a number of Catholics from other cultural traditions, such as the Africans and Vietnamese.

Less obvious but no less complex is the cultural problem of white Catholics. The suburbs were not, I suspect, filled with Roman Catholics just before and during World War II. Many Catholic parishes still consisted mainly of blue collar workers whose children might be the first in their family to go to college (or even, to high school). Greeley has reminded us that today's American Catholics are among the better educated and more upwardly mobile population:

> When the Second Vatican Council began, Catholics had achieved rough equality with white Protestants. Twenty years later they have achieved economic occupational superiority. Parish priests facing a typical Catholic congregation on Sunday must realize that they are now preaching to a group which is or is about to become, with the exception of the Jews, the most affluent denominational group in American society.[29]

These facts help us to see in sharper profile many of today's Catholic parishes in this country and to appreciate the changes in cultural as well as sociological terms. In the last quarter of a century, in which the liturgical changes of the council have been in place, it is the makeup of the parish that has quietly changed.

## Parish as Microcosm of the Local Church

The Catholic church in nineteenth-century America has received high marks from historians for its pastoral creativity and sensitivity to both the spiritual and cultural needs of the waves of European immigrants that flooded our shores. At that same time, the church's response to Mexican and African American Catholics, as we saw in chapter 2, was less than adequate. How has the postconciliar American church measured up to the challenges of its time?

The Notre Dame Study presents a profile of personal attitudes on the purpose of religious belonging. Some Catholics' religious concerns are focused on themselves and their needs ("agentic") while others see their religious praxis as sensitizing them to the needs of others ("communal"). Using these categories, the study concludes that 39 percent of core Catholics are exclusively agentic or individualistic (e.g., have concerns about self-improvement, reward and punishment, etc.) while only 18 percent are primarily communal (e.g., have concerns about peace and justice, social disharmony).[30] Even when parishioners use the postconciliar ecclesial descriptions of parish as "the people of God," they still employ self-centered language when dealing with priorities, decisions and values.

Philip Murnion's study of some 350 parishes in the archdiocese of New York seems to reflect similar results. He found that 29 percent of these parishes had a careful balance between community building and outreach to the larger community ("the theopolitan parish"), while 17 percent concentrated on their mission to the world ("the public action parish"). Another 25 percent were active but inward looking ("the sectarian parish"), while 28 percent provided sacramental participation but not a sense of mission ("the sacramental service parish").[31]

Although there is nothing surprising in these figures, they would, at least initially, seem to indicate that American individualism has had some influence among Roman Catholics. If we compare this picture with the one that Robert Wuthnow gives of the American Protestant churches of the same period, we can find some similarities and dissimilarities with the Roman Catholic community. Wuthnow describes the general trend of the American denominations as "a service agency for the fulfillment of its individual members."[32] Although he maintains that Roman Catholics were less affected by this trend than other groups, there is certainly some resonance with the praxis of many Catholic parishes. The findings of the Notre Dame Study and Murnion seem to indicate that the bonding of the parish communities derived mainly from individual devotion and from pastoral care principally directed toward individual needs.

Not surprisingly, Wuthnow views this American religious individualism as a mode of cultural adaptation.[33] American culture's emphasis was focused on the individual's internalized commitment and responsibility. As a case in point, Wuthnow cites the American bishops' letter of 1947: "The moral regeneration which is recognized as absolutely necessary for the building of a better world must begin by *bringing the individual back to God* and to an awareness of his responsibility to God."[34] While the passage may be read as an example of fostering American individualism in religious terms (as Wuthnow seems to), another reading might be a classical expression of the call to conversion, which always leads to the participation in the church community. But, given the period in which it was written (1947), Wuthnow's interpretation is probably correct.

What was new in the approach of the American Protestant churches in the post–World War II period was a fresh concern for socialization as the best way of reinforcing values.[35] The Roman Catholic reaction was somewhat similar, though for different reasons. John Coleman has pointed out that the favorable American ambiance for Catholic advancement evoked a relatively approving, if not unprophetic, attitude on the part of the American church leadership toward the American political, social, and economic ethos.[36] He cites Richard Hofstadter's judgment that American Catholics up to the 1950s had not so much influenced but rather been influenced by the American environment.[37]

One of the most disputed of American cultural traits is individualism. In looking at the postconciliar church in America, some studies would describe the church as individualistic, but others would strongly object to this characterization. This question might serve as a good example of a potential clash between our culture and God's Word. It will also be crucial for arriving at some idea of what the American Catholic understands by a parish community.

## American Individualism and the Gospel Challenge

I take individualism, as used in this discussion, to mean an excessive preoccupation with self that relegates the needs of others to a secondary level.[38] Robert Bellah and his colleagues have argued that American individualism with its emphasis on private concerns has spawned basic discourses or languages of excessive self-interest in our culture.[39] Language is, after all, an important expression of a culture, for it accurately reflects the values and meanings of the culture in which it is used. Language also affects the way we listen to others as well as the way in which we speak to them. It is not surprising, for example, to find an anthropologist like Mary Douglas examining the speech patterns of different social groups in London because they mirror the sociocultural codes of those groups.[40]

In the case of our American culture, Bellah and his colleagues have argued that our economic, political, familial, and religious languages have assumed cultural shapes. (Language is employed here as a moral discourse with its own vocabulary and moral logic.[41]) Most middle-class Americans, they argue, speak two languages: the first language is the principal discourse of American individualism, while second languages gather up some of our other American moral traditions (the biblical and republican traditions). These critics insist that American individualism wants moral language to reflect exclusively the needs of the self-centered individual.[42]

Once this demand is accepted, there is no moral language left in which to confront seriously the problems of community, of justice, of caring for others and of being authentically religious. Groups of individualists would have their vision restricted to mutual needs and shared life-styles.[43] In fact, Bellah and his colleagues charge, as noted earlier, that American individualists confuse life-style enclaves with authentic community. On the other hand, some would argue that individualism may also connote a strongly motivated and self-directed person who, as a result, can be more compassionate. Mother Teresa would be an example of this understanding of individualism.[44] This type of individualism would also be conducive to community (e.g., the vigorous religious community of sisters that have been attracted by the strong charism of Mother Teresa.)

As already noted, white American Catholics have moved from the socioeconomic and educational margins of our society to becoming an increasingly affluent and well-educated group.[45] This is in sharp contrast, for example, to the financial situation of Hispanics.[46] Presumably, upwardly mobile American Catholics might be more susceptible to the temptations of individualism. Catholics who have had a religious education and who still hear the Word of God proclaimed each Sunday might conceivably retain the key vocabulary and practices of their faith without being necessarily challenged in their individualistic concerns. The social and moral concerns of such groups would eventually be reduced to the least common denominator. But is this true?

In the ongoing debate that *Habits of the Heart* has generated, much ink has been spilled over the question of what is meant by "community." Some critics discern a certain nostalgia for the "little community" in this debate. They then proceed to criticize such people for running away from the complexity of contemporary living and the refusal to accept the ambiguities that come from freedom.[47] Others would argue that it is the notion of society, and not that of community, that has held Americans together.[48] Without trying to resolve this debate, we can profit from the discussion. The basic question is whether the church has an understanding of community that is not only authentically biblical but also one that is viable in the complex cultural setting of the United States.[49] Do Catholics share with their fellow Americans a form of individualism that tolerates belonging but not authentic community? Obviously, the way in which individualism is defined is crucial. Further, no matter what definition is used, it will have to account for the highly positive profile that Greeley and others give of the American church. We will return to this question in subsequent chapters.

## A Community of the Word

During the 1960s and 1970s in this country, a therapeutic model of community became quite popular. This model took the notions of mutual healing, growth, and intimacy and constructed the notion of community around these therapeutic elements. The caricature of such a community was a group of needy and self-absorbed people who spent their time holding each other's hand. Christopher Lasch and other social critics excoriated this model of community as being inward looking and unrealistic. Some theologians, on the other hand, used this therapeutic model to construct the notion of a church community. The result was usually an unrealistic and privatized description of a sect that had little to do with a mission to the world.

When Vatican II retrieved the rich multidimensional notion of church as found in the New Testament and the writings of the theologians like Augustine and Origen, the pastoral result was to experiment with different ecclesial models that took into account the particular sociocultural situations of people. The so-called base communities in South and Central America provided one successful example of such experimentations. In this country there were efforts, for example, to subdivide parishes into smaller units or cells in order to facilitate more interaction and responsibility among parishioners. Religious communities in this country also experimented with different models of community that would engender a more evangelical style of life and prayer.

What is the result of this postconciliar search for community? As both Greeley and the Notre Dame Study testify, many American Catholics seem more aware and challenged by their current parishes than perhaps their parents were. This does not mean that they have found some ideal parish, but it does indicate that even imperfect pastoral structures can successfully call out the generosity and service of more people than one might think.[50] But parishioners' satisfaction with their parish is only one side of the question. Allowing for different kinds of emphasis in different kinds of parish (e.g., a parish of mostly retired people as compared with one that mainly comprises young families), does the structure of the church community enable it to draw out the gifts of its parishioners and to give witness to the world? This is not to make the church a sect but rather to insist that there is both a mission dimension and a public dimension to American church life.[51] To return to Rahner's insight, the liturgy of the church is tied to the liturgy of the world.[52]

There is perhaps something to be learned from the process employed by the committee of American bishops who drafted the letters on the economy and nuclear disarmament. The bishops were aware that such topics which are not considered strictly religious (or religious at all, in the minds of some), would involve visceral reactions as well as intellectual positions from American Catholics. In contrast to their usual procedure, the bishops invited participation in dealing with these complex and disputed issues. They listened to interested parties and tried to arrive at some consensus in these matters in view of Christ's teaching. Naturally this kind of process entails listening to conflicting groups of experts and of interest claiming a Christian perspective on the economy and nuclear disarmament.

The result is not perfect consensus but does represent a number of people dealing with gospel commands in new and demanding contexts. Such an endeavor also takes seriously the charisms of Christians both individually and communally. Further, the bishops hoped that their examination of these moral questions might not only make some contribution to the discussion in the public forum but also arouse the conscience of Catholics on these issues. Hollenbach sums up their effort: "the bishops are seeking to retrieve the central values of biblical faith and civil virtue in order to contribute new moral purpose to American economic and cultural life."[53]

Implicit in the process employed by the bishops is the conviction that a large number of American Catholics struggle with their consciences and their Christian experience has been marked by such struggles. Although many Catholics may not be aware of the technical questions surrounding the economy and nuclear disarmament, they have had to deal with the repercussions of these questions in their own lives. Therefore, they bring their narratives of these struggles to their hearing of the gospel. The process of consensus building used by the bishops was not an invitation to vote on moral issues but rather to engage in a dialogue about problems whose solution critically affects Catholics' understanding of what it means to be a disciple of Christ. Such dialogues invite honest Catholics to welcome the ongoing conversion that such evangelization brings with it. Such dialogues also indicate what is involved in a church community.

Community, as already noted, is premised on such shared meanings. The liturgy of Word and sacrament invite people to struggle with and appropriate God's meanings and to live them out in a particular culture. This is a form of community that differs from some of the institutional models of parish we have already discussed. This model of community recognizes complexity in the makeup of a typical parish as well as the complexity of living the gospel in the American cultural situation. But liturgy as symbolic participation is quite capable of dealing with such complexity, if given a chance.

In the liturgy of the Word, a community, not simply a group of individuals, is empowered to hear and to respond to the living Word of God. The practical matters of how that Word is lectored and of the quality of the homily are important. Greeley and others have, with good reason, decried the poor quality of preaching in the American church.[54] (I have sat in the pew on Sunday morning often enough to testify to the frequency of unprepared and irrelevant homilies to which Catholics are regularly subjected.) But there is another related problem: Does the way in which the liturgy of the Word is celebrated invite a response from the community?

## Communities of Narrated Response

Evangelization never takes place without narration. The Word invites members of a community to remember their struggles to understand and live out the gospel values in the American culture. That Word also recalls God's saving actions in their lives. The paradigm for this process is the Emmaus account. The risen Lord does not convince his disillusioned disciples of the meaning of the cross by a textbook argument. Rather Jesus argues from the religious experience of these disciples that God has indeed redeemed them through the shame of the cross. They later admit to one another that their hearts were burning within them as Jesus invited them to appropriate God's meaning for their lives.

This type of listening to God's Word is obviously much more demanding than simply taking up pew space during the reading of the scriptures. Because this is a liturgy of the Word, it is a symbolic process that requires some participation of the listening community. In addition to the personal and interpersonal experience of each listener, there is also the experience of the parish community. This latter experience is usually a very ordinary account of how this community has helped them to perceive and find God. As we shall see, these narrations cannot be told or remembered without implicating ourselves in "owning" our experience.[55] The listening community and its individuals bring all this experience to symbolic participation. But this experience, in turn, has been shaped and modified by the American culture in which it took place.

A great deal of our symbolic interaction with our own culture passes largely unnoticed, because it forms so integral a part of our lives. This does not diminish the importance of symbolic interaction but simply verifies the axiom, we know more than we care to tell.[56] A major cultural example of this interaction is television. Television couples the telegraphic system of communication (the nineteenth-century revolution in communication) to graphic images (the result of that century's photography). Television's symbolic codes affect every area of public discourse, including the religious sphere.[57] (One wag has suggested that Americans may be more active symbolically in front of their television sets than in their churches.[58]) With the advent of television, the public discourse of American culture was transformed from a reading to a viewing culture. The cultural impact of television on our own American culture is such that Neil Postman has claimed that "television is our culture's principal mode of knowing about itself."[59]

The negative corollaries of this medium are well known: sharply reduced spans of attention, the oversimplification of complex moral and social problems and relationships, fragmented and uncontextualized information (e.g., the typical plots of the television "soaps"), the fostering of a consumer ethic (e.g., the control by the advertising world), and a passive viewer's presence. (Some commentators have suggested that television therefore provides the appropriate symbolic environment for individualists.[60]) But the potential for positive and active symbolic participation is also widely acknowledged.

Robert Wuthnow, for example, has analyzed the viewer reactions to a widely watched televised drama, *Holocaust,* depicting the genocide of Jews under Hitler. He suggests that the program is an example of a symbolic-expressive event that "communicates something about social relations in a relatively dramatic way."[61] (In Wuthnow's language, culture is described as symbolic-expressive when it implies much more than it actually states.[62]) Such messages are being constantly transmitted culturally through rituals and languages.

Wuthnow's thesis is that a moral ritual, such as the televised *Holocaust,* invites action. The moral dimension of the program is a vivid dramatization of the evils of social and moral chaos. (Recall the medieval liturgical plays, which originally were part of the liturgy of the Word at mass and functioned as a moral commentary on the meaning of the scriptures.) Wuthnow then argues that the moral dimension of *Holocaust* also begs for comparison with potentially similar situations in our own society. The narrative structure of the ritual/drama permits different groups within the American scene to examine their own positions and to arrive at multiple meanings for their own situations. In brief, Wuthnow is saying that the viewing of *Holocaust* not only connects the event with values of the community (not only for the original German participants but also for contemporary American people) but also provides an opportunity for the viewers to take moral responsibility for the values needed to resolve such a situation. In effect, the American viewing public is being asked not only what they might have done in that historical situation but also what current events in their own lives involve similar responsibility.[63]

In other words, Wuthnow argues that a moral ritual/narrative, such as the televised *Holocaust,* invites action and interaction. The moral dimension of the program is a vivid dramatization of the evils of social and moral chaos. At the same time, for the American audience it also begs for comparison with potentially similar situations in our own society. The narrative structure of the ritual permits different groups within the American scene and multiple meanings to be addressed. It also spells out the moral obligation of the viewers to assume moral responsibility about the values implied in such a story. *Symbolic narration invites transformed communal and individual participation.* The audience, in effect, is asked to survey their own life praxis and to reassess their life situation. (The personal narrations that form such an important part of Alcoholics Anonymous meetings and similar support groups might be considered another form of symbolic narration for this very reason.)

If this type of performative response is possible from a televised drama, how much more may be expected of the symbolic celebration of God's Word? From the Christian viewpoint, the death and resurrection of Christ have forever changed the way in which believers listen to the scriptures.

Everything leads to and from these key events in our redemption. The Word of God gathers a disciple community around this paschal mystery, a mystery whose narration ultimately takes the form of thundering and provocative questions about the answers that our own culture and interests suggest. These are not rhetorical questions that invite passive listening but direct questions that provoke a reassessment of our own values and vision.

Karl Rahner reminded us that the presence of God in Word is encountered in stages and throughout the span of our communal and individual lives. The focus and intensity of God's Word, he noted, are also affected by other elements such as the particular commitments of the hearers and unique existential situation.[64] The local church accepts as part of its ministry of evangelization and liturgical proclamation the responsibility to enable its communities to hear God's questions in an undistorted and honest way and gradually to appropriate God's mission and vision. The liturgical celebration of the Word provides a symbolic environment for the prophetic reexamination of the meanings and values of our culture. Because God's Word is symbolically expressive, it does not restrict itself to the intellectual dimension but addresses the whole spectrum of pervasive and unexamined feelings, attitudes and biases, and unacknowledged horizons that characterize any community of flawed and inculturated disciples. In brief, God's Word speaks to the narratives and textures of our shared and individual experience.

Contemporary pastoral examples of how this can be implemented are not hard to find. In response to the encouragement of the Latin American bishops at Medellin in 1968, numerous "basic Christian communities" have been formed in which sometimes ill-educated Christians gather to reflect on God's Word, using the guidelines (familiar from the Young Catholic Worker movement earlier in this century) of "seeing, judging, acting." These are people who struggle with the meaning and the implementation of that Word within their own culture.[65] This same process has been employed with impressive pastoral results in difficult situations. The Jesuits, for example, at the Dolores Mission in Los Angeles minister in a parish of perhaps twelve to fifteen thousand potential parishioners living in housing projects, mainly Mexican Hispanics with refugees, the undocumented, youth gangs, and the very poor. In addition to such outreach ministries to the undocumented, the homeless, and to gangs, the parish has fourteen basic Christian communities that meet every week for prayer, scripture reading and reflection, and outreach service.[66]

The practical corollary of this discussion is a fresh look at what it means to be a gathered Christian community in the United States. *Shared meaning, as the foundation and test of all community, is always meaning for which people have struggled not once but many times.* While our American culture may not always facilitate such struggle, it can provoke it technically, by our advanced systems of communication, and religiously, by the conflicting values of our American way of life (e.g., materialism versus the willingness to die for freedom). God's Word has never addressed its transforming message to Christians who were in ideal cultural situations for building gospel community. But Wuthnow's example of the televised *Holocaust* is one example of the positive features of our culture that have not destroyed, and probably have strengthened, the moral awareness of many Americans. To be sure, there are other examples that might be cited to argue the opposite view. My point would remain: the struggle for gospel meaning is a better indicator of Christian community than fears about individualism and privatism, even if those fears are justified.

Another way in which the Christian community recognizes how God has also gifted other communities is the way in which it "receives" the gospel insights and practices of worship of such communities. When Vatican II, for example, spoke to the local churches throughout the world in its decrees and liturgical reforms, these communities had the task of "receiving" these gifts. How well did the American church "receive" the teaching and liturgies of Vatican II?

## The Gift of Reception

Have Vatican II's liturgical reforms been merely implemented or actually "received" by the U.S. church? "Reception" is a technical term in ecclesiology that generally refers to how the local church accepts and appropriates some aspect of worship or doctrine as expressing its own living faith experience.[67] The term "implementation" as used here describes the external acceptance and adaptation of rituals without necessarily appropriating their underlying values. Such a question intends not to denigrate the sincerity of the U.S. church but rather to take seriously the complex pastoral challenge of liturgically "meaning what we do" within our specific American culture. Although there are several forms of reception, we will limit our discussion to ecclesial reception.[68]

Ecclesial reception describes how one believing community or church is enriched by the faith and praxis of another such community. In other words, one church adopts some thought or action of another church because it believes that it will enhance and deepen their own gospel life and worship.[69] There are two aspects of this process of reception. First, reception implies adoption by a community through a process of acknowledgment and appropriation. But it is also an act of interpretation in which the community comes to some new awareness that should assist it in living the gospel life. This is interpretation not only in the theological sense but also in the cultural sense of a reorientation of that community's values and vision. (One historical example is how the church of Jerusalem developed a series of prayer services and vigils at the historical locations where Christ was supposed to have had the Last Supper, and so on. These celebrations were eventually adopted by other local churches in Europe and elsewhere.)

The theology of reception rests on a keen appreciation of how the risen Lord and his Spirit are present in a disciple gathering or church. In the early Christian communities the Greek terms indicating "receiving" and "passing on" (e.g., of the Eucharist and of the New Testament canon) are cited as normative examples of such gatherings.[70] Obviously these early Christian communities felt that what they received from other churches would help them in the work of the gospel. The sociocultural context of the community also affects reception. The Pauline churches, for example, had to receive the teaching on circumcision/baptism within their Gentile situation. Paul argued to the church in Jerusalem that circumcision was not necessary for the salvation of the Gentiles. On the other hand, the church in Jerusalem, while agreeing with Paul's point, continued its use for Jewish converts for sociocultural reasons.[71]

## Liturgical Reception

As already indicated, the New Testament churches provide examples of liturgical reception. Paul reminded the Corinthians of the eucharistic practice and doctrine they had "received" (1 Cor. 11:23). What eventually became the canon (or official list) of the New Testament writings was generally first received and read within liturgical assemblies. In fact, the development of sacramental life within the church cannot be discussed apart from reception. As people were evangelized and "gathered" as a church, they were given not a book of rituals but rather an injunction to celebrate the dying and rising of Christ in initiation and Eucharist. Furthermore, the cultural context of a particular Christian community affected how it received the "law of worship" from another community.[72]

But, for our purposes of cultural analysis, we should note a subtle shift that took place in the later history of liturgical reception. A much-cited example of liturgical reception is that of a German liturgical book, the

Mainz Pontifical, as received by the Western churches in the tenth century.[73] As Kilmartin notes, the reception of this Pontifical and some of its negative consequences is a prime example of a culturally conditioned usage uncritically received. In this case, the German cultural usage of handing over the symbols of secular office had been introduced into the ordination ceremony of presbyters (the handing over of the paten and cup). The result was a shift of emphasis from the ordination prayer and laying on of hands by the bishop with its implicit ecclesial meaning to an understanding of ordination as a personal power "enabling the candidate to consecrate bread and wine even outside the context of the ecclesial celebration of the eucharist."[74]

Two remarks seem in order here. First, uncritical reception can provoke negative consequences.[75] An example of such consequences is the Mainz Pontifical, where a privatized notion of priesthood replaces an ecclesial understanding. In such cases, a ritually deficient *lex orandi* (law of worship) has led to a distorted *lex credendi* (law of belief). Reception should be a clarification and perhaps a development of that in which the receiving church already has some initial experience (e.g., the leadership dimension of priesthood in the example given above), and some distinction should be made between what is culturally and theologically received (e.g., in the Vatican II reforms, the "kiss of peace" has a long cultural as well as theological history). This initial experience, in turn, has been shaped by the justifying power of Christ, which both gathers the community and enables us to worship.

Second, reception is always more than ritual appropriation. Throughout the centuries rituals have been produced by individuals such as Hippolytus in third-century Rome[76] and by committees such as the postconciliar commissions of Trent and Vatican II. But the meaning of salvation is more profound than any ritual text can encompass. Liturgy that effectively symbolizes this meaning is much more than the texts it uses. Reception as a dynamic process also involves an appropriation that ultimately facilitates the conversion and mission of the community. The post–Vatican II reform of the Eucharist, for example, is much more than the translation of texts into the vernacular and the simplification of very elaborate rituals: the Eucharist now provides easier access to the mystery of Christ's death for us and our appropriation of that mystery in our lives.

The warning to post–Vatican II churches is important: Do not confuse implementation of rituals with authentic reception and appropriation of the redemptive meaning announced in such rituals. Without denying the value of ecclesial obedience given to a liturgical praxis or to a teaching originating with a council and approved by the pope, liturgical reception must mean more than this. The ultimate purpose and test of reception are the resulting fruitfulness of witness and mission in the receiving local church. A merely externalized reception would result in what Kilmartin aptly calls an immunization of what is received by superficial adaptation.[77] That is why it is so important in research such as the Notre Dame Study that the attitudes and actions of a parish are examined in addition to its implementation of Vatican II's reforms.

What would some of the criteria be for judging whether liturgical reception was indeed fruitful? First, *the local community's interpretation of its own particular gospel tasks should be clarified by the renewed liturgical celebrations that have been received.* (In response, for example, to the question about the main purpose of the parish, 33 percent of the Catholics interviewed thought that charitable work was the answer, while 28 percent thought of the parish as a place for worship.[78] One way of reading this result is to see post–Vatican II Catholics as having their values in correct order.) Second, *liturgical reception by its very nature cannot be a passive acquiescence but rather asks the community and its individual members to enter intentionally and more deeply into what they celebrate.* This attitude follows the classical sacramental injunction of "intending what the church intends" (*intentio faciendi quod facit ecclesia*). The ministries of the church should help people to deepen their intentions in prayer and worship (e.g., the manner in which the minister of communion presents the Eucharist to another can model an attitude of joy or commitment; a good homily can challenge the intentions of participants; and so on).

Third, *reception is a lengthy theological and religious process that encourages a local church or parish to appropriate gradually and more deeply what has been given to it.* As an ongoing process, evangelization helps a community look at its cultural background more critically and to live the gospel life more creatively. This ongoing process in turn enables the community to be more open to further tasks of mission and to be more critical about its reasons for reception. (For example, reception of the postconciliar greeting rituals for various sacraments and the kiss of peace would challenge the cultural individualism of a local church if the full religious meaning of these rituals were appreciated.)

## The American Parish: Test of Reception

Liturgical reception should be analyzed within the total pastoral practice of a community. A particular American Roman Catholic diocese or parish not only is the potential "receiver" of the liturgical reforms of Vatican II with their implied theology of church but also historically embodies pastoral strategies and ministerial styles that carry their own implied theology of church as well as highly structured cultural elements. Robert Wuthnow speaks of these cultural elements as moral codes that explain the nature of commitment to a specific course of action.[79] Now some of these moral codes might be in tacit contradiction to the religious meanings implicit in what is liturgically received (e.g., the liturgical "kiss of peace" can easily be reduced to another form of superficial social greeting in a culture that is highly individualistic).

Wuthnow also offers a warning to those involved in rituals: "unobservable values may be replaced by observable activities."[80] In other words, because we do the action does not necessarily guarantee that we share the meaning that was attached to that action. "Going to church" on Sunday, for example, is theologically tied to belonging to the body of Christ. For some people, however, "going to church" is part of a private conversation with God that has little or nothing to do with being part of the church, except in the most superficial way. (In our American culture, "belonging" to groups in a superficial way can be perfectly acceptable.)[81] This is not a question of bad will on the part of such a person but of limited expectations about the meaning of the action they are taking part in.

These observations on "liturgical reception" should make us appreciative of the real postconciliar changes that have taken place in American parishes and, at the same time discerning the differences between observable activities and unobservable values. Andrew Greeley's description of the American Catholic as "the communal Catholic . . . a new paradox of American pluralism" is quite accurate.[82] When he insists that these Catholics also have a social bond with their neighborhoods and contribute to political and cultural life of their communities, he is persuasive.[83] Both the Notre Dame Study and Philip Murnion's research emphatically state that the American church has profoundly welcomed and appropriated the liturgical reforms of Vatican II.[84] In other words, there has been more than implementation of the conciliar reforms. On the other hand, Murnion and others have been insistent on the individualistic character of American Catholics.[85] But the value of a closer look at the meaning of liturgical reception is that it provides a reasonably demanding assessment of how the local church lives the gospel. A local church must be able to generate a realistic and credible way of life, based on the gospel and attuned to the time and culture it inhabits.[86]

## Some Conclusions

A gathered church is much more than a gathering. While its language and symbolic actions are redolent of its culture, the local church and its parish communities are centers of God's communicative action, which proclaims and enables the peaceable reign of God. Vatican II did all that could be expected at the time in describing the characteristic profile, actions, and worship of such a church. But it also reminded us that all this had to be lived out in specific cultural contexts. The Word of God is one way in which a local church is enabled to hear and respond to its mission within its encultured situation. The community itself must enflesh that Word in culturally attuned ways that celebrate and extend God's compassion and challenge. One example will have to suffice.

In 1984 the Vatican initiated its own study of why so many Catholic Hispanics were deserting the church for sects.[87] In summarizing some of its findings the report said:

> Some suggest a rethinking of the classic Saturday evening/Sunday morning liturgical patterns which often remain foreign to the daily life situation. The Word of God should be rediscovered as an important community-building element. "Reception" should receive as much attention as "conservation." There should be room for joyful creativity, a belief in Christian inspiration and capacity of "invention," and a greater sense of communal celebration. Here again, inculturation is a must (with due respect for the nature of the liturgy and for the demands of universality).[88]

Although it might seem easier to implement such suggestions among Hispanics and African Americans than among white Americans (who are often characterized as individualists), there are a number of outstanding examples of parishes of every ethnic profile where such efforts have been successful.

The American church might also benefit from the quite positive experience of lay preaching in the German church. Like us, the German church has a fairly large number of laity who have done an intermediate degree in theology and are currently working in pastoral ministry. The German bishops allowed such people to preach occasionally in their parishes, with certain restrictions. The American bishops have issued guidelines for lay preaching in this country. These guidelines require real necessity for such preaching as well as the necessary theological education.[89] But the great potential for creatively using these dedicated and gifted people should be examined.

Liturgical reception is a process that demands a fairly lengthy period of time for a community to appropriate the meanings and values behind the new rituals. What is usually received is not entirely new, but it does contain a challenge to the receiving community to welcome the ongoing conversion of the gospel more deeply. One important example from the reception of Vatican II is the importance of the Word of God. The idea is certainly not new, but the ways in which the Word is celebrated (e.g., the normal postconciliar celebration of any sacrament involves a liturgy of the Word) do require the community to reassess its own conception of the gospel life and its practical corollaries in the American culture. Given the size of the Roman Catholic church in the United States, we would expect that different local churches or dioceses would have received the heritage of Vatican II in different degrees, depending on their cultural as well as their sociohistorical background.[90] (Prophetic Christians, such as Mother Teresa of Calcutta or Dorothy Day, seem to transcend such categories because, although they may have appeared to retain a Tridentine ecclesiology, their lives are prime examples of self-gift and radical discipleship.)

The American church, with whatever faults it may have, seems to be generally a healthy and vigorous church. At least some of this should be attributed to the liturgical and doctrinal heritage received from Vatican II. But there are problems. The voluntary character of American belonging seems to betray itself when there is an overly individualistic use of sacrament or when a parish or diocesan community seems to lack a critical stance toward economic, racial, and cultural assumptions. There is much in American culture that encourages some volunteer public service but that in no way sees the life of service as a requisite for being a moral, much less a Christian, person. Such charges, of course, cannot be overgeneralized and must be addressed in the following chapters.

For the moment, it might be useful to recall that other local churches in other eras have struggled with various forms of individualism, both social and ecclesial, and managed to achieve a strong sense of mission. Nineteenth-century French theology and spirituality, for example, were in some important ways highly individualistic, as was the culture.[91] Yet this church managed to have a strong sense of evangelization which resulted in the formation of a number of religious congregations of men and women with various apostolates and gave that century some of its best missionaries. The point of the example is not to dismiss the serious problems that individualism generates for a praying and missioned church that is constantly defined as a community. But it is classical teaching to insist that the praying church is always given all that it needs to be a missioned church, no matter the culture, the theology, or the historical era. When individualism becomes a seriously distorting factor in a local church, then that church must ask how prophetic and enabling its ministries are.

In any case, authentic liturgical reception encourages and enables an ecclesial community to make the serving Christ more visible in its specific cultural world. When John Coleman suggests that the renewal of moral theology cannot be separated from the need for groups of Christians who are "critical communities of truthful and emancipatory societal practice,"[92] this should not be restricted to religious communities or houses of the Catholic Worker movement. There are not, after all, two classes of the Body of Christ: each Christian community "receives" what is necessary for its witness to its world. Young Christians provide a good example and test of this assertion.

Younger Catholics (eighteen to twenty-nine years of age) have only known the postconciliar liturgy. In general, this group is less likely to consider the church important in their lives, to attend mass weekly, and to support the church financially.[93] Some researchers would locate at least some of these young Catholics in the "cultural Catholic" group, that is, people for whom Catholicism is a cultural identity more than a distinctive morality and worship.[94] On the other hand, the importance that Andrew Greeley has attached to Catholic education continues to be verified by others. Patrick McNamara says: "As seniors, volunteers clearly showed the positive devotional effect of all-Catholic elementary schooling . . . the more pre–high school Catholic schooling, the stronger the religious behavior as seniors."[95] Thus, the importance of factors such as the extent and quality of religious education influence the questions of liturgical and doctrinal reception. But there is also the paradox that many young American Catholics, when challenged to share their gifts, are willing to do so. Any Catholic college can attest to how many students not only volunteer for weekly outreach programs near their campus but also give a year or two after college to living and working among the poor in this country or abroad.

Several answers might be given in response to the question of how much liturgical reception has fostered a dialogue with American cultural values and vision. The insertion of many Catholics into the mainstream of American life, with its upward mobility, is not necessarily more of an obstacle to cultural self-criticism and ecclesial awareness than the ethnic preoccupations of nineteenth-century immigrant Catholics in this country. A more serious problem may be the continuing dichotomy between moral teaching and sacramental life in the American church. In effect, we seem to have a pattern in which there is a spirituality for sacramental participation and a morality for personal and public actions. A notable exception is the American bishops' call for a deeper awareness of the connection between worship and the world of work[96] and their classical assertion that "in worship and deeds of justice, the church becomes a 'sacrament', a visible sign of that unity in justice and peace that God wills for the whole of humanity."[97]

Finally, the pluralism within the American church suggests a certain untapped richness of liturgical participation. Just as we can legitimately argue from the documents of Vatican II that aspects of ecclesial reality are to be found in other Christian non-Roman communities, so too more ecumenical learning is possible on both sides. The devoted concern of other Christian churches about the celebration of the Word of God provides a teaching moment for the American Roman Catholic church. Moreover, the Hispanic and African American Christians have much to teach their white sisters and brothers in terms of community, celebration, and reception. In the end, postconciliar liturgical reception is not an end but a means to help those gathered in Christ's name to worship in spirit and truth.

The best assessment of any American Roman Catholic community, once gathered, will be its sense of time. There is, I would argue, no more unique cultural characteristic of our culture than the meaning and value we attach to time. The American sense of time would seem to be in direct contradiction to the liturgical sense of time, and to this issue we now turn.

# CHAPTER FOUR

# American Time and God's Time

Time is the gift of God's creation. Transformed time is the gift of God's new creation in Christ. Time becomes transformed when we begin to understand why God gives us time. In the previous chapter, we discussed how God gathers a community who will witness to the world the love of God and the purposes of the new creation. When Karl Rahner insisted that the liturgy of the church must be tied to the liturgy of the world, he presumed that we would not leave time out of the discussion.

Each culture has its own sense and meaning for time. Americans jokingly refer to certain cultures where time does not seem to be as important as it is in our culture. After all, we are the culture that has shown the rest of the world the meaning of the proverb Time Is Money. Long before we could define time or even read a wristwatch, our American culture was teaching us the importance of time in subtle as well as obvious ways. Many of the cultural meanings for time remain unexamined for most Americans. These meanings are so much a part of us that we take them for granted. It may take a crisis to make us aware of how fragile our hold on time is—the death of a child, a doctor's diagnosis of a life-threatening illness, watching parents grow old.

As Christians we follow a liturgical time as well as a civil time. The liturgical year is a practical way for us to remember and, more importantly, to celebrate the saving mysteries of God in time. There are two theological assumptions behind the Christian sense of time. First, time is an unearned and measured gift of God for which both nations and individuals will one day be held accountable. This assumption, as we shall see, is directly and indirectly contradicted by the belief and practice of American culture. Second, we are pilgrims not only in this world but in this time. In other words, a practical test of Christian commitment is the way in which the gathered church uses time. The liturgical year is a continuing reminder of these assumptions; yet we theologians and liturgists are sometimes tempted to speak too glibly about the Christian sense of time. A liturgical calendar does not ensure a Christian sense of time. Celebrating Christian communities can move through the liturgical year with more ritual flair than religious commitment.

When Paul VI urged the church to evangelize human culture in a profound way, he noted that salvation has its beginning in time, but it will only be fulfilled in eternity. Recalling the classical "already but not yet" tension between our present situation and the fully realized kingdom of God, he then insisted that evangelization must deal with our sense of time in view of our eternal destiny.[1] Evangelization not only requires time to listen to the message of Christ; it demands a radical reordering of our time priorities. The praise of God, as well as time spent in service to others, requires a redistribution of our already limited time.

The Christian sense of time, then, does not exist in a vacuum. Just as the gospel should transform our culture, so it must also challenge our cultural sense of time. To put it differently, Christians should not presume that our American sense of time is necessarily the meaning that God gives to time. What, for example, might God think of the proverb Time Is Money? The question of American individualism, which was discussed in a more theoretical fashion in the previous chapter, becomes quite specific when we ask how time should be used. On the other hand, when many Americans are found to be fairly generous in the giving of their time for volunteer work, it might suggest that we need a more nuanced idea of what late twentieth century American individualism might be.[2]

Our inculturated and liturgical sense of time forms part of the fabric of our lives together. As Christians, if we are really on the path of conversion, one major test of that process will be our changed sense of time and its meanings and purposes. The person who realizes that time is an unearned gift of God will use time in a different way than someone who does not. In this chapter, I will argue that the redemptive sense of time that liturgy celebrates and theology articulates must take into account the contemporary, and more specifically, American cultural sense of time. The Christians who crowd our churches on "Sunday" are continually affected and shaped by the goals and concerns of their cultural sense of time throughout the rest of the week. Just as evangelization must deal with particular cultures, so must evangelized Christians confront their inculturated sense of time in late twentieth century America.

But before we can discuss the Christian sense of time, we need to review some of the components of our American sense of time and some examples of this kind of time telling. This section will serve as a point of comparison with the Christian approach to time as both present and future feast, and the reflection of Christian thinkers, such as Karl Rahner and Paul Ricoeur, on time within the narratives of our redemptive experience. But the test of this entire discussion on the cultural, Christian, and liturgical sense of time is the way in which our intentions give a direction and a shape to the time we have left.

## American Time

Charlie Chaplin's ironic and prescient film *Modern Times* caught the accelerated rhythms and dissonant textures of "industrial" time and its effect on people's lives. The classic scene in which Chaplin is temporarily made prisoner by the very machines he runs captures not only the dilemmas of the machine age but also the tempos and times that accompany it. The term "American time" serves, first of all, as a reminder that our ideas and experience of time have changed radically in the past hundred years because of far-reaching technological, historical, and sociocultural changes.[3] "American time" has also become synonymous with lack of leisure time. For those who work in pastoral ministry, it might help to recall how difficult it is to schedule any activity (e.g., parish council, parish renewal, youth meetings) during the week. Two of the major reasons for this are the lack of free or leisure time and the fear of nighttime in urban areas troubled with crime.

Space exploration in these past decades has also made us aware of how inadequate our sense of time is when we deal with the beginnings and the end of creation. Stephen Jay Gould, for example, speaks of "deep time" as "an almost incomprehensible immensity, with human habitation restricted to a millimicrosecond at the very end."[4] In fact, our sense of time has been revolutionized by advances in other directions as well—the scientific, philosophical, artistic, and technical discoveries in the last half of this century. Our sense of time is so embedded in our sociocultural experience that we find it difficult to know our own assumptions about the uses and purposes of time.[5]

One way in which to perceive the rapid change in our sense of time is to recall what is known as "World Standard Time." Even though our international plane schedules and nightly news are based on this practice, it is easy to forget how recent standard time is.[6] Successively the railroads, telegraph, the telephone, supersonic travel, and satellites have also changed our perception of time and history. The nightly televised news cultivates our sense of immediacy and simultaneity, the sense that we are there. An ironic twist of our time experience, on the other hand, is that many Americans spend more time, for example, traveling to and from work (and sometimes, in worse conditions) than their parents did.

With this notion of a universal and irreversible public time, however, came a sense of private times created by the individual in a number of spheres.[7] These marked-off time zones (e.g., lunch hour, parents' time when the children are asleep, television time, weekends, "quality time," etc.) are temporary buffer zones in the whirlwind of public, professional, and social datebooks and calendars. In fact, our cultural experience is shaped by a particular sense of time. Because no two cultures share an identical sense of time, their perspectives on life, to that extent, are different.[8] Our American culture, for example, seems to have the distinction of having coined terms such as "personal time" and "quality time."

Some sociologists, in attempting to map out the routinized patterns of daily life, will employ the term "time-geography."[9] Since embodied people move through time and space and experience limitations because of these factors, researchers attempt to analyze peoples' social actions in a sort of three-dimensional way. A banal activity such as food shopping, for example, assumes a new profile in a supermarket open twenty-four hours a day. If viewed as a microcosm, this market displays social lives contextualized in time and space, and, as A. Giddens suggests, in "intersections of presence and absence."[10] On the other hand, many senior citizens, for example, can shop only at certain times because of constraints of transportation, fear, and so on. Further, parish life in certain urban situations is directly affected by people's unwillingness to attend functions on weeknights because of long commutes to work or safety factors.

Because there are many cultures operative in the United States, there are many "American" times. In the American situation, for example, the experience of time for the marginal and poor may be quite different from what it is for professional and successful people.[11] The scarcity of time and concerns about "saving time" preoccupy not only the industrial world but also, in quite different ways, the elderly, the upwardly mobile, and an increasing number of families where both parents work.[12] Paradoxically, the upwardly mobile economic groups in our country may find themselves with less time, because of professional expectations, than blue-collar workers. For such people, the "weekend" assumes an importance that might rival the notion of "sacred time" in other cultures.[13] "Thank God it's Friday!" has become the eschatological cry for many in the American culture.

Time is influenced by explicit and implicit priorities and shaped into a number of "private times." A Chicano anthropologist describes part of his cultural sense of time in this way:

> There were times that we let loose with these expectations among ourselves— at times of ritual, at times of dancing and drinking, at times of gaiety and happiness. . . . Times when we would strut and show that we were worthy, that we were human, but inevitably someone would disagree with our assessment. . . . Somehow during these times we came to know ourselves and others and the content of our "stuff."[14]

These are a few of the areas that make up our American sense of time, and there are several practical corollaries that emerge from this brief tour. First, technological changes in our sense of time (e.g., a transatlantic flight of six or seven hours may feel tedious to someone now accustomed to the Concorde flight of three hours) have been matched by the increasing rapidity of historical and social changes (e.g., the "disappearance" of the Soviet Union and its replacement in a matter of weeks by a number of independent states). We usually experience these changes indirectly (e.g., television telescoping the Soviet events into much shorter time periods). The practical result of such changes may be that time becomes more "unreal" and external to us. Second, to the extent that time thus becomes "larger than life," we may experience ourselves as less responsible for time since we are apparently in less control of time (e.g., when television news shows us in a thirty-second clip vast numbers of displaced and famine-ridden people). Third, since much more may be accomplished in less time (e.g., a computer search for extensive detailed information), it is easier to move from a qualitative and intentional use of time to a quantitative use of time. On the other hand, such capabilities also permit new and better uses of time. The final result of such changes in awareness of time may be a difficulty in symbolizing deeply and intending responsibly in time.

As Americans, we have vested but often unexamined interests in maintaining these cultural time patterns and commitments at any cost. This might seem unreasonable until we realize that such a sense of time gradually relieves us of responsibility for time. When the televised evening news, for example, can show us the misery and crime of the world in less than thirty minutes, the reaction of the viewer, whether impervious to or overcome by such scenes, can be: "There's nothing I can do about it." Guilt over the "loss" of time can often be much more traumatizing than any guilt over the waste of material things. Time Is Money is not necessarily a call to more responsible living, but it certainly can be a sentence of guilt for contemporary Americans. Yet many Americans have learned not only to cope with "American time" but to create productive and satisfying lives for themselves and others.

In brief, our theologies of time and our pastoral strategies and plans remain very naïve if the challenge of our cultural sense of time is not taken seriously. Time is a practical test of some of our most cherished values, secular or religious. An unchallenged cultural sense of time is inevitably accompanied by an unrealistic notion of salvation. We will return to this question, after giving some specific examples of this sense of time and its corollaries for the Christian understanding of time.

## American Time Graffiti

Hugh Daziel Duncan once noted that "nothing is more painful to endure in American life than our blind belief in the 'tradition of the new.'"[15] His examples are familiar: the doctrine of Manifest Destiny in American history, which claimed that the future was ours and that therefore we might do what we would to the Native American; the thoughtless replacement of the old and beautiful by the new and tawdry; our cities of the future already poisoned by the excesses of the present. His examples also implicate our sense of time. There are ways of thinking about the future that seem to excuse us from dealing responsibly with the present. When Frederick Jackson Turner explained American history in terms of his "frontier thesis"—that is, that the enthusiastic individualism and self-sufficiency needed to confront each new frontier forged the American spirit—he might have added that it also helped to create the American sense of time as unlimited possibility. Duncan and Turner bear witness to the weaknesses and strengths of the American sense of time.

A few examples might help readers to think of their own experiences and to concretize some of our religious concerns about time. Because so many demands are made on the time of the average American, time is a highly prized commodity whose distribution accurately reflects the values held. American marriages, for example, must inevitably face the question of time and its allotment. In a two-career marriage, time is not only a point of scheduling but also a test of the couple's affective life and their "quality time" together. The decision to have children entails a reassessment of values and demands a radical redistribution of precious time.[16] Recent studies of stages in life have discovered how surprisingly early the sense of "time running out" begins in a young person's life. Parents and their children sometimes have set such demanding career goals for themselves that their time is already highly scheduled. It is not uncommon for high school students to have athletic practice or glee club rehearsal at 6:00 or 7:00 A.M. because of other scheduling conflicts after school. Parents who have spent years chauffeuring their children to school and to other events are well aware of the problem of time.

Another example of our American cultural sense of time may be found in our attitude about the future. If, as Christopher Lasch insists, the American expectation of the future is becoming progressively pessimistic, then his conclusion should be noted: "A profound shift in our sense of time has transformed work habits, values, and the definition of success. Self-preservation has replaced self-improvement as the goal of earthly existence."[17] In many cases, career changes have been motivated by the lack of personal or family time or by the amount of time needed to commute to work. Early retirements have become more appealing to people who have become keenly aware of the number of years they might have left to enjoy grandchildren, travel, hobbies, or simply free time. Children of "successful" parents may choose a less-demanding career because they have had firsthand experience of what the lack of time has done to parents.

We do not have to accept this assessment totally to be aware of the ambiguous attitudes of American youth toward the future as well as the past.[18] Daniel Bell has pointed out that our society has yoked time to such specific purposes that young people are under constant pressures to advance, succeed, and conquer.[19] The very fact that young Americans today are a television and audiovisual generation means that time manipulation has been part of their formative background. Television programs are divided into eight minute segments to accommodate the mobile television users and their shortened span of attention.[20] "Virtual reality" in the audiovisual world implies not so much a suspension of time as a different sense of time from our work-a-day world. American television regularly either presents complicated stories in a simplistic and trivializing fashion (because of the half-hour or hour format with its commercial breaks) or overextends thin story lines into "mini-series" (a manipulation of time for predominantly economic reasons).[21] On the other hand, young people also belong to a "computer generation," and they are accustomed to creative use of timed information which has transformed the possibilities of teaching and learning.

A final example of the American framing of time can be found in what J. Rifkin evocatively calls "time ghettos."[22] People who must live with a narrowing sense of time, for political or economic reasons, experience limitations in these temporal ghettos that are as devastating as any physical ghetto. Two examples of "time ghettos" in our American culture are the growing worlds of unskilled workers and of the homeless. The situation of both these groups usually condemns them to an uncreative and limited use of time that is focused on the present. "Unskilled and semiskilled jobs require little past knowledge and even less predictive or planning skills. . . . Lack of economic opportunities undermine hopes for a better future and willingness to plan ahead and set long term goals."[23]

Robert Wuthnow has studied Americans' willingness to help others, which is also a question of time. He notes that eighty million persons—45 percent of all Americans age 18 or over—participate in some form of voluntary caring activity (e.g., taking meals to the elderly, working in a homeless shelter or for nonprofit organizations, and so on).[24] In addition, there are the unrecorded acts of kindness and compassion that demand both time and attention from the donors. But Wuthnow cautions that an equally large percentage of the population feel that both success and failure depend on the person ("people generally bring suffering on themselves") and place self-interest as a high priority.[25] Wuthnow's study would also suggest that "by a margin of 35 percent to 26 percent, Protestants are more likely than Catholics to be involved currently in charitable or other social-service activities."[26] Rather than draw any immediate conclusions about individualism or the charity of particular Christian traditions, I call attention to an unspoken component of this data—the cultural and religious attitudes of the participants about the purpose and "ownership" of time.

In brief, Americans can be exceptionally generous not only financially but also in volunteering their time when they are properly motivated. But there are a number of obstacles in our culture which make such generosity increasingly difficult to maintain (e.g., the lack of leisure time). American Catholics, moreover, as they move into the upper echelons of our society find a number of legitimate demands from all sides being made on their diminishing free time. Some of these Catholics already may feel that they make something of a sacrifice in spending one hour a week at their parish for the Eucharist. To ask such people to get involved in a homeless shelter, a parish council, youth work, or a retreat can seem an unfair, if not an unreasonable, demand. To challenge such people to reconsider their priorities in their use of time might seem naïve when these people feel that they are no longer in control of their use of time. In the typical, busy American parish or parochial school many feel that they are already "overextended"; that is, not only energy but time has been used up.

Ongoing conversion must always challenge our use of time since it is God's gift to be used for God's purposes. There is always a temptation to think of religious time as personal time set aside for worship and "good works" and to forget the invitation to change radically our perspective on the larger Christian purposes of time. When the American bishops, for example, speak of "leisure" in our culture, the use of time is the central focus. They candidly admit that if the Christian sense of time is retrieved, then "the use of leisure may demand being countercultural. In leisure, the Christian tradition sees time to build family and societal relationships and an opportunity for communal prayer and worship, for relaxed contemplation and enjoyment of God's creation, and for the cultivation of the arts which help fill the human longing for wholeness."[27] Even prayer may be seen as countercultural by some in American society, since its practical results are questionable (e.g., the contemplative life of the Trappists).

There is some consolation in remembering that the use of time has always been a difficult part of Christian living. But there has also been a classical conviction that it is in the celebration of the liturgy that Christians learn how to tell God's time. It is not by accident that many ancient societies (e.g., the Egyptian or Mayan cultures) expected their priests to be the expert guardians of their calendars since time and religion were closely associated in their minds. In the Christian perspective, God's future feast at the end of time is the context for our present praise and gratitude, since Christ's death and rising make that feast possible for us. The next logical step, then, is to reexamine the meanings of liturgical time and how our cultural sense of time might help or hinder the living out of these meanings.

## Feast as God's Time Celebrated

The meaning of liturgical time has continued to provoke much creative discussion among scholars.[28] Robert Taft cites *1 Clement* as the earliest Christian text attributing a symbolic value to times of the day: "We see, beloved, that the resurrection was accomplished according to the time. Day and night make visible to us a resurrection. Night goes to sleep, the day rises; the day departs, night follows" (*1 Clem.* 24:1–3).[29] The sanctification of time, as eventually celebrated in the hours of the Divine Office (generally, a combination of psalms, prayers, and readings), symbolizes a time transcended.[30] Throughout day and night, Christians would consecrate time by their fixed hours of prayer of praise and thanksgiving. In other words, the Christian community has always been relearning the larger purposes of God's time and the practical corollaries of such insights.

Taft puts his finger on an essential point when he remarks that, while the ritual moment is a synthesis of past, present, and future, the New Testament looks to the fullness of time.[31] This seems to be borne out in the regular ending of classical liturgical prayers of the Eucharist, where Christ's reign is described as "through all ages of ages" (*per omnia saecula saeculo-rum*).[32] In the paschal mystery of Christ's dying and rising for us, this full-ness has a transforming immediacy. As a result, our celebrations are animated by God's saving power being actualized among us. Both gospel and liturgical feasts share a common task of actualizing this redemptive power among us as a present reality that enfolds our lives in Christ.[33] Since redemption and the reign of God are intimately connected, liturgical time is never simply a repetition of saving events but each year brings us closer to God's timeless time.[34]

These beautiful insights, however, suggest a very different sense of time and its purposes from the cultural sense of time in the United States that we sketched earlier in this chapter. While it might seem utopian to think that this liturgical sense of time can prevail in our culture, we should remember that we learn this sense of time not as an intellectual idea but as part of a symbolic action. Participation in this action requires a changed sense of time. Because symbolic actions open up communications between God and us on a deepened level, our motivations and intentions are directly challenged by those of God, and our vision of reality and its time can be transformed by God's transforming presence.

But to intend some action is not only to commit time to that action but to shape our present by our choice of a future. Once again, the liturgy measures time's purpose by Christ's victory over death. In particular, the events of Holy Week and Easter project God's view of time in many power-ful but nonverbal ways (e.g., the stripping of the altar, new fire, Easter water, etc.) that celebrate the self-gift of Christ in time. One explicit litur-gical example occurs in the Easter Vigil when the first and last letters of the Greek alphabet (*alpha* and *omega*) are drawn at the ends of the cross on the Easter candle to remind participants that Christ is the beginning and the end of time.[35] The accompanying prayer is to the point: "Christ, yesterday and today, the beginning and the end. Alpha and Omega, all time belongs to him and all ages to him be glory and power through every age for ever. Amen."[36]

In our culture, for example, birthdays (i.e., celebrations that mark the passage of time) can be highly charged symbolic moments precisely because of their celebration. Well-celebrated birthdays may enliven our sense of time and even prompt a new and better use of it. Liturgical cele-brations do much more: in one way or another they make present the self-gift of Christ and enable us to "have the mind of Christ Jesus," that is, radical attitudes about living our lives in time for the sake of others. When Paul explains the paschal mystery ("Christ died for us so that we might no longer live for ourselves but for him who died for us"), "no longer" indicates both a change of direction and of the use of time. One cannot happen without the other, and neither can happen outside our culture.

## A Different Kind of Memory

This liturgical discussion of time obviously presumes a biblical understanding of "memory." Recent biblical research has deepened our awareness of this Semitic approach to the connection between time and feast.[37] Israel is constantly being called to *"remember* that you were once slaves" (Deut. 5:15) and *"call to mind* what the Lord your God did to Pharaoh . . ."* (Deut. 7:18). These are not exercises in historical memory. In more recent biblical research "to remember" (Hebrew *zkr*) has been shown to be a dynamic process: a saving past is actualized so that every generation might participate in the same redemptive time. "When Israel observes the Sabbath in order to remember the events of her redemption, she is participating again in the Exodus event. . . . *Israel in every generation remembers and so shares in the same redemptive time."*[38] Biblical memory invites people to participate in a time shaped by God's purposes. Within such a sense of time, cultural meanings and time can also be present and celebrated. The Jewish celebration of Passover, for example, is a synthesis of this religious and cultural sense of time. Christmas, on the other hand, in our culture has been almost overpowered by the cultural sense of consumer time and nostalgia time.

This sense of time transformed by God's saving acts continues in patristic teaching as found, for example, in a typical Christmas homily of Leo the Great:

> Although every individual that is called has his own order, and all the sons of the Church are separated from one another by intervals of time, yet, as the entire body of the faithful being born in the font of baptism is crucified with Christ in His passion, raised again in His resurrection, and placed at the Father's right hand in His ascension, so with Him they are born in this nativity.[39]

Notice that Leo recalls Christmas not as a historical event of the past but as a redemptive event celebrated in the present for the sake of this generation.[40]

This same conviction is demonstrated in Leo the Great's repetition of certain words that serve as themes in his eloquent preaching. "Today" (*hodie*) is one of his more frequently used and highly nuanced terms. "Today" for Leo is the present time transformed by a saving event. On the feast of the Ascension, for example, Leo says to the liturgical community: "For *today* we are not only strengthened as possessors of paradise, but we have even penetrated into the highest heavens with Christ."[41] In other words, "today"[42] spans the past, present, and future in a saving way and finds its effective expression in liturgical action and word.

The paschal mystery, then, as welcomed in the ongoing conversion of the Christian community and celebrated in its worship, transforms the community's sense of time. The presence of the Lord sums up these interwoven ideas of redemption and the reign of God in such a way that whenever the Eucharist is celebrated, it becomes an actualization of the Christian understanding of time.[43] How could it be otherwise since, as Paul reminds his reluctant hearers, "*every time* you eat this bread and drink this cup, you proclaim the death of the Lord until he comes" (1 Cor. 11:26).[44] In brief, this paschal dying and rising overturn our perspectives on time while continuing to operate within the historical and sociocultural categories of time.

The biblical understanding of time, then, rests on a radical appreciation of how our lives are played out against the background of time. These discussions represent perspectives on time that are radically different from those of our American culture. Our important choices and decisions always involve the use or abuse of time. The practical test of any conversion is the decision of what one will do with the time that is left, and so we turn to theology for insights into the purposes of time in our lives.

## Once Upon a Time or God's Time

Augustine, in response to his own question about the meaning of time, replies that he knows what it means until asked, but when asked, realizes that he does not know the answer.[45] Contemporary theology makes a similar admission: people experience time because they are involved in it, but they do not master time. In contrasting time and eternity, Karl Rahner helps us to appreciate the importance of time for the Christian. In a wonderful essay entitled "Experiencing Easter," Rahner points out that many people think of the period after their death as a "lasting on" of their earthly existence. In that case, the reign of God would be an improvement on but not a completion of time. Rahner then gives a beautiful image for the meaning of eternity as beginning in time but eventually emerging from it like a ripened fruit. For him time is the starting point for the spirit and its freedom that will someday give birth to eternity.[46]

In Rahner's thought, freedom and liberation are the goals toward which all time should tend.[47] For if we are to understand ourselves and our vocation as Christians, it is crucial that we understand the awesome freedom we have to be our authentic selves in time. In contrast to people who have only a "wristwatch" or superficial sense of time, Christians learn to shape time by their intentions and the actions that flow from them.[48] Rahner's authentic Christian has encountered the crucified and risen Lord much as those disciples on their way to Emmaus after the resurrection. Christ's free and unreserved acceptance of death for the sake of others becomes the model for a courageous freedom that is exercised in time.[49] To experience the paschal mystery, therefore, is to use our freedom, acquired for us by Christ, to decide to live and die for the sake of others in the time we have left.

There is another aspect of Rahner's thinking that is less noticed: the link between his understanding of the Eucharist as the unrepeatable sacrifice of the cross and our own appropriation in time of that same paschal mystery. Rahner pictures the individual participating in the Eucharist against the vast backdrop of world history where a graced creation is to be found ("the liturgy of the world"). The celebration of the Eucharist reminds us of God's liberation of humankind precisely because the Eucharist proclaims, not repeats, the perduring "mysterious presence in the world" of the cross of Christ.[50] But what should be the participant's response to this proclamation of the cross? Rahner's answer is a transformed sense of time. The result is that the Christian participant "experiences every day in that this every day life is sustained by the movement toward God."[51] In other words, ongoing conversion, as a choice of direction toward God and the use of time as that direction is lived out, transforms the civil calendar.

What has Rahner added to our understanding of feast as God's time celebrated? Rahner's insights sharpen our awareness of the connection between time and worship. First, liturgical time (e.g., Christmas, lent, and so on) becomes blurred if it is not experienced within the Christians' ongoing dying and rising with Christ in ordinary time. As already mentioned, Christ's cross and resurrection are the practical model that God gives us to imitate. In that model Christians begin to realize that Christ gave not only of himself but of his time: Christ consecrated time by living and dying in it for the sake of the world.[52]

Second, Paul's practical test of redemption as "freedom" (*eleutheria*) is highlighted by Rahner as the individual's willingness at different periods of time to become freely all that God intended.[53] This understanding of Christian freedom implies a sense of committed time, time "on account of others." Such freedom is both founded on and motivated by the paschal mystery, where time is revealed as part of God's new creation in Christ. Within the world created by God with its time we are to become a new creation in time. Thus, the Eucharist with its proclamation of the paschal mystery challenges our tendency to revert to a static and highly individualistic sense of time. Our very hope, as Christians, to participate in the reign of God urges us to share the present in view of that shared future.[54]

Third, these implications need to be appropriated by the church community as well as by its individual members. The mission of Christ remains a theological abstraction until the whole community is willing to reprioritize its sense of witness and service within the American sense of time with all the difficulties and sacrifices that may represent. The U.S. bishops' statement, cited earlier, that our use of leisure time may have to become countercultural should be understood within this context. What passes for compassion in American culture can never be simply equated with what Christ asks from the ministry of his body, the People of God.

The average Christian might find this discussion of time abstract and impractical. With a moment's reflection, however, that same average Christian can recognize time as the most precious of gifts. Every human action takes place in time. One way of writing a biography or autobiography is to tell what people did with their time. We turn now to seminal thinkers whose thought on time can help us reevaluate our own sense of time and thus, from one perspective, tell us how deeply conversion has taken hold of our lives.

## The Tenants of Time

From the beginning, Christians forged a vocabulary to remind themselves that only the reign of God will endure. Here is the paradox for the Christian. Because we believe that God created time and that Christ was enfleshed and redeemed us in time, we esteem time and its purposes. On the other hand, we also believe that there is nothing in time that can completely satisfy the human spirit. No surprise then that Christians, in recalling the passing character of space and time, described themselves as "pilgrims in this world." A contemporary version of the same thought might be "tenants of time," with its reminder that we do not own time. Both phrases gently hint at the fleeting impressions we ourselves make on the sands of time.

Those scholars who write about human action have also had to deal with the related question of the human sense of time. As already mentioned, biography has to make connections between our narrative experience and our accompanying sense of time. The title of Paul Ricoeur's study *Time and Narrative* comes, then, as no surprise because the two ideas are so closely linked. A major theme in Ricoeur's work is that time becomes human through narrative while narrative has its full impact only within a temporal existence.[55] Ricoeur employs Aristotle's notion of "plot" coupled with Augustine's concept of "time" to arrive at a richer appreciation of how actions move through time in complex sociocultural contexts. (At the beginning of the chapter we spoke of how inculturated our sense of time is.) Ultimately, plot must connect the beginning and end of time and thus assure the triumph of concord over discord.[56] The opening and closing books of the Bible, in effect, integrate the meaning of God's action in history and thus retrieve the meaning of time by its purpose in view of eternity.[57]

In the last chapter, we spoke of the parish as a community of narrated response. The Word of God invites and enables a response from the gathered Christian community, not just of intellectual assent but of practical purpose. The Word of God puts in perspective how God has acted in time to save human beings and how God sees human destiny. The Christian community cannot make sense of what is happening currently if it does not pay attention to what has happened in the past and what is planned for the future. In fact, such narration is constitutive of community: "What is grasped as common experience can be met by common action."[58]

Christian communities and their individual participants respond with their own narratives of how the many liturgies of the church and the world, already celebrated, have had a saving impact on their own lives and their outreach to others. This shared experience and its celebration in praise and thanks are formative elements of Christian community. The book of Revelation offers a model in its narrative of the seven Christian communities it judges. These accounts may be seen not only as a commentary on the actions of the community but also on their use of God's time for the mission they have been given. To use Ricoeur's insight, plot and time are linked in the story of how these communities lived and witnessed.

Ricoeur and Rahner have similar concerns. Eternity understood as "the fruit of time" becomes concretized in the praise-filled narratives of the Christian community and its celebrations. The theme of such narratives ("Come, Lord Jesus!") also serves as the background for the narratives of those who freely choose a way of living that transforms their time experience (a point we will return to later in this chapter). In brief, Ricoeur's careful delineation of the different kinds of time within the fabric of a narrative prompts some searching questions about the sense of authentic time within our liturgical and personal narratives of redemptive praise.

The sense of authentic time is suggested in English by two contrasting phrases, "marking time" and "telling time." "Marking time" takes its meaning from a marching step in which the feet are alternatively raised and lowered in rhythm without moving forward. In its applied meaning, those who mark time make no progress for the time being. There is only the impression of spirited movement. Rahner and Ricoeur are concerned with ways of "telling time," not "marking time." Their work centers on the rediscovery of why time is given to us.

This rediscovery, however, entails honest narratives of what God has done for us and the consequent praise that comes with this "memory" of such saving "times" in our lives. Such narratives are not to be confused with our curriculum vitae, that is, with an objective description of our familial and professional life with dates attached to each entry nor with a schedule of parish activities and worship. Our narratives must deal with the "moods and motivations" (Clifford Geertz's phrase, cited in chapter 1) of our American culture within which we dealt with ourselves and others. But there are no adequate words for many of the most important events in our lives—the unspoken contexts of the births and deaths, successes and failures, change and fear of change in our lives.

Calvin Schrag has suggested a wonderful image for recounting such nonverbal complexity in our lives—"texture." Think of the texture on the canvas of an oil painting or the texture of the "thick" orchestration in a passage from a Brahms symphony or the texture of richly woven tapestry. All such textures are an important part of the total artistic effect. In our lives, think of the textures of feeling, of ambitions, of friendships—in other words, of all the crucial nonverbal parts of our narratives that only texture can convey. Our narratives are not simply a text but a performance which has a certain "feel" to it (texture).[59] In such narratives the individual is seen as "a living present, coming from a past, and projecting into a future."[60] Our actions disclose not only ourselves but the ways in which we belong to our social world and the time frames within which these actions have their meaning. What we responsibly preserve from our past should not be separated from the creative construction of our future.

Christian communities worship out of their own experience of a redeeming Lord who has already touched their lives as community and as individuals. Worship, because it is a symbolic action, has the ability to take that redemptive experience and to retrieve its textures and times in such a way that celebrating Christians have deeper and better reasons to praise God than before. This process resembles what cultural celebrations and narrations do when, in recapturing past times and events, they forge a new unity among the participants (e.g., the televised funeral of President Kennedy or an anniversary celebration). But this process of worship far surpasses those celebrations because it affords Christians a new experience of God's future that changes the way the past is viewed and the present is lived. In other words, fruitful liturgical celebrations enable Christians to scrutinize their timed actions and to intend better uses of their remaining time.

## Our Intentions and the Sense of Time

Honest and fruitful liturgy occurs when our intentions begin to resemble those of God. God's fundamental intention, according to New Testament writers, is that all people might be saved. The paschal mystery of Christ's death and resurrection put into action God's intention of universal salvation. What remains to be done is that we make God's intentions our own. When Augustine argues against the Donatists, who question the validity of sacraments that are not celebrated by holy people, he asserts that sacramental actions are valid if their celebrants intend what the church intends even in a general way. His reason for this assertion is that sacramental actions are the work of God, not of the celebrant.

But Augustine then goes on to point out that a valid sacrament is not necessarily a fruitful sacrament: to *possess* a sacrament (validity) is not necessarily to *profit* from it (a thought he will repeat in dozens of ways in his work *On Baptism*). There are catechumens, he reminds his opponents, who are more Christian than the baptized (e.g., *On Baptism* 4.21). Fruitful sacraments always have one practical and visible result: people's lives are profoundly changed because God's purposes for life and time are gradually being appropriated.

This précis of liturgical intentionality is a necessary prelude to any discussion of the purpose of time or, more precisely, of the time that is left to us. Our intentions shape and give direction to our use of time. One of the most revealing tests of honest conversion is the extent to which our use of time coincides with God's will that all people be saved. To put it more concretely, it would be hard to imagine Mother Teresa getting up in the morning and wondering what she should do with a new day! She will continue to do what she has already been doing for a long time—care for others. In Mother Teresa's practical formation as a Christian, the liturgical year has contextualized worship and sacraments with powerful "reminders" of God's saving actions through Christ in historical time. Since all Christ's saving actions are for the sake of others, this intention must shape that of any follower of Christ. "My time is your time" becomes thematic for any Christian who has learned that eternity is indeed the "fruit of time."

How often does the liturgy plead that "through the *temporal feasts* that we celebrate, we might merit to attain eternal joy"?[61] How easily do we call God "the powerful and beneficent *moderator of our days and times*"?[62] In celebrating liturgy, we are constantly asking God to enable us to be honest in time and to be purposeful in its use. But if, as we have argued, we are to do this within our own cultural and subcultural situations, then we must have a critical awareness of our cultural assumptions about time. If our eucharistic narratives with their accounts of the wonders that God continues to work among us are to ring true, then our sense of time will need to be prophetically contested.

## Conversion and Its Liturgies: Test of Time

We alluded, in the preceding chapter, to the debate on American individualism and its impact on the American church. More recently, in response to a study of liturgy in some American parishes, Aidan Kavanagh, O.S.B., one of this country's most respected liturgists, said: "I see very little that is countercultural in the parish liturgies reported in the study." He cited with approval the judgment that "liturgy is increasingly sanctifying middle-class skills of joining, acting, and proclaiming in public."[63] This interpretation probably represents the majority view of commentators at the moment and should be taken seriously. There is also much discussion of the assimilation of Catholics into our middle-class American culture.[64] A historical example of such assimilation would be the nineteenth-century immigrant Catholics who slowly absorbed the cultural language, values, and goals of this country. The assimilation process, therefore, might explain the gradual appropriation of individualism, privatism, and consumerism, but it also might explain the positive values of pluralism, democracy, and loyalty. Changes in society such as the sexual revolution, youth culture, and women's rights movement would also have to be factored into any explanation of Americans' current approach to others.[65] Unfortunately, as accurate as these observations may be, they are of little help when the local church has to reassess its directions.[66]

One practical test of both liturgy and culture is their sense of time. The sense of time is both a cultural creation and a Christian conviction. As shown earlier, our American culture attaches certain meanings and values to time. Our faith presents time as God's gift with certain responsibilities.

Conversion in the Judeo-Christian tradition has always implied a re-directed use of time as well as actions in view of God's purposes and goals. If individualism and privatism have become *distorting* factors in the American church's mission and liturgy, one practical test of that thesis will be its use of time. (In the next chapter I will discuss some potentially positive aspects of individualism.)

By that I do not mean, for example, simply counting the number of hours that are spent in volunteer work but rather trying to assess the sense of time that motivates parishes and dioceses to move in one direction rather than another, that inspires individual Christians to commit precious time to help others and to reassess their personal use of time. If such assessments are considered unnecessary or impractical, I fail to see how any realistic assessment of liturgy is possible. There is an implicit warning, I would suggest, in what some sociologists call "symbolic ethnicity."[67] This theory refers to a new stage of inculturation and assimilation in which the present generation adopts cultural practices of former generations that may be "easily expressed and felt, *without requiring undue interference in other aspects of life*" (e.g., taking part in the feast of St. Anthony as celebrated each June in the Italian section of Greenwich Village, New York City).[68] Similarly there is a way of participating in liturgy that allows a continuing Catholic cultural identity without necessarily appropriating the values that liturgy celebrates. Often enough this is not because of bad will but because the local church has not known how to connect liturgy and life or eternity and time.

## American Youth: A Test of Conversion and Time

One practical test group for these remarks on conversion and the use of time is the young people of this country. Young people are often used as examples of American individualism, privatism, and consumerism. Daniel Yankelovich, in his influential book *New Rules,* cites the case of one successful young married person who illustrates these tensions in terms of time:

> Not having enough time becomes such an artificial and important barrier to people who want to live and experience. Our culture seems to treat time as the overriding consideration for everything—when a job is done, when to meet with somebody, how long to talk, how long to have fun. I am trying to get out from under that; but we are all controlled by it, so it is very difficult to do.[69]

Yankelovich is describing members of a younger generation who have an abundance of choices with which to fulfill themselves but have trouble knowing which to choose.[70] Self-fulfillment requires choices and the time in which to pursue those choices. On the other hand, young people are capable of extraordinary generosity, especially in giving time to others, if properly motivated (e.g., many collegians who give part of their limited time to teach or work with the underprivileged).[71] There is, of course, a narcissistic self-fulfillment that distorts the sense of time and the meaning of choice, and Yankelovich points to such trends. But there is also the self-fulfillment that has its meaning only in relation to others—Augustine's thought that we are made for God and will not be completely self-fulfilled until that union. So perhaps it is not so much the cultural problem of time we should ultimately attend to but rather what and how effective are the catechetical[72] and moral strategies for teaching a sense of "shared time" as a corollary of liturgical time. This is where conversion works itself out in practical time.

The church has a classical model for this type of Christian formation called the catechumenate. As an early model for forming adults in the practical steps of conversion, the catechumenate offered prolonged exposure to the Word of God, a Word to be prayed over and then acted upon. In brief, the catechumenate proposed new ways for spending time and new motivations for doing so that were quite different from their previous cultural view and use of time. Although many of these catechumens had "spent time" in pagan temple worship, they learned a new way of being together in time as they heard the Word of God; they were prayed over and blessed; and they were anointed with the oil of the catechumens. Unlike a pagan gathering in a temple, this community was forged by the unifying presence of Christ and the mission Christ gave this gathering. This same conversion process was later built into the monastic life with its *horarium*, or schedule (Latin *hora* means hour)—that is, the way the twenty-four hour span of time was to be spent in praising God and living the gospel life. Monastic prayer was divided and named after the hours of the day and night (matins, prime, sext, etc.). In the Middle Ages, the proliferation of feast days not only validated, to some extent, a religious dimension of time but in actuality provided leisure time for overworked masses of people to praise God. In this country, the Young Catholic Worker movement and CYO (Catholic Youth Organization) before and after World War II were two quite different but fairly successful attempts to offer young Americans ways of spending time together in profitable ways both culturally and religiously. In the past three decades, religious communities and Catholic universities have sponsored successful programs that train and send young people to help the less fortunate in this or other countries. These volunteers give a significant amount of time to this commitment, ranging from a summer to one or two years. In other words, the church has had to be creative in dealing with the cultural sense of time if Christians were to persevere on the path of conversion.

## Conclusions

At the core of every Christian celebration is the firm belief that the reign of God is the final purpose of creation and time. If the reign of God, however, still seems blurred and unreal after all our celebrations, could it be that our cultural sense of time has yet to be challenged and transformed by God's purpose in giving us time? In a sense, the answer is given in the last book of the scriptures, the book of Revelation. The author describes the worship and praise of God and the Lamb, no longer in time but in an eternity that is indeed the fruit of time. This worship is given by those who found the meaning for their times and lives in the following of the Lamb, the crucified and risen Lord. The church in its present liturgy is always looking forward to that future liturgy. Thomas Aquinas, in his beautiful prayer "O Sacred Banquet" (*O Sacrum Convivium*), connects the past death of Christ, the present remembering of that death in the Eucharist, and how it is God's promise of future glory. In theology, we call this sense of all time moving toward God's future as eschatology. But it is not an easy sense of time to acquire in the American culture, where time's purposes can become blurred by cultural schedules of how time should be spent.

This sense of God's future, which changes the way we live in the present and look at our past, is the fruit of conversion. Once again, notice how Christ, in the Emmaus walk, connects the past events of his death with the present disbelieving situation of the disciples and the future salvation that God has planned. These disciples have a change of heart, a conversion. But today's Christians do not work out their conversion in time by themselves any more than the Emmaus disciples. It is the worship of the community that always initiates the Emmaus walk once again. It is the specific local church in its living out of the gospel in a particular culture and time that guides its members in the new wilderness.

But that church must have pastoral creativity as well as cultural awareness if it is going to invite Americans of any age to give more than an hour of worship on Sunday. This pastoral and cultural insight is all the more important when the American church stands in the public forum to witness to the practical corollaries of the Christian vision and its values. In the next chapter we will look more closely at some of the advantages and problems of being a church whose liturgy in church always recalls the liturgy in the world.

# CHAPTER FIVE

# In the New Wilderness

The Puritans found some of their most creative metaphors in biblical imagery. One early colonial writer, John Higgenson, in speaking of God's providence in leading so many believers to seek the kingdom of God in America, instinctively employs the exodus images of a "desert land" and "wilderness." But, unlike the first exodus people, Higgenson's "new wilderness" people, the Puritans, are seen as a true covenant community that has made the most of the New World's opportunities for the sake of the reign of God.

"New wilderness" is still an appropriate metaphor to describe the unique potential of being a Christian and covenant community within the American culture. In fact, our discussion of creation and new creation in chapter 1 takes a much more realistic form when we speak of the American church in the "new wilderness," for it suggests both the dangers and the opportunities in realizing a credible community of witness and worship. Just as the biblical images of creation and new creation remind us that God's transforming vision always occurs in the world, so the new wilderness focuses that same vision more sharply on the complex American culture and subcultures at the end of the twentieth century.

The preceding chapters have been leading in this direction. The biblical themes of creation and new creation in chapter 1 served as a measure for judging how well the American church has evangelized its culture while also benefiting from it. From this conversation two important guidelines emerged. First, the mutual impact of culture and church community must be examined more critically. Otherwise, creation and new creation remain interesting theological ideas that have no complement in reality. Second, the specific mission of the local church depends, in part, on a keen assessment of the strengths and weaknesses of the host culture. In other words, there is no mission without cultural discernment since evangelization and culture are closely linked.

Chapter 2 provided the opportunity to test these ideas historically by concentrating on the immigrant period with its achievements and failures. In regard to the European immigrants, the church was ecclesially and liturgically creative, while in the case of African Americans and Hispanics there was a flawed and sometimes disturbing dichotomy between liturgical ministry and American cultural life. The assessment of our current American Catholic presence is more difficult, not only because we lack total objectivity in the matter but also because it is a good deal more complex in every respect. The generally positive interpretation of the American church by influential critics such as Andrew Greeley is reassuring but still leaves us with the questions of future tasks and challenges for that church.

Since worship and sacrament are rooted in specific communities of faith, chapter 3 took a closer look at the American church's operational understanding of community. We might call this a praxis ecclesiology, that is, a description of what is actually happening in the local church rather than what should be happening. One controverted question is whether the American church is so individualistic as to undermine the very notion of what it means to be an ecclesial or church community. We might expect the current practical ecclesiology of the American church to have been radically reformed by the teaching and practical reforms of Vatican II (or, to use the technical term, the "reception" of Vatican II). These questions remain in play in these last two chapters.

Finally, in chapter 4 we examined one of the most practical measures of both church mission and a healthy culture, the sense of time. The sense of time always accurately reflects the meaning and values of the culture. On the other hand, the American sense of time has been so thoroughly revolutionized in the past century that its effect on the culture is still being analyzed. Liturgy and sacrament function within a liturgical year that interprets the religious meaning of time. One question that arises when the liturgical sense of time and the cultural sense of time interact is, How countercultural must American Catholics be in their use of time? Certainly from a theological perspective there is no authentic conversion that does not require a change in the use of time as well as a change of direction. Ultimately these are not academic discussions. What is possible to achieve in any American church community is directly tied to the cultural sense of time and how successfully the religious meaning of time has been able to challenge it.

In this chapter we turn to the question of the "public presence" of the church in America. Expressed differently, how well does the local church effectively radiate a positive message about the reign of God when so much in our culture seems to contradict that message? Worship and sacrament, after all, do not proclaim their message about God's reign independently of the church or of culture. What are the unique charisms of the American church that help to ground its worship in a given situation and parish? Must the church be countercultural to be effective in its message about God's purposes for our creation and our culture?

## The Public Church

Before we can discover the particular meaning of "community" that the American church seems to personify, there must be a common ground for discussing "church" in general. Jean-Marie Tillard has pointed out that once we accept the church as the place of truth and faith there is a profound connection between that faith and "the way in which each believing community puts into practice in its daily life in the world and celebrates in its liturgical gathering the gift received from God." Each local church must be "the announcement-of-the-facts," a witness, and a revealing event of what God is doing for all people in the world.[1] On reflection, of course, the church is "public" not primarily because it openly takes a stand on certain moral issues but because liturgy, by its very nature, constantly thrusts the church back into God's world to witness as well as to praise and thank God.

In other words, it is the vocation of a believing community to be an effective symbol and sacrament of all that God holds important so that God's creation and new creation may one day be perfectly realized. Such a gathering is a Christian community because it shares most intimately the values and meanings of a crucified and risen Lord. Once a particular church, however, begins to take this job description seriously, it comes up against its particular "world," that is, the complex cultural world of a farming area or an inner-city parish or of a white affluent suburb.[2] Descriptions of this church community as "witness" and "revealing event" suddenly take on a much sharper and more challenging aspect. (One need only compare the responses from rural and suburban areas in the Notre Dame Study to be convinced of such differences.[3]) Each community begins to experience the indifference and hostility of their "world" only when that community begins to be more than a culturally acceptable sign of respectability.

David Roozen has suggested that the religious presence of a church community in its mission to its particular world provides a sharp profile of what that community understands "church" to be. Roozen and his colleagues closely examined some of the Protestant and Catholic parishes of Hartford, Connecticut, to develop this notion of religious presence in mission.[4] Since the church celebrates God as creator and redeemer of this world, the practical corollaries of living the gospel in civil and social life must be articulated (e.g., the Civil Rights Act of 1964). These researchers argued that one way to interpret the particular community is to analyze its relation to the broader community, that is, its mission orientation. (In chapter 3 we began to look at American parishes in this way.) A further question is whether the community would take a public stand on certain issues or not. From these starting points, these researchers then distinguished four orientations: activist, civic, sanctuary, and evangelistic.[5]

The activist orientation sees the world as the normal place in which church exercises its prophetic mission and shares in the public work of creating a better society, while the civic approach, though sharing some of the same activist convictions, feels that the community must discuss the issues but the individual must take responsibility for implementing any corrective or prophetic action. The sanctuary orientation perceives the ecclesial community's otherwordly role as one of teaching and worshiping, while relations with society are maintained by civil obedience and patriotism. The evangelistic outlook also shares some of the sanctuary convictions, except that it encourages its members to insert themselves into the world, not to correct its social aberrations but to preach the gospel.

Roozen notes that people in a particular church community may be theologically illiterate and yet not necessarily morally bankrupt. The church needs to educate its members on the application of the gospel values to the current social issues. In other words, formation of conscience entails both the personal and the public sector. But if the church itself is not a participant in effective actions to implement its convictions, then how can it credibly educate its members?

These abstract descriptions of church community become real in the detailed descriptions of two Catholic parishes in Hartford. The first, St. Margaret's, is discussed as having an activist orientation. The parish is a mixture of Anglos and Spanish-speaking members. The well-celebrated liturgies are described by parishioners as the core of their parish life. At the same time, the community has outreach programs of every conceivable kind and has managed to energize a basically traditional kind of Catholic to envision the larger needs of the world. As one of the parish staff remarks,

> The Mass is where life starts. If the church wants to teach values that are not paramount in the society, then the team of the parish must teach them to

look at life as the Lord does and utilize their talents for more than themselves. . . . This is countercultural, because it is not what the culture around us teaches.[6]

St. Margaret's is in somewhat startling contrast to the other Catholic parish that Roozen and his colleagues discuss. St. Felix's is given as an example of a sanctuary parish. The people are either white, blue-collar workers or low-income families that live in rundown community housing. St. Felix's does not have outreach programs. The pastor sees the parish as having a basically sacramental mission to its members, who see their liturgical participation as the door to personal holiness. People understand the role of the parish as spiritual and physical care for its members. Although a few parishioners do have a larger vision of the mission of the church, this is not shared by most Catholics at St. Felix.

These same differences are reflected in the Notre Dame Study, which questioned American Catholics on the purpose of their belonging to their local Catholic church. Some people's religious concerns, as noted in chapter 3, are focused on themselves and their needs (agentic), while others see their religious practice as sensitizing them to the needs of others (communal). Using these categories, the study concludes that 39 percent of core Catholics "are exclusively agentic or self-centered and individualistic" (i.e., have concerns about self-improvement, reward and punishment, etc.), while only 18 percent are exclusively communal (i.e., have concerns about peace and justice, social disharmony).[7]

If these findings, however, are isolated from other data, we might have a distorted picture of the American parish.[8] The study also shows communal and personal dimensions functioning together in Catholics' definition of the purpose of their parish. In other words, when these dimensions are operative in the same person, the theologian's neat categories of the church "as herald" or "as servant" may not fit. These American Catholics do expect the parish to serve others, "but charitable works can also be done comfortably, particularly in a middle-class, American mainstream religious body."[9] (Americans' willingness, for example, to volunteer their services and money for secular charitable organizations, such as CARE and the Red Cross, is well known.) Another factor is that there is no single model of the American parish: Catholics are affected by the particular emphases and goals of their community.[10]

The initial question that emerges from the discussion of the public presence of American local church may be somewhat different for a Roman Catholic community from what it is for Protestant communities. The Roman Catholic tradition has always insisted on a strong ecclesiology, that is, on a demanding description of what it means to be "the Body of Christ" with a mission to a particular historical and sociocultural situation. No matter what type of classification is used to describe such communities, it is generally understood that most parishes are never purely "activist" or "sanctuary" types. Even the term "community" has always had some distinctly different dimensions for gatherings in different historical and cultural times. What is important, however, is that the local community—while being shaped, to some extent, by its social and cultural contexts—must also transcend it.

In the quarter century since Vatican II, the experience and notion of "being church" have changed for most Roman Catholics in America. How that change is described can vary considerably. For some, the change consisted in a movement from inward-looking and parochial preconciliar Catholics to squabbling and divided postconciliar types.[11] These observers do not necessarily see a better sense of community even if American Catholics now use phrases such as "the People of God" to describe themselves.

A more positive assessment, while acknowledging the turmoil of the post-Vatican II period, would describe the same population as loyal and sympathetic to its Catholic heritage while being "curious as to what the Catholic tradition might have that is special and unique in the contemporary world."[12] These critics seem to find a good sense of community in the preconciliar church, which is still alive and well in the postconciliar age: "The American neighborhood parish is the Sacramental Imagination . . . working its way in the set of circumstances in which it found itself in the big cities of North America."[13] Other commentators have employed the phrase "the Catholic moment" to describe a certain "personalistic communitarianism" that could prove crucial for maintaining an authentic American republic in an interdependent world.[14] These writers tend to view contemporary American Catholics with their emphasis on community as "the only game left in town."

In the two preceding chapters we began to examine the charge that Americans are highly individualistic and privatized in their notion and practice of religion and that Roman Catholics are no exception. If this charge were true, would it not essentially change the Roman Catholic conception of "being church"? Would not such a change, in turn, represent a radical redefinition of the purposes of liturgy and sacrament? One of the practical corollaries of linking creation and new creation is that we cannot simply cite "secular" writers for the public dimension of the question and theologians for the ecclesial dimension. If individualism is in the air, then American Catholics breathe it as much as anyone else.

### Individualistic Catholics in Ecclesial Garb?

Terms such as "individualistic" and "privatized" not only seem to have as many meanings as there are authors but also may suggest pejorative overtones. As a positive characteristic of Americans, I understand "individualism" to refer to the unique, self-sufficient, and God-given profile of a person and that person's right to function and value herself or himself as such. Robert Wuthnow designates three cultural pillars or values of American individualism: the freedom to do what we want, to struggle for individual success, and self-interest. But he points out that three-quarters of the American people also insist that helping the needy is very important and two-thirds regard the giving of time for this purpose as a priority.[15] Do we ultimately have two sets of values on a collision course with each other? Or do such data indicate that there are two quite different understandings of individualism? Before attempting an answer, some of the current discussion should be noted.

In one sense, an "individualistic" person is self-sufficient in ways appropriate to a difficult environment but still needs community. Frederick Jackson Turner's famous "frontier thesis" argued in a somewhat similar way that each American frontier has been settled by people who were self-sufficient enough to overcome its hardships even while they sought to build its communities.[16] More recently, some church historians have suggested that Turner's thesis might apply to the American church. In this view, the early national church of Carroll's time as well as the frontier church of the west of the nineteenth century would differ from the mainly urban immigrant church of cities from Boston to Chicago and Baltimore to St. Louis.[17] Thus, it was not by coincidence, for example, that the liturgical renewal originated at St. John's Abbey in Collegeville, Minnesota.[18]

As noted earlier, Andrew Greeley would characterize American Catholics as "communitarian" in their moral approach to the world, while others would label them "individualistic."[19] In the larger discussion, Herbert Gans has chosen the phrase "middle American individualism" to describe middle-class—that is, working-class—Americans who cherish a combination of cultural and moral values for coping with daily life and a set of goals for encouraging personal and familial growth.[20] They view their work lives as a necessary evil that affords them the standard of living that their parents never had. These Americans will endure public squalor for the sake of private affluence. But, once their incomes begin to decline noticeably, their usual benevolence toward the poor also tends to diminish.[21] Gans argues that this group has developed more individualistic attitudes about the function of faith and church in their lives: "When Catholics discover that ending weekly Mass attendance does not feel like a sin to them or their friends and that they can still be religious, a new, more individualist relationship to the Catholic church has begun."[22] Although I do not agree with Gans's last remark, it illustrates how varied the use of the term "individualism" can be.[23]

Once again, Wuthnow has added some precision to the discussion by taking the value of "caring for others" as a test of American individualism. In his survey, 73 percent of Americans said that "helping other people in need" was absolutely essential or very important.[24] On the other hand, Wuthnow adds that an equally large number of Americans in his survey prize the characteristics that describe individualism.[25] One such example, also cited by Bellah and his colleagues, is that 76 percent of Americans feel that you can be a good person without belonging to a church or synagogue.[26]

There is some correlation between being an active church member and volunteerism. Yet regular churchgoers demonstrate no more caring in the workplace than more indifferent churchgoers.[27] Wuthnow's assessment is that "the evidence on religious participation suggests . . . that churchgoing does not seem to generate convictions about caring that carry over into all realms of the believer's life."[28] In observing some of the differences between Protestants and Catholics in these areas, Wuthnow notes that Protestants were more likely to feel that they could depend on the members of their congregations than Catholics (though the larger size of typical Catholic parishes may be a partial explanation). There is also some data to indicate that Protestants are more likely to act on the values of caring and compassion than Catholics.[29]

Robert Bellah and his colleagues, as already noted, have given similar warnings to the mainline American churches, especially the Roman Catholic church. They point to the acceptance of "thin" theories of good that indicate moral and religious tolerance, if not collusion, with more shallow value systems. Personal choice and value consensus, even for these believers, are private matters lying outside the public realm. The practical result of these attitudes is an operational distinction between a community and a life-style enclave. While community demands a unifying value system that connects public and private life, life-style enclaves replace values and meanings with a shared life-style, and collective support substitutes for authentic community.[30]

The particular strength of churchgoers has ideally been their ability to walk a narrow line between their appreciation and absorption of a culture's best values while maintaining a prophetic stance against the weak-

nesses of that same culture. Bellah and his fellow researchers admit that
individualism will remain an important and even appropriate part of the
American religious experience, but they argue that it must be anchored in
a church that continues to hear sectarian warnings against compromising
gospel values.[31] Gans, however, challenges the unrealistic nostalgia for the
town-meeting and church-fellowship styles of community advocated by
Bellah and his colleagues because they ask far too much: "Because getting
people to work together is extraordinarily difficult, Bellah, like other
American reformers, has placed a heavy load of cultural and political
expectations on community and on actual communities which neither
can bear."[32] This judgment from an eminent sociologist cannot be
bypassed and I will return to it later in the chapter.

Andrew Greeley characterizes Bellah's charges about individualism and
the church as an oversimplification of a highly complex situation. While
admitting important strains of individualism in the American culture, he
rightly points to equally important strains of communalism and to
resilience of the neighborhood city parish as a source of community.[33] If
our church gatherings have not always been as communal as they should
have been, the underlying problem may be that they have not known how
to draw out the best from their American culture.

But perhaps Greeley's strongest point is his insistence that the sacramental imagination ensures that Catholics will continue to value community. In the discussions of Gans and Bellah, the cultural dissolution of
community can too easily be equated with the religious dissolution of an
ecclesial community. Yet there is one important difference between the
two: even in the most desperate of cultural situations, the powerful and
rich symbolic actions of the liturgy have continued to invite and empower
Christians to look beyond the concerns of their own salvation.

One historical example that illustrates this last point is Europe in the
aftermath of the barbarian invasions. The last four hundred years of the
first millennium were witness to the loss of the practical civilization that
Rome had established, which resulted in constant famine, the loss of the
magnificent road system of the empire, and the destruction of the main
centers of culture and learning, the monasteries. In this worst of times,
great bishops such as Chromace of Aquilea were dealing pastorally with
what can only be described as a considerable loss of symbolic competence
on the part of worshiping Christians.

This is apparent in the increasingly allegorical interpretations by theologians not only of worship and sacrament but also of the Eucharist. Most
people were concerned with survival, not with culture or symbols. Yet

symbolic participation managed to survive in the experiences of pilgrimage, in the development and exporting of the more dramatic rituals of Gaul and Jerusalem, in the many forms of popular religion, and even in the otherwise misleading miracle stories about the Eucharist. These were not ideal ways in which to "be church" and participate liturgically, but they were probably the best that one could expect in such conditions.

Several definitions of individualism, sometimes more complementary than competitive, seem to be in play in our American history and practice. Tocqueville's use of the term included self-interest and a sense of community. Turner's frontier people are individualistic in this sense. (With the rise of the industrial revolution, the term could also describe a self-interest destructive of community.) The current profile of Americans as described by Gans, Wuthnow, or Greeley seems to retain these same characteristics in a somewhat dissonant way. In other words, depending on the people themselves and the character of the Christian communities they are a part of, either self-interest or a sense of gathered community may predominate. This may mean that instead of consistently blaming American culture for the selfish individualism of Catholics, the actual practice of being church and participating liturgically in a specific local church should be examined more critically. We turn to an interesting example at the turn of the century in New York to suggest that appearances of individualism may be deceiving.

## The Madonna of 115th Street

The conditions for being a Christian community in mission have seldom been pastorally ideal. But the gathering of Christians has often been effected and strengthened by the most modest fusion of cultural and Christian practices and situations. In examining another situation closer to our own time and culture, both historians and sociologists are revising some of their initial conclusions about the cultural and religious dimensions of nineteenth-century migrations to this country. Timothy Smith, as noted in chapter 3, has persuasively argued that immigration is fundamentally an uprooting and theologizing experience in which many different ethnic groups were confronted with the same challenge: to choose God as a pilgrim people and to make a covenant to walk with God.[34] Immigrants had to make a conscious decision to become more deeply involved in their religious community. With this new appropriation of and participation in their old religion, old rituals then began to take on new meanings. Smith insists that these reappropriated rituals and customs are not necessarily individualistic: "though they made faith a profoundly personal experi-ence, *their aim and outcome was to bind individuals to new communities of belief and action."*[35]

A particularly telling example of this process can be found in the model study of Robert Orsi, who examined the feast of the Madonna in the Italian Harlem section of New York City (1880–1950).[36] He sketches the incredibly difficult working and living situations of Italian immigrants living in uptown Italian Harlem at the end of the last century. Equally important are the connections he uncovers between the territoriality of Italian neigh-borhoods and their local clubs and their representation of towns in Italy. Four of the major problems these immigrants had to face were urban pathology, neighborhood isolation, degradation in the view of outsiders, and persistent poverty.[37] For these people, the feast of the Madonna, which they instituted and celebrated in the streets and courtyards of tenement houses (not in the church) was closely linked to the pervasive influence of the family (*domus*). Other important factors were the Italian immigrants' distrust of the secular clergy, the place of a saint as part of a *domus,* the eat-ing of traditional foods as the "sacrament" of the *domus,* and the convic-tion that the *domus* was the source of conflict.[38]

This description of Italian immigrants seems to confirm the stereotypes of them as superstitious and nonecclesial pagans who used some of the trappings of Christianity without embracing any of its central doctrines or liturgical meanings. But the great merit of Orsi's study is his insight that the feast of the Madonna not only summarized the traumatic experience of the immgrants' dislocation but also supplied a link between Italy and East Harlem. Further, this connection provided the necessary security that the immigrant experience had deprived the people of.[39] The celebration of the feast enacted highly condensed rituals that strengthened the *domus* and facilitated the necessary reconciliation, renewal, and remembrance of these groups.[40]

In brief, what might appear at first glance to be another personal devo-tion that was fundamentally antiliturgical and individualistic was, in fact, a ritually effective way to overcome the isolation of the Italian ghetto (out-siders were welcome to the feast) and to reaffirm the social core of their lives, the *domus*, and the personal and social identity it provided them. If there was to be any sense of an ecclesial community, it would have to come from the effective experience of the *domus*. The efforts of the Pallotine Fathers who staffed the local church to have the statue of the Madonna placed in the church (rather than kept in the tenements) reflect their awareness of how the feast functioned in the larger community. Orsi's study also substantiates the contention of Smith that such rituals, far from being necessarily individualistic, enable individuals to link themselves to new communities of belief and action.

This outlook suggests that Bellah and Gans represent two sides of the same discussion. Bellah and his colleagues are reminding American churches that might assume too much about Christian community that there are forces of individualism and privatism in our culture inimical to such a community. Gans and Greeley, in different ways, are insisting on the viability of such communities, even though they will never take the idealized forms that some ecclesiologists might suggest.

American Catholics have traditionally identified the church community in its institutional forms: the Catholic educational system, the Catholic hospital systems, the Catholic charitable organizations, and the Catholic parish system. The role that these institutions may play in the future of the church in America is complicated and disputed and has been discussed elsewhere.[41] For our purposes, it is more important to pursue the question of the presence of the American local church in terms of its narrative and performance.

## Do You Have Words for the Song?

The gathered community speaks best of what it knows best—the action of God in its midst and the implications of that action for the larger community. The dying and rising of Christ, the paschal mystery, is an experience that shapes the Christian community and constitutes its basic message to the world. The new creation, spoken of in chapter 1, is the transforming result of that same paschal mystery. But since the paschal mystery is an experience, not just an idea, it is best performed and communicated rather than simply talked about and repeated.

The local church as a celebrating community is the normal posture of Christians who have been touched time and again by the power of Christ's dying and rising. That same local church as an evangelizing and prophetic community is the expected response from those who are being redeemed in redeeming others. But the preceding discussion should have reminded us that such a community is ordinary in its cultural appearance and language while extraordinary in its ecclesial performance and message. As the Christian community struggles to hear and apply the Word from the cross, their communication might be described as a rhetoric of persuasion—"a showing, a making manifest through the evocation of new life-styles and new ways of seeing the world. . . . its movements are sketched against the broader background of the habits, customs, and social practices of the polis."[42]

The best example of this rhetoric of persuasion is the Sunday Eucharist. I might visit and observe four parishes in different parts of the United States which are considered moderately successful examples of the post-conciliar liturgical reform. I can foresee that the liturgical responses of these four parishes will resemble each other in postconciliar gesture and text, but there will be two important differences that will set each parish apart: the communal and personal intentions of each parish as well as their cultural and social background. Actions are expressive of the concerns and values of inculturated individuals and communities and go beyond what these groups may understand as the meaning of their actions.[43] The practical pastoral corollary of such actions is that much more is taking place than the outside observer or the community realizes.

Although communications theory may insist on the far-reaching, expressive consequences of our actions, theology should and does demand much more of those same actions. The gathered Christian community in its liturgies always participates in symbolic (and thus, communicative) actions in a public situation for public reasons that are always larger than the specific celebrating community (as the Greek root of "liturgy" reminds us). More simply, no liturgical celebration is solely an "in-house" affair. In particular, the celebration of initiation and Eucharist, by its very nature, communicates publicly that God wills the salvation of all and graciously provides what is necessary for an effective proclamation of that good news by the gathered church.

Worship and sacrament, as communicative actions, link the church with the world in a unique way: "The sacrament of baptism articulates the belief in a Creator and with it a view of the world as God's creation; the baptized renounces evil and enters the world in a quite defined relation."[44] In those same actions, the sense of past, present, and future is radically redefined. In the experience of the celebrating community, for once our shared ultimate meanings and goals are more sharply defined in God's terms, and so our experience of the gift of time is radically refocused.[45] Long before Vatican II, Baroness de Hueck, in speaking of the youth program of her Friendship House, expressed this idea in a very practical and pastoral way: "We base all our work on the liturgy—our cornerstone is the Mass. Then we try to balance, in the order named, the spiritual, educational, recreational, and sports programs."[46]

Therefore, in the case of the four parishes mentioned above as well as of any local church or parish, the communicative nature of liturgical action addresses two of the concerns that we have been discussing in this chapter. First, in the face of whatever individualism may be part of the American culture, liturgical action is, by its very nature, an ecclesial as well as a personal empowerment to do the work of the gospel in the sociocultural and historical situation in which the community finds itself. If this is so, why does the American church sometimes seem to have been at least infected by individualism? The answer might be that the ministries of the church have, as one of their functions, the creative pastoral direction of all the charisms that God has given the community. In chapter 2 we reviewed historical examples of both prophetic and unprophetic direction of such gifts. In the contemporary situation, the prophetic tone of the American bishops' letters on the economy and on peace or their Pro-Life activism still must be preached and appropriated on the local level by those who participate liturgically.[47] Otherwise, the liturgy of the church and that of the world have once again been separated.

Liturgy as communicative action is also the foundation for the narratives of the community. Narrative is based on the shared experience of people in a specific historical and cultural situation, not on a theory of such experience. Communicative action informs and challenges the narratives of a gathered people. One liturgically expressive way, for example, in which the praying community does this is in liturgical response. The "amens" and "and also with yous" of the liturgy are premised on the Spirit's work in the community and express some basic awareness and openness to that action. Narrative need not always be a text. It may shine out through any communicative action.

To ask, then, what is the narrative of each of the four parishes in our example is to request more than their history. Certainly two important theological poles of each community's narrative will be the community's origin in the death and resurrection of Christ and its ultimate goal, the reign of God. The parish community can also give a "biography" of its founding, growth, and current status. But it is the actions of the community that also provide an essential text for its narrative.[48] These actions include the liturgical expressions of the community as well as other expressions of belonging, outreach, and mission. It is this actional dimension of the community that best encompasses its complexity and mystery. No verbal text could hope to describe comprehensively the full meaning of these actions. The rhetoric of persuasion is expressed in these actions like the deeply textured strands of a rich tapestry.

When I, as the outside observer, visit these four parishes, my most lasting impressions will be the narrative of the community which is experi-

124 · An American Emmaus ·

enced rather than simply read.[49] Robert Orsi's Madonna of 115th Street captures this whole discussion. Some of the richness of Orsi's account is due to the diaries and oral histories of parishioners, but it is the action of the procession of the Madonna through those streets of long ago that still expresses most persuasively what no written text could capture—the complexity of a community of Italian immigrants who are also a flawed but real American Christian community in terms that no current theology of church employs.

Such a rhetoric of persuasion, while as flawed as the community that celebrates it, also speaks convincingly of God in its midst. As the community not only hears what God has done for others but narrates, in turn, how God has been "seen" in Boston or Boise as well as in Ur of Chaldees and Jerusalem, the expressive and persuasive character of their story witnesses to their world, even as it clarifies the praise of that community. The liturgical action and word of a community in the new wilderness are shaped by the very texture of their narrative, a narrative unlike any other not only because of the individuals involved but also because of the specific cultural tasks and consequent ecclesial mission.

Ultimately, a rhetoric of persuasion is the same type of witness Paul VI spoke of so forcefully—a handful of Christians whose understanding and sharing of life with others "radiate in an altogether simple and unaffected way their faith in values that go beyond current values."[50] Such Christians provoke irresistible questions in others about the source of their motivations, inspirations, and goals. This silent witness, Paul VI notes, is a very powerful and effective one because it is not repetition of a salvation story but the evangelizing experience of a saving event that is actualized in the midst of the community. This special type of "memory" as the presence of a saving event is regularly found in the liturgical contexts of the Hebrew Scriptures. As noted in the previous chapter, to "remember" what God is doing in one's midst is an invitation to participation in praise and thanksgiving.[51]

Some homely examples of the rhetoric of persuasion come to mind. In the pre-Vatican II church, where there was usually no place for Catholics to express themselves in church, the Miraculous Medal novena, a devotional favorite in this country, allowed for the reading out of petitions and thanksgiving from anonymous parishioners. It was always a moving experience, not only because of its uniqueness at the time but also because, if only for a moment, the hidden lives, faith, and needs of a community were expressed and there was a sense of silent participation on the part of everyone present.

Another example was provided in a recent documentary about the Shakers that was seen by many people in this country on public television. An elderly Shaker woman, when asked by the interviewer how she was taught to pray as a child, rose to her feet and with the grace and agility of a young person began to sing and dance the Shaker song "It's a Gift to Be Simple." It immediately recalled Johannes Metz's use of Martin Buber's hassidic stories to illustrate how narrative is not telling but doing.[52] The evangelization in the catechumenal process provides another example. This gospel formation of catechumens relies, in part, on the living witness of the baptized about their lives of faith and worship in their particular communities. Such narratives foster deeper community because they are affective as well as historical.[53]

The irony is that many American readers will be aware of what is meant by a rhetoric of persuasion and narrative performance from such "secular" models as Alcoholics Anonymous, group therapy, and groups whose members share devastating diseases such as AIDS or drug addiction or who care for those with these problems. No one doubts the efficacy of such sharing and witness because its remedial effects eventually become apparent.

## Presiding or Leading within a Servant Church?

The priest celebrating the Eucharist is still a model of leadership for many people in a highly liturgical church such as the Roman Catholic community. However, as more parishes in the United States begin to experience "priestless Sundays," because of the shortage of ordained priests, when a deacon or a lay person will lead a liturgy of the Word and communion service, this image may change.[54] In the directory from the Congregation on Divine Worship (1988) and in its application to our situation by the American bishops (1989/1990), there is concern not only about the scattering of a priestless parish but also the separation of Holy Communion from the mass and the loss of a sense of ordained ministries in such a parish.[55] The third section of the bishops' statement does recall the various ways in which Christ is present (in the Word, in ministers, in the Eucharist, and in other liturgical celebrations), but as John Huels has pointed out, "it is easy to infer from this discussion that all the symbolic aspects of Christ's presence in the eucharist are also found in the non-eucharistic celebrations with communion: assembly, word, minister, and consecrated hosts."[56] Huels also notes that any remedy for the problem of a shortage of priests, apart from praying for vocations, is not discussed.[57]

The Eucharist celebrates Christ's dying and rising in a unique way, and it constantly enables the participating community to be the Body of Christ. Again, Augustine's words insist: "If it's you that are the body of Christ and its members, it's the mystery meaning you that has been placed on the Lord's table; what you receive is the mystery that means you."[58] Augustine, like Paul, is speaking of the communion received in the celebration of the Eucharist. Therefore, if the immediate future of a growing number of parishes in the American church is a communion service of one type or another, there is a serious problem that does not admit of an ideal solution but may force us to reexamine the connections that Paul and Augustine make.

The American bishops also reasserted that the gathered community without a priest is also a primary symbol. And it is indeed. Just as Paul explained the unity of the community by the power of the Eucharist to the Corinthians, so in a later chapter he described that same community in all its various charisms for its "up-building." But Rosemary Ruether's observation on this point should remind us of the practical consequences of this: "Most church liturgies are dead precisely because they have no real reference point in a community that has a collective sense of its identity and a social praxis that expresses that identity."[59] She is not, I believe, denying (any more than Paul does) the reality of the Eucharist but rather insisting on the responsibility of the gathered church to live out its consequences not only on a personal level but also in its world. To return to Rahner's image, those who do liturgy in church should be the first to do liturgy in the world.

In the Notre Dame Study, it is not surprising that the highest-rated reason for parishioners' attachment to a parish is related to the number of activities they participate in and the highest-scored reason for attraction to a particular parish is "the opportunities for parishioners to participate in community service." The quality of pastoral care and concern provided by parish priests is rated third, after the "quality of friendliness and/or concern among members of the parish."[60] Opportunity for becoming a lay leader in a parish is the fourth highest rated reason for attraction to a parish, followed by the two liturgical reasons: the style of worship and the quality of preaching at mass. These priorities do not denigrate the importance of the liturgy but rather contextualize it.

But leadership, narration, and calling people to ministries and mission within American Catholic communities are complicated by the average size of parishes, often ministering to between twenty-five hundred and five thousand people.[61] Another important factor in this discussion within the American context is the role of women. Since women are already part of many parish staffs and collaborative ministries, it is not surprising that "58% of those outside the pastor who were named as leaders are women."[62] In hospital work, women are often the more visible minister for the Eucharist, counseling, and praying with the sick; and people value them in these roles. What Maria Pilar Aquino says of women within the Hispanic church might be said of other Catholic women:

> It is undeniable that the concrete activity of the Church is supported by women: in pastoral action, evangelization, catechesis, bible groups, sacramental preparation, basic communities, liturgical participation, school, parish, committees for peace and justice . . . and even the very administration of a parish.[63]

But many of these women are deeply dissatisfied, if not angry with the church: "the anger of Catholic 'feminists' is the result of conflict among images of the Church, past and present, Women, past and present, and God and Housewife, present."[64]

Even if one puts aside the question of women's ordination, there seems to be a growing rift between many American Catholic women and the leadership of the church,[65] a rift that is theological, liturgical,[66] and cultural.[67] The crucial role of Hispanic and African American women, for example, is a cultural strength that has yet to be fully appreciated for the ministerial effectiveness of the American church.[68] It touches directly the gathered community because it questions not only how we minister but what we celebrate.[69] Moreover, within our culture, women bring certain qualities to liturgical celebration that seem to be sometimes culturally difficult for many American men: embodiment, expressiveness, devotion, nurturing, a strong sense of community and ministry, and affective commitment.[70] Such charisms model for men certain important dimensions of community and celebration that we need to appropriate more deeply.

## Conclusions

The tentative suggestion of this chapter is that a form of American individualism and a strong practice and theology of church as God's gathered community may not simply coexist but may indeed strengthen and purify one another. Perennial theologies of church do not assure ideal ecclesial communities, but they challenge each generation of Christians in their particular cultural situation to gather an imperfect but credible community of witness and of worship. If, for example, one reads the theological works of St. Augustine without reading his letters and some of his homilies, one might erroneously conclude that his church at Hippo was an ideal Christian community. It was not. But within the complicated sociocultural context of fifth-century North Africa, Augustine's church community did proclaim the reign of God in an impressive and often effective way.

Any such credible ecclesial community, however, is the result of ongoing struggle and challenge from two major sources—the host culture and the gospel. The "new wilderness" offers a suggestive metaphor for the desert experience each community must undertake to clarify and purify its reasons for being gathered in Christ's name. The American church is currently in a transitional stage. In a pastoral situation somewhat similar to the nineteenth-century immigration crisis, the American church is attempting to deal with the vast numbers of Spanish-speaking Christians as well as many more recent groups of immigrants. These immigrant Christians bring with them rich and diverse cultural heritages as well as their own experience as Christian. Their own exodus experience can deeply bind them to Christian communities of belief and action, as in the cases of their nineteenth-century predecessors.

Christian communities in one way or another should be expected to narrate more often what God has and is doing in their midst. (The Search retreats, for young people, for example, modeled on the Cursillo weekends, evoke narrations from participants about their individual and their shared experience as a faith community.) Greeley's reminder about the symbolic imagination of American Catholics should encourage communities to start looking at themselves in more positive and critical ways. One case in point is the position of American women in their church. It is one of the great gifts of American culture to the wider world to have affirmed the unique roles of women in our society. The American church would not have much of a history without such women.

In the final chapter, we will examine the classic liturgical notion of participation as a way of looking at the Christian community in the American culture. Is this classical idea viable in the postindustrial United States on the verge of a new millennium?

# CHAPTER SIX

# American Sacramental Praxis

In both Eastern Europe and some South American countries, where repression and war have recently claimed victims, spontaneous rituals of reaction and protest have frequently marked certain locations with photos, flowers, or candles. People have participated, sometimes at the risk of their lives, in these memorials by simply standing in silence or by bringing their own gifts of flowers. If a television reporter were to ask one such participant what she was doing, she might well answer that it should be obvious. But what is obvious to the participant, is not necessarily obvious to the observer, as Clifford Geertz and others have pointed out. These ritual enactments are "not only models of what they believe, but also models *for* the believing of it. In these plastic dramas men attain their faith as they portray it."[1] There is nothing mechanical or automatic in these rituals. On the contrary, there is a powerful addition of new meaning to the way the participant normally makes sense out of her world.

Staying with our example, some of these participants have doubtless used flowers in more peaceful times to commemorate their dead relatives on special days in the religious or civil calendar. What marks off the first ritual from the second is not only the dramatic situations of war and repression or the unusual site but the way in which the participant's world and its meaning, disturbed by these destructive events, must be renegotiated. The changed situation and its meaning are put into perspective by the experience of this ritual of flowers or photos in its new setting, by which the individual participant has reestablished an important connection with the larger community.[2]

In the previous chapters we have tried to show how Christians and their communities are interconnected with their cultural world. In the last chapter, in particular, we saw how different types of parish communities reflect different sociocultural backgrounds as well as different operational theologies for being together. But communities need not be prisoners to one way of being together. The rhetoric of persuasion is a reminder that new perspectives and new worlds are religious and cultural possibilities. Even in the worst of situations, the retrieval of meaning is possible, as our example above shows. New insights and greater freedom have paradoxically been found even in the concentration camps and war-torn cities of the world.

In this final chapter, we must look more closely at the specific liturgical and sacramental celebrations of the American church. In one sense, this chapter is a reflection and meditation on the previous chapter, for worship and sacraments are never separated from the community that celebrates them. From this intimate link between rituals and the celebrating community we draw another axiom: *the more ritualizing a church is the more it should look to its intentions in such celebrations.* The reason for this warning is that communities do not always mean what they do! Augustine, with his usual flair, expresses it this way: "Don't be surprised, either, at how many bad Christians there are, who fill the church, who communicate at the altar, who loudly praise the bishop or priest when he preaches about good morals. . . . They can be with us in the Church of this time; but in that Church which will come into being after the resurrection, they will be unable to be gathered in with the saints."[3]

In this final chapter, the nature and art of liturgical participation must be discussed. Ritual participation, after all, may be a way of either welcoming or avoiding meanings new and old. One question that emerges from such a discussion is whether we participate in culturally displaced sacraments, that is, sacraments that are not effectively connected to our American culture, so that they are not as prophetic and clarifying for our larger world as they might be. One way in which to test these observations on participation and effective sacraments is to look at the pastoral practice of the sacraments of initiation in the American church.

## Participation and Rituals of Change

The word "participation" has several meanings in English, ranging from superficial involvement to committed cooperation. Television talk shows, for example, often have a master of ceremonies whose job it is to work the audience up to a fever pitch before the star of the show appears. During the course of the show, he will signal the audience for certain kinds of pre-arranged responses. The master of ceremonies, we say, is responsible for "audience participation," that is, for a type of fairly superficial reaction to what is happening on the stage.

On a deeper level, sociologists remind us that participation is a condition of community. Within a community there are groups of people with different needs, for which they must bargain with one another.[4] Whether it is a question of a PTA meeting or a hearing on school busing or environmental concerns, different points of view have to be accommodated in some way. The results of such participation will have an effect on other groups, and so the question arises: Should a particular segment of society be allowed to act as if its actions did not affect others (e.g., abortion vs. right-to-life groups)?

Unity within our American culture occurs when there is some shared purpose that is persuasive enough to bond people (e.g., efforts to help AIDS victims). But organized programs and cooperation with them (e.g., work in an office or factory) do not of themselves assure shared meaning. Formal organizations, such as the Knights of Columbus, require participation only in the sense of accomplishing the specific purposes of the group. Sociologists sometimes classify churches as formal organizations in that they serve the needs of worshipers.[5] "Participation" exists in some of the practical activities of the parish community (e.g., liturgical ministers, religious education teachers, ushers, etc.). This external cooperation in the necessary projects and tasks of the parish certainly indicates some commitment, without necessarily demanding a deeper appropriation of meaning that might lead to a more profound unity among the participants.[6]

Participation in a sociological sense, therefore, entails some common effort and some type of sharing in a common purpose or motive. The American cultural conception of participation encourages some commitment to the activities of the group without necessarily appropriating the underlying motives. Thus, a eucharistic minister or a lector is certainly participating in the important "work" of the parish, presumably because he or she agrees with at least some of the purposes of that parish. But there is a danger in our society, as Robert Wuthnow notes, that "unobservable values may be replaced by observable activities."[7] Thus, a parishioner may give twenty years as a minister or lector without having necessarily made the underlying Christian value of service a part of his or her life.

In brief, there are several widely used meanings for the word "participation" and all these meanings can be found in the life and activities of any parish community. Each of these meanings is legitimate as long as it is not confused with a more demanding use of the word. Thus, when Vatican II in the Constitution on the Liturgy asked for a "full, conscious, and active participation in liturgical celebrations" as the "primary and indispensable source" of the Christian spirit, another more demanding meaning of participation was obviously being employed. In view of what was said in the last chapter, participation is the appropriation of a communicative action and its implications. It is to that conciliar understanding of participation that we now turn.[8]

## Participation as Ongoing Renewal

Participation, in the biblical and theological sense, is a response to God that changes and renews us. Leo the Great often used the term in the same sense as Paul: "What is *participation* with Christ's death for us unless that we cease from being the way we were?"[9] In other words, participation is ongoing conversion that unites us more closely with Christ (in his incarnation and redemption) and with the rest of his body.[10] Leo has retained the christological and the ecclesial dimensions of sacramental participation by being faithful to the Pauline understanding of the term.[11]

In 1 Corinthians 10 Paul uses two Greek terms (*koinōnia, metechein*) meaning "participation" to criticize the Corinthian Christians for their uncritical acceptance of some of their culture's values. If they had followed the gospel values, the poor Christians would not have been embarrassed by their rich fellow Christians in the love feast that preceded the Eucharist. The cultural practice in question seems to be the quite different eating habits of the rich and poor in Corinth and the general custom of rich hosts to provide better food for their colleagues than for their poorer guests.[12]

The centerpiece of Paul's argument against this practice is his tensive use of the term "participation" to contrast the unity that stems from liturgical participation with the Word or with demons.[13] The full import of participation in the paschal mystery is captured in two forceful lines: "Is not the cup of blessing that we bless a sharing (*koinōnia*) in the blood of Christ? And is not the bread we break a sharing (*koinōnia*) in the body of Christ? Because the loaf of bread is one, we, many though we are, are one body for we all partake (*metechomen*) of one loaf" (1 Cor. 10:16–17).[14]

The profound Pauline awareness of the ecclesial and personal implications of participation warns against any superficial reduction of the term to external ritual activity or privatized notions of sacramental reception. The Body of Christ cannot be separated from the act of participation which constitutes it.[15] Paul assumes the objective and gratuitous action of God in the sacramental celebrations of the local church at Corinth while calling its ministers to a more responsible and prophetic role in ensuring honest and fruitful participation. The criterion for fruitful participation, Paul insists, is the appropriation of the meaning and power of the death of Christ for us. It is the power of that death which restores the possibility of unity with God for us and with one another. Thus, the sociocultural and religious disunity in the Corinthian community is a telltale sign for Paul of flawed participation in the worship of the community: "Paul's chagrin was not that the Corinthians were profaning a holy rite but that they are fragmenting a holy society."[16]

At the end of the twentieth century we still have the same pastoral concerns as Paul and Leo the Great. Just as Paul's understanding of participation has been sharpened by the flawed sacramental appropriation of the Corinthians, so Leo's theology and prayers reflect the profound need of the celebrating community to enter more deeply into the paschal mystery as the gratuitous and saving action of God. In other words, participation always prophetically reminds us that "Christ is always present in his Church, especially in its liturgical celebrations"[17] at the same time that it warns us to come to worship with the right dispositions and ready to be more generous in our response to the gospel "lest they receive it in vain."[18]

The vigorous Pauline idea of participation as a complete and transforming investment in the paschal mystery began to disappear only, it would seem, in the early Middle Ages. As more juridical interpretations of the liturgy had an impact on sacramental theology, the term "participation" seems to have been used only occasionally in theological discussion. But practical moral issues of the early Middle Ages, such as simony (the selling of something spiritual), provided more than one occasion for examining "participation" in a new light. In response to how sacramental ministers should assist the faithful in the honest reception of sacraments, theologians once more followed Paul's lead and drew out the implications of the cross.[19] As in the original Pauline teaching, these theologians reiterated that God's action in the liturgical situation does not depend on us, but this assurance does not excuse us from having the proper dispositions for receiving a sacrament.

## Pastoral Implications of Participation

Vatican II found in Paul's teaching about participation a powerful challenge to the religious and cultural disunity of our own century. The council's teaching could be summarized in one sentence: *Participation engenders an authentic worship of God and a profound ecclesial unity rooted in the death and resurrection of Christ.* But the postconciliar commissions that worked on the liturgical reforms were keenly aware that the council expected this teaching to be translated into pastoral forms that people could understand and appropriate. The kiss of peace is one such liturgical reform that concretizes this teaching about participation.

When the kiss of peace was restored to the celebrations of the Eucharist, it quickly became a popular action in most parishes in the United States. One reason for this popularity might be our American cultural propensity for easy social introductions and greetings. In any case, the kiss of peace is usually an occasion for greeting other Catholics who are around us in the church. But is this the principal purpose of this rite? In other words, is this another example of a cultural ritual transposed naïvely to a religious setting?[20]

Historically, Christians were accustomed as early as the second century to exchanging this sign of peace after the prayers of intercession that closed the liturgy of the Word. The position of the rite in the Eucharist usually helps to explain this meaning. When the kiss of peace is done just before the offering of the bread and wine, it might serve as a natural conclusion to the liturgy of the Word or as a response to Jesus' injunction to be reconciled with our sisters and brothers before we offer our gifts at the altar (Matt. 5:23ff.). By the fifth century, however, the sign of peace was usually given immediately after the Our Father to unify and reconcile the eucharistic participants before communion. Augustine explains the rite to the newly baptized in this way: "What is indicated by the lips should happen in the conscience; just as your lips approach the lips of your brothers and sisters, so heart should not be withdrawn from theirs."[21]

The sign of peace in both positions in the Eucharist symbolizes unity and reconciliation. The prayer immediately before the rite recalls the postresurrection scene in which Christ bestows his peace on his reconciled disciples. The General Instruction of the Roman Missal also understands the rite in this way: "Before they share the same bread, the faithful implore peace and unity for the Church and for the whole human family and offer some sign of their love for one another."[22] The kiss of peace ritualizes eucharistic participation and honest worship of God, which imply unity with our sisters and brothers.

But if this rite simply becomes an extension of our cultural rituals of greeting, then its meaning has been considerably reduced. What distinguishes this rite from our American rituals of greeting and friendship is its ability to deepen our intention of wanting to do what Christ asks for—to reconcile and be one with others. For Paul, sin always implied disunity and division; thus, the heart of the church's mission was to reconcile and unify all in Christ (2 Cor. 5:11–21). When flawed Christians honestly exchange this sign, their imperfect but real unity and reconciliation are a powerful witness to the coming reign of God, a reign of total peace and unity.

Such unity, however, is the result of an ongoing conversion of the Christian community and its individual members, and this always occurs in a specific culture. Evangelization provides the initial call to conversion, which is intensified in each celebration of Word and sacrament. This experience of conversion reveals the disunity that sin causes and at the same time the gathering of God's people that redemption initiates. This is the obvious intent of the eucharistic plea that the celebrating community might become one body, one Spirit in Christ. A Christian community that gives even an imperfect witness of such unity makes God's promise of a new creation quite real. On the other hand, without such witness, the present purposes and the future promises of God's salvation will remain obscure. In brief, if the reign of God is usually described as this definitive and mutual presence of God and us with one another, some credible testimony must be given in our own time and to our own culture. The sign of peace, as one example of participation, is potentially a powerful symbol of imperfect but real reconciliation and unity.

When liturgical participation is analyzed within a particular culture and historical era, another level of complexity is introduced which makes the witness of such unity difficult to assess. At the beginning of the chapter, I noted the range of meanings associated with the term participation. The cultural use of this term in our country is much less demanding than the theological meaning we have just discussed. A sociologist knows that participation is necessary for community, but have we Christians yet realized that a deeply unifying participation is what Christianity is all about?

## Who Challenges the Christian Community?

Participation is about the fruitful and effective celebration of liturgy. But the fear of pelagianism, understood as some sort of self-propelled spiritual improvement, has always haunted any discussion of the meaning of fruitful participation. Ever since the time of Augustine in the fifth century, theologians have worried that any discussion of a fruitful sacrament might be an invitation to forget that God is the source of all such participation. A similar concern has also plagued the study of the interpretation of meaning (hermeneutics). For example, on a Sunday morning, as a parish community celebrates the Eucharist, an observer might ask what meanings are being celebrated in this ritual and how those same meanings are effectively shared among a group of people. To respond to these important questions, another axiom is offered: *Participation challenges the worshiping community's intentions and meaning and serves as a reminder that God is the source of all salvation.*

Any community must begin with people sharing the same meanings. Christian community begins with the meaning of the death and resurrection of Jesus and continues with the celebration of that meaning. Observers of our Sunday Eucharist cannot confine themselves to what is going on in the minds of participating parishioners. Meaning can also be found in what these people are actually doing, in the ritual practices.[23] In other words, when we look at the practice of a community, we discover not the private but rather the shared meanings fleshed out in the shared practice of this group of people. The practical corollary of this observation is that we must look at what people are doing as well as what they are saying (expressed more technically, the observer must look at the texture of their actions as well as the texts of their words).[24]

Participation, then, does not discuss how lively our rituals are but rather how spirit-giving our meanings are. There is no liturgical celebration at which God does not invite us to "own" more deeply the implications of Christ's death and resurrection by sharing symbolic liturgical actions and words. In responding to this invitation, there is also a deepened sense of community among us. But we must not forget that these particular celebrating Christians are also Americans (or whatever cultural group is in question). Creation and new creation in Christ are not simply international ideas that have no cultural resonance. Our American culture, like all cultures, provides a certain way of listening and responding with which we hear God's invitations and meanings as well as anyone else's. The powerful but often implicit meanings of our culture may at times be in tension, if not conflict, with God's meaning, especially as found in the death and resurrection of Christ. On the other hand, that same American culture can often provide a better vantage point from which to welcome God's insights. Our human actions, which so often carry cultural meanings (e.g., the kiss of peace and its secular counterpart, our American greeting rituals), can also provide a tensive and clarifying dialogue with gospel meanings and values (e.g., the civility implicit in public greeting rituals versus the Christian recognition of others as the family of God in the sign of peace).[25]

Mary Collins has commented on this crucial problem of authentic participation in looking at the celebration of the feast of Our Lady of Guadalupe. Her eloquent and prophetic analysis merits its full citation:

The Christian liturgical assembly which fails to reveal the reconciling power of the reign of God is a flaccid manifestation instead of a dying Body of

Christ. In Mexico City on the feast of Our Lady of Guadalupe the powerful ecclesiastical and civil elites gather inside the basilica with US tourists to eat at the eucharistic table. Outside, thousands of peasants remain marginalized even on this patronal feast, performing ritual dances in the square to memorialise the coming of the Spanish conquistadores who shaped their world and diminished their humanity. There is no hint in either of these assemblies that anyone present believes in the power of baptism and the Church's Eucharist to overcome this division.[26]

To summarize, participation is both a practical witness of the gathered Christian community and a liturgical response to God's redemptive and unifying work. Authentic and fruitful participation is also an interpretive action that clarifies God's meanings and values for our lives. Communities of liturgical celebration are involved in interpretive actions that disclose what God is doing in our lives and world, and the practical implications for living as Christians within our own culture. Such celebrations also invite and enable us to appropriate more deeply God's purposes as realized in Christ and the work of the Spirit. But if participation involves interpretation, then is it only the community's version of the gospel that we share?

## Participation as Musical Performance

When we look more closely at the Sunday morning community participating in the Eucharist, it might seem that everyone is perhaps doing the same ritual actions but each one appears to be in her own private devotional world. Where is the unity in such a situation? To deal with this possibility, I would like to propose a metaphor to help us look at the problem of participation as interpretation—the performance of a musical classic.

If one goes to Lincoln Center to hear the New York Philharmonic play Beethoven's *Fifth Symphony* under the direction of their conductor, Kurt Masur, one must remember certain things. First, the orchestra has played this symphony many times under a number of distinguished conductors, none of whom interprets this familiar music in exactly the same way, despite the fact that they all read the music from a fixed and detailed score or text. This should not be surprising, since the *Fifth Symphony* is a classic whose "meaning" cannot be exhausted.[27] Second, no matter how many insightful performances of this work the musicians have already given, they must reinvest themselves in performing this classic if they are to have another successful interpretation of the music. Third, if the audience is not to waste their money and time, it must also enter into this process of interpretation, not by playing the music but by truly listening to it. Finally, in a musical performance players and audience move from a text (the musical score) to the action of performing or listening.[28] On this particular evening, then, if the conductor, the players, and the audience enter into this dynamic process of interpretation of Beethoven's music, *they will indeed become a community of interpretation.*

This metaphor is based on the important work of Paul Ricoeur. I have no intention of rehearsing here his whole theory of interpretation since it has been insightfully done elsewhere.[29] Briefly, Ricoeur has explained how our discourse and its written form, a text, can open up a new world of references.[30] Interpretation of the text is the first step in entering this new world. He has pointed out that appropriation is the final stage of interpretation since it actualizes or makes present the text for the reader. But there is one condition for this happening: I must become a "disciple of the text."[31] In other words, I must be completely open to the meaning in the text. When I appropriate the meaning of the text, a new and more active way of looking at reality is afforded me. The text provokes powerful questions that bridge its past with the reader's present and thus clear the way for new understanding.

Ricoeur provides an illuminating metaphor to describe the process of appropriation of meaning in a text: it is like the performance of a musical score.[32] If the reader reviews what was said above about a musical performance, it should be apparent that this is a wonderful comparison because it entails a constantly new and more insightful reading of a classic that can never be exhausted. This approach does not forget the historical and social background of the text or the music, but reminds us that there is more to the text than that.[33] The classic does not disown its cultural contexts (e.g., in Beethoven's case, nineteenth-century Vienna and the composer's role as a bridge between the classical and romantic periods of music) but rather transforms them into a universal language. The twentieth-century New Yorker does not need the cultural background of the nineteenth-century Viennese in order to enjoy and appropriate Beethoven's *Fifth Symphony.*

At this point, we can return to the Sunday morning eucharistic community and their participation in the liturgy. In Word and sacrament they are given God's classic, the paschal mystery. God's gift enables them to participate in this paschal mystery "knowingly, actively, fruitfully." Liturgy, more than any other classic, invites and provokes Christians' interpretive performances or participation. Such performances, while appreciative of the original setting of this classic, are carried out and listened to within the current historical and sociocultural contexts of this Sunday morning community. The community must also be willing to continue the process of interpretation and reinvestment in the meaning of the Eucharist each time they assemble. This community, more than any concert performers or audience, is invited in each liturgical action to become once again a community of interpretation. This interpretation cannot be limited to some theological or devotional ideas about the liturgical actions and text being celebrated, since God's presence in the liturgy reaches every level of the participating community's and individual's being. Unity in this community is thus deepened because God's meanings are shared in more profound ways. This interpretive dimension does not detract from the teaching office of the universal or local church but rather is a response to that teaching. But how deeply does this unity permeate the actual sacramental practice of a specific parish community?

## As Your Sacraments, So Your Church?

As discussed earlier, Paul linked sacramental praxis in the Corinthian community with their conception of what it meant to be the body of Christ. That classical Pauline connection still provides a theological guideline today. In the last two decades I have spent a considerable amount of time speaking at religious education and liturgical congresses throughout this country and working with their offices in particular dioceses to implement sacramental programs. I have great admiration for the highly professional preparation and the creative and generous service of so many American Catholics in these ministries. The following remarks, then, should be interpreted not as a critique of what has been accomplished by these ministries but as a reflection of acknowledged problems and of the sometimes unappreciated creativity in many American pastoral situations.

I would phrase the problem in this way: it is not uncommon to find specific sacramental programs in the same parish which are at odds with one another in their requirements but which also "cue" parishioners to an incomplete idea of what it means to be church. Take the case of a typical parish in a large urban setting. Such a parish might have a Rite of Christian Initiation of Adults (RCIA) program, an infant baptism program for parents, a confirmation program, a marriage preparation program, and a penance and reconciliation program for children. In the best possible scenario we can presume that the staff of each of these programs has been carefully trained. This parish is obviously concerned about an active and fruitful sacramental participation, as called for by Vatican II.

Since initiation is the foundation of the other sacramental programs, we should begin there. The RCIA program permits interested adult inquirers to have contact with the larger faith community and acquaint themselves with the worship and teaching of the church. (Of the 1,099 parishes surveyed in the Notre Dame Study, only 32 percent had an organized RCIA program.[34]) The program usually follows the school year calendar of approximately nine months, and candidates are normally baptized at the Easter Vigil. Taking into account holidays, the program might last about seven months. In a parish, the catechumenal team might include a priest and several sufficiently or highly trained parishioners.

The basic commitment demanded of candidates in the RCIA program might be a willingness to attend the weekly two-hour sessions and some participation in the discussions. The election of the candidates for the initiation sacraments is the normal expectation of both the team and the candidates. The contact of the parishioners with the catechumens is limited to the specific ceremonies during lent (e.g., the dismissal of the catechumens after the Liturgy of the Word) at one of the Sunday Eucharists. The catechumens' principal formation to the Christian life is instruction in the basic doctrine of the church and the familiarization with the worship of the Roman Catholic communion. Time is provided at each session for questions of the catechumens. There is a weekend lenten retreat for the team and candidates in preparation for the reception of initiation and Eucharist. There is no post-Easter (mystagogical) followup for the newly initiated Christians.[35]

I have tried to describe the catechumenal program of an above-average parish.[36] Just as initiation is the door to other sacramental participation, so it also embodies the implicit theological and pastoral model for other sacramental participation. This observation is borne out in the history of sacraments such that I would propose an axiom: *As the praxis of initiation, so the praxis of the other sacraments.* (I will return to this point shortly.) Praxis of initiation includes not only the doctrine and the words of the ritual but also the actions of the community as well as the actions of the ritual. The proverb Actions Speak Louder Than Words has a particular force in a liturgical situation.

In analyzing the requirements of this program for commitment, I would make the following observations: (1) This implementation of the RCIA requires a considerable expenditure of time on the part of staff and candidates, and because of this fact the staff may find it difficult to address the unique situation of each catechumen. (2) This process affords the catechumens no real experience of the church community. (3) The program reflects the parish in that it offers little sense of mission, while service is understood in mainly institutional terms (the lack of a followup period after initiation is but one sign of this problem). (4) Doctrinal information, though important, is confused here with evangelization, a much more demanding ecclesial and personal process. (5) This parish may instruct, but is it also learning from the commitment of the candidates? (6) The demands for commitment, aside from the time spent in meetings, seem to be minimal. Weight Watchers or Alcoholics Anonymous would demand more commitment in terms of time and change of life-style. This catechumenal program may not be realizing its full potential as a major force in the Christian renewal of this parish.

The central dynamic of the RCIA, as described in the introduction to the rite, is ignored, and thus the process is in danger of being reduced to a program: "The initiation of catechumens is a gradual process that takes place within the community of the faithful. By joining the catechumens in reflecting on the value of the paschal mystery and by renewing their own conversion, the faithful provide an example that will help the catechumens to obey the Holy Spirit more generously."[37] In this succinct statement, the ecclesial process of conversion, in which the growing commitment of candidates calls out new commitment from the initiated even as the candidates are challenged by the community's witness and mission, is eloquently described.

If the process of adult initiation provides a positive norm for other sacraments, we might expect to find similar expectations in other sacramental preparations. In point of fact, we might well find quite different expectations in other programs of the parish. The preparation for infant baptism, for example, makes certain demands on the parents in order to ascertain that they have at least some minimal Christian commitment. The parents may be expected to come to three catechetical group sessions and to one meeting with the pastor or one of his staff. If the parents do not cooperate, this may be viewed as a lack of minimal commitment, and the baptism of the infant may be deferred in a kindly but firm fashion.

Even though less time is involved in meeting demands of infant baptism than those of the catechumenal process, the parish in our example obviously has much clearer criteria for infant baptism than for the RCIA. The parish also seems willing to stand firm on the deferral of baptism, if necessary, even though this is always a potentially explosive pastoral situation. On the other hand, as in the catechumenal program, instructions may have substituted for evangelization of the parents. Many young couples have yet to appropriate their faith, and the occasion of their infant's baptism is a unique opportunity for them to reconsider their own position.

Another point of comparison is the marriage preparation in the same parish. After the initial interview with a priest, in which a first contact and paperwork are completed, the couple might be asked to attend the diocesan pre-Cana conference, which involves four evening sessions or a weekend. Although there is some general inquiry about the faith of the couple, their willingness to answer the canonical questionnaire and to attend the pre-Cana talks may well be equated with readiness for the sacrament.

Although the classical theology for the sacrament of marriage is based on an ecclesial ideal (Christ's love for the church is mirrored in the love of the couple [Eph. 5:25–28][38]), the actual praxis described above assumes readiness for a sacrament on generally inadequate grounds, which in no way reflects the concerns of a responsible initiation theology or ecclesiology. While bishops and marriage tribunals bemoan the number of applications for annulments, little is done about the root cause—an inadequate conception of and commitment to the faith required for a fruitful sacrament.

In setting up these comparisons, I am keenly aware that Roman Catholic parishes in the United States might have different descriptions of their praxis for each sacrament. This disparity of praxis does not vitiate the model's purpose, which is to illustrate operational and somewhat contradictory approaches to three sacraments within the same parish—a not uncommon phenomenon in my experience. Readiness for a fruitful, and not just a valid, sacrament must rest on the ecclesial nature of symbolic participation: "For it is through the liturgy, especially, that *the faithful are enabled to express in their lives and manifest to others the mystery of Christ and the real nature of the true Church.*"[39] This traditional teaching is sometimes difficult to believe in the midst of the pastoral realities of ministry. But it is one of the major reasons why we continue our ministry in confidence, whatever our cultural and religious situation might be.

The import of the council's teaching in this last excerpt is quite classical. Augustine himself (who gave definitive direction to the distinction between a valid and a fruitful sacramental participation) constantly insisted on the symbolic responsibility to show forth this mystery of Christ: "So if it's you that are the body of Christ and its members, it's the mystery meaning you that has been placed on the Lord's table; what you receive is the mystery that means you."[40] In the context of the homily, it is quite clear that Augustine does not refer to merely ritual reception of the Eucharist but to symbolic appropriation and ecclesial responsibility for the mystery of Christ.

Once again, the point of these remarks is not to denigrate the long hours and hard work that pastoral teams in so many American parishes and other ministries expend. On the other hand, the council was not offering theories about how parishes should be run. Rather, the same point that was made in chapter 5 is being made here: the liturgy empowers the gathered local church and its individual members to be and to do much more than they might care to believe. Pastoral expectations understandably can be lowered by the apparently poor reception of so much hard work. As Forster and Sweetser point out, in summarizing their parish evaluation polls over the past twenty years, the fact that parishioners are in favor of a particular parish activity does not mean they will take part in it.[41] But here is where the danger of liturgy is: once more, observable actions may replace, rather than empower, unobservable intentions.

## The Spirit over the Waters?

A better-known example of this problem of different sacramental programs that give confusing, if not contradictory, signals about the nature and mission of the local church is the praxis of confirmation. For well over a decade, there has been a growing debate in this country between those who favor the liturgical sequence of initiation sacraments (baptism, confirmation, Eucharist) and those who emphasize the faith maturity of the candidate for this sacrament (baptism, Eucharist, confirmation). (This debate, I should add, is not an academic affair. In my own experience, it often engages the liturgy office and the religious education office of the same diocese, who are working at cross-purposes.)

The Notre Dame Study notes that there is no general praxis of confirmation in the American church. Of the thirty-six parishes closely surveyed, all demanded some form of sacramental preparation. Parents were required to participate with their children in such programs in 61 percent of the parishes in this group. The two average age groups for the sacrament (twelve to fifteen years, and sixteen and older) are represented rather evenly across the spectrum of parishes. To complete this varied picture, the study observes that programs last from six weeks up to three years with the conferral of the sacrament being given in the senior year. Furthermore, even adult baptism is not usually accompanied by confirmation and first Eucharist in the representative sample.[42] Obviously, there are different conceptions of confirmation behind the different practices.

My purpose here is not to solve this debate but to point out an assumption that is made on both sides of the question. This assumption is ecclesial in nature and is best expressed as a question: Is there a credible community into which to receive the confirmed? Not only initiation but all the sacraments take place in the midst of the Christian community. This is a principle that the history of sacramental praxis would consistently affirm: without a credible Christian community, the pastoral celebration of sacrament becomes very difficult. When there is a parish that is not yet a community, the sacraments given are valid and, let us hope, individually fruitful; but in terms of the full meaning of the sacraments, where are the first signs of redemptive, and not merely ritual, unity that manifest to others the mystery of Christ and the real nature of the true church?

Dispensing sacraments does not of itself automatically produce a church community. This is Paul's point, even as he speaks of the unity of the body of Christ to a disunited community. Paul's forceful teaching about the thrust of all liturgy as well as of all charismatic gifts provides a fundamental ecclesial principle: "Since you have set your hearts on spiritual gifts, *try to be rich in those that build up the church*" (1 Cor. 14:12). "Building up" (*oikodomē*) the church is not an organizational term but rather the description of an ecclesial process in which God gifts the individuals of the community for the sake of the specific mission of that community. Franz Josef van Beeck sums up this aspect of all liturgical and sacramental life: "Christian worship also involves the Church's relationship with the world. Hence, it must allow its worship to be tested and verified externally as well. By making Christians witnesses, worship involves them in a commitment to the life of readiness in anticipation of the judgment, in the imitation of Christ."[43]

In the American situation, where individualism, if not tempered and redirected by the witness and mission of the church, might hamper the development of authentic Christian community, Paul's reminder that God's gifts will work their purpose if we cooperate with them is still relevant today. There is no situation, no cultural context, in which God's promise cannot be realized. If the honest answer to the question about whether there is in fact a community in which to receive the confirmed, is doubtful or even negative, this situation does not have to continue. The celebration of the sacraments of initiation, which include confirmation, provides a moment of ecclesial honesty in which the community remembers what God has given them and why it has been given. But if the community does not entertain such questions regularly, some of the cultural and personal obstacles to a fruitful reception of confirmation will not be corrected. Michael Warren touches on the core of the problem when he insists that in discussing confirmation it is the community's commitment to watch over the faith-growth of this person that is crucial.[44]

Another assumption often made is that there are problems with confirmation but not with the other sacraments. The sacramental system is a whole piece of cloth, not patches sewn together. A total sacramental and pastoral strategy in which there are some common ecclesial values growing out of a sense of mission can reorient a parish community. The conservative but effective neocatechumenal movement in Europe and South America, for example, has dramatically proved this. This movement is based on the conviction that the RCIA models a total process for Christian community. In place of the parish mission, a team of evangelizers comes into a parish for a period of a few months and, in effect, invites all the members of the community to go through a catechumenal process as a way of renewing the shared gospel values and vision of everyone.

Compare this approach with the situation even in many of our better parishes where groups of parishioners gather around a particular work or cause (e.g., St. Vincent de Paul Society, Pro-Life, etc.) but do not interact with the rest of the parish. Or, to express the same problem in another area, do the individual sacramental programs help to tear down some of the artificial barriers that our American culture can sometimes foster even in Christian communities, for example, the separation between the young and old, or between ethnic groups within the same parish?

## Collaborative Ministry and Participation

Paul VI gave a surprising test for those who are truly evangelized: they evangelize others in turn.[45] This evangelization may take many different forms, but they are all ministerial and engender participation in one way or another. One pastorally effective model of such evangelizing participation is collaborative ministry, which invites a wider participation in and responsibility for the work of the parish community. This model takes seriously the teaching of the church that the initiation sacraments bring all Christians into a shared and holy priesthood. The People of God are indeed a priestly people.[46] The ordained ministries of the church which have the charism of leadership are linked to the nonordained ministries and charisms of all the baptized.[47] Paul's frequent references to his "co-workers" refer to Christians with varying ministries.[48]

Collaborative ministry implements this teaching and its implications. At the same time, this model may be one approach to dealing with some of the problems that must come with the projected declining ratio of priests to people: "According to the data presented here, steady growth in church membership and precipitous decline in the diocesan and religious clergy are practically inevitable. Consequently, it is highly probable that the layperson to priest ratio in the United States will double in size from 1,100 Catholics per active priest in 1975 to 2,200 in 2005."[49] But collaboration is more than an institutional response to a looming pastoral crisis.

Such collaboration assumes that the local church has a mission to the larger world and that the liturgy of the world and that of the church are connected, as argued in previous chapters. It also assumes that the various ministries of the church are not in competition with or in fear of one another. To ensure clear pastoral objectives for the ministries of a parish community, a process of "refounding" is often employed. Religious communities that have used this concept return to the originating insight of their founder.[50] On the parish level, such refounding would involve a re-examination on the part of parishioners about the goals of the community and their implementation based on some reeducation about the theology of gathered church.[51] An ensuing dialogue of ordained ministers and laypersons focuses on their particular sociocultural and religious situation and what pastoral strategies and programs are needed. Each local ministry implicates these lay people in decision making and promoting their ministries.

The Hispanic local churches have realized a similar model of collaboration on a larger scale, a process called *encuentro* (encounter).[52] The National Conference of Catholic Bishops in their pastoral letter on Hispanic ministry (1983) urged the Hispanic people "to raise their prophetic voices to us once again" and convoked III Encuentro "so that together we can face our responsibilities well."[53] They envisioned a process that would begin with the basic communities and parishes, move to dioceses and regions, and culminate in a national gathering. Each delegation was to have a limit of two priests with one farmworker or laborer, two women, and one young person. There was not only a cross-section of Hispanics of different ethnic origins but also of all sections of the ordained and non-ordained.[54]

A process of arriving at consensus was realized through working groups and subgroups who dialogued on pastoral guidelines, commitments, and followup and then returned to plenary sessions.[55] Liturgy and other prayer forms were an essential part of each day's gathering. The results are impressive: prophetic commitments from "a people who are a minority without economic means or a sufficient number of specialized pastoral agents, with few leaders, and without satisfactory support. . . . The starting point in this process is the socioreligious reality which is analyzed and judged in the light of the Gospel and the teachings of the Church and then acted upon in this same light."[56]

This model of collaboration is not always an easy one to implement because it requires some honest self-evaluation on the part of the local church and a belief in the complementary charisms of God's people that is carried into practice. But there are a number of American parishes that already function this way without having formally adopted a collaborative model.[57] Collaboration also puts into practice a frequent theme of concluding prayers of the eucharistic celebrations: "You give us a share in the one bread and the one cup and make us one in Christ. Help us to bring your salvation and joy to all the the world" (Fifth Sunday in Ordinary Time).

Perhaps the bridge between the liturgical life of a local church and the sociocultural life of an American Catholic is to be found in the classical liturgical idea of *devotio,* that is, taking into account affections and feelings as well as the other dimensions of the praying person.

### Devotio Futura?

Our contemporary American life is filled with some obvious and some more subtle kinds of ritual (e.g., the rituals of football games as opposed to the more subtle "cues" we give people who bore or interest us). If anything, young Americans seem to need ritual even more than their parents did (even a cursory viewing a television channel that caters to the audiovisual needs of young people will provide examples). Many of these rituals are popular because they permit and promote the expression of feelings and affections (e.g., standing while singing the college school song). Religious devotions have the similar purpose of allowing the whole person to address God with thoughts and feelings, as an extension of one's liturgical prayer. Popular religious devotions are particular forms of prayer that more directly use folkways and rituals in their expression (e.g., the stations of the cross involves the actual walking from station to station in recalling the incidents of Christ's passion).

In the aftermath of the council, the word "devotion" sometimes took on a pejorative meaning, indicating an untheological and self-centered style of praying. The word, however, has a rich ecclesial and liturgical history.[58] In its early use in liturgical prayer, *devotio* often indicated the action of offering to God.[59] By the medieval period, the term took on the more affective meaning of praying with fervor, that is, "where what is said agrees with what is thought, where the mind is at one with the heart."[60] When popular religious devotions began to substitute for a liturgy that was becoming ever more distanced from the people, the privatized notion of religious devotion began to predominate.

Following Vatican II, many such religious devotions of questionable value were quietly discontinued (e.g., devotions that concentrated on getting something from God). Yet even today, devotions among American Catholics can hardly be said to have disappeared. Even a cursory reading of the surveys we have mentioned in this book reveals a surprisingly active devotion to the rosary and to certain saints.[61] To dismiss such piety as popular devotion in the pejorative sense is to lose some insight about liturgical participation as an expression of our whole selves.

Vatican II did not forbid devotions but asked that they be in accord with the liturgical year, that they draw their inspiration from the liturgy, and that such practices should lead people to participation in the liturgy.[62] Paul VI gave a practical example of these guidelines in regard to Marian devotions. He pointed out that while the Orthodox have maintained this devotion to Mary and the Anglican communion has a place for her in its theology, many other Christian communities as well as some feminists have honest problems with such devotion. Paul VI remarks that in the history of Marian devotions at their best, there has always been a connection between the expression of devotion and the cultural and historical genius of the people.[63] Finally, he notes that an authentic devotion to Mary is always one that leads people to a more committed gospel life.[64] How might these guidelines be worked out in our own culture?

Certainly, the devotional life that Archbishop Carroll encouraged among American colonial Catholics was quite different in expression from that urged by the American bishops for the immigrants in the nineteenth century.[65] Carroll as a student, and later as a Jesuit, had acquired great admiration for English Catholic piety, which essentially fostered a liturgical spirituality rather than an individualistic pietism.[66] Carroll's successors in dealing with the immigrant tides favored a different devotional piety, where there was sometimes a misplaced emphasis on indulgences and petition, typical of some nineteenth-century devotions.[67] In the context of those times, when immigrants suffered loss of their country, traumatic voyages, and crushing social conditions in this country, the emphasis on the sufferings of Christ and the life of the Holy Family was a pastoral attempt to respond to these experiences and to connect them with the prayer of the church.[68]

Furthermore, Joseph Chinnici has pointed out how the innovative pastoral use of popular devotions in the nineteenth century, such as those to the Sacred Heart and the Holy Spirit, indicates the social and cultural implications of Catholicism in the American situation. In the post–Civil War period, there was an intense effort "to fashion a religious expression reflective of experience." The result was devotions and prayer forms that symbolized the American Catholic view of politics, society, the church, and Catholics themselves.[69] (An excellent example of such devotion and its more profound ecclesial effects was the Madonna of Italian Harlem in the late nineteenth century, which we discussed earlier.)

An early pastoral example in this country of religious devotions connected to the liturgy is the pioneering work of Monsignor Martin Hellriegel (whose contributions were discussed in chapter 2). Hellriegel took cultural actions such as family meals and birthdays and suggested actions as well as prayers that might sanctify the occasion in the home. In the Hispanic cultures, the customs associated with the liturgical year combine the devotional and the ecclesial dimensions (e.g., in the days preceding the feast of Christmas, *Las Posadas* ["the inns"], in which the community is rejected as they move from one home to the next until they are finally welcomed to some hospitality).[70] After Vatican II, for example, the American Franciscans, whose churches were always crowded for the popular St. Anthony devotions, revised the novena prayers to express the conciliar theology in a popular way and gave new importance to a more biblical style of preaching in the novenas. Gatherings of young people that combine prayer and song so that affective and expressive dimensions are included in liturgy and devotion have proven popular and effective.[71]

Among the postconciliar rituals, the communal anointing of the sick has proved to be an unlikely but popular liturgical celebration in this country. Even for those who are not "sick" but who crowd into such celebrations, this liturgy represents an important meaning in their lives and can potentially renew their ecclesial vocation. Because American culture lives with the paradox of having an exaggerated emphasis on youth coupled with an elderly population that is living longer, the experiences of sickness and death present troubling questions. The celebration of anointing, with its liturgy of the Word, penitential prayers and intercessions, the blessing of the oil, and the anointing, effectively connects the praying church with the late twentieth century concerns of American Catholics. There is in the ritual the element of evangelization on key Christian themes, such as suffering and a sense of time linked to vocation. The penitential dimension is coupled with care and concern for the sick, the responsible care of one's own health, a Christian challenge to socially shunned diseases such as AIDS and other contemporary problems. One cannot take part in such celebrations without becoming more keenly aware of the ecclesial needs of our brothers and sisters. Finally, these celebrations effectively teach us to look forward to God's future reign with hope and to use the present time for the advancement of that reign.

In brief, the communal anointing of the sick is an example of liturgy that is also popular religious devotion in the best sense of the term. Such celebrations challenge our cultural assumptions and fears. The American culture of the twentieth century, for example, regularly shuns areas of human living where finitude and mortality are encountered. This celebration, on the contrary, teaches positive Christian values and draws countercultural lessons of hope from the cultural fears of our day. David Power has addressed this point with great insight in discussing blessings: "The fundamental meaning of blessing, whatever form it takes, is that God's power redeems the powerless. Earliest Christian communities . . . found their way of dwelling on earth and using among themselves the things of the earth by reason of their strength in Christ. This depended on the strength of being a community in him."[72]

The communal anointing of the sick has been offered as a pastoral example of linking liturgy with more popular religious devotion. Such celebrations can open up the vistas of the Christian vocation in our culture, which might seem to have little time for the service of others. Such celebrations also follow the spirit of the conciliar reform: "For well-disposed Christians the liturgy of the sacraments and sacramentals causes every event in human history to be made holy by divine grace that flows from the paschal mystery."[73] The liturgies of Vatican II invite our integrated response, which includes the affective. And, as David Power has noted, affective wholeness confronts the darkness that accompanies symbolic awareness.[74]

To the extent that Christians are able to integrate their acculturated experience into their devotional and liturgical prayer, they will discern their mission in the community of Christ. The title of this section, *"Devotio Futura,"* refers to the future unending liturgy described by the book of Revelation, with the implication that such future devotion should transform the ways in which we worship in the present time. *Devotio futura,* then, in whatever form it takes should teach Christians something about their current tasks within their ecclesial communities. Those tasks, however, cannot be understood apart from their own cultural as well as personal situation.

## Some Concluding Remarks

The American Emmaus is the walk that renews and changes the community and its individuals. If the walk consists only in a theological lecture, there would be no assurance that anything might change. But a walk that makes peoples' "hearts burn within them" is surely an invitation to conversion once again. The fact that the walk takes place in an American setting frames the scene and its meaning of conversion in very specific ways for late twentieth century Christians. After all, a long history of both transforming grace and radical sin separates the first Emmaus walk from the current ones. And the American reluctance to walk this road will not resemble the mindset of early Christians in every respect. For conversion within the American scene has its own set of problems that question the meaning and value of the cross.

What about the questions we have asked in the course of this book? In chapter 1 we asked whether our post-technological American culture and society help or hinder us as we gather to praise and thank God. That question could not be answered without asking in turn what we believe the implications of God's creation and new creation in Christ are for our time. Such a question is more difficult to face in an era in which the world is on the verge of being turned into an environmental slum.

The scriptural answer is both hope-filled and challenging: God will make all things new. New creation is creation transformed by the surprise of the redemption. Such answers take away our excuses and restore to us the responsibility of being fully human according to God's plan. If our worship is responsible, our moral witness before the world can only be challenged and enriched. If our worship is honest, then, as David Power has reminded us, there will also be an element of lament in our worship.[5] The American "new wilderness" has been and continues to be the home of a generally enthusiastic and generous church, whatever faults it might have. The same culture that has spawned individualism and consumerism has also been able to nourish to an unusual degree a spirit of freedom, toleration, and even generosity that is unique. The American church has benefited from all this.

The final remarks in chapter 1 provided some of the questions for chapter 2. Have the liturgical life and the moral witness of the American church had some positive impact on our culture? Our predecessors in faith and citizenship have left us both examples of unprophetic collusion with the worst in our American culture and challenging examples of creative and countercultural living of the gospel. In the rigors and potential of the new wilderness, these American Christians gathered into communities that struggled with the meaning of the gospel for their times. But no previous period in American church history can match the possibilities of our postconciliar times. The very pluralism that seems at times to be tearing apart the seamless robe of Christ is also the strength of the American church.

American Catholics are often generous when confronted by the gospel invitation to go the extra mile and to give the shirt as well as the coat that was begged for. On the other hand, one can still wonder what impact liturgy has on the middle-class American Catholic in matters of peace and justice. One NCR/Gallup poll found that most Catholics were not aware of the U.S. bishops' 1983 pastoral on peace or the economic pastoral of 1985. This is, of course, not the fault of the people in the pew but of the preaching and teaching ministries of the church. But the results of the poll are revealing. Of those who had read the peace pastoral, 57 percent agreed with it, and 71 percent backed the economic pastoral.[76] But agreement is not necessarily formation of a more responsible conscience.

The number of Americans who go to bed hungry, who are homeless, who lack basic health care or education is a scandal to the nation but also a reminder to Christian communities who do liturgies but not the other work of the gospel. When the dignity and charisms of women or minorities are glibly ignored, this is not the silence of the liturgy but of cultural collusion. Liturgy evocatively recalls that we are part of a communion of the saints, living and dead. The practical corollaries of this liturgical teaching are not explicated often enough.[77] To say we celebrate our communion with God, the saints, and our sisters and brothers and yet ignore a large segment of God's people all around us is to deceive ourselves. American Catholics who participate liturgically are empowered to discern the hidden Christ in their midst. To do less than that is to jeopardize our praise.

Chapter 3 took up the question that continued into succeeding chapters: Has American individualism taken the place of ecclesial communities? There is obviously an individualism that is so self-centered that it mutes the gifts and needs of others. Examples of such individualism are not absent from our cultural and ecclesial life. But there is also an American individualism that builds new frontiers: it honors the unique gifts of God in each person and urges their use for the sake of others. To the extent that the American church only pays lip service to such gifts, the local church will be the poorer. If the present upward mobility and affluence of middle-class American Catholics are seen only as pastoral problems and not as gifts with a purpose, we will once again be fighting pastoral windmills. Meanwhile, the Hispanic and other churches do possess a prophetic voice, as the American bishops have said. Their cultural heritage, value systems, and familial structures often are more intact than those of their more favored fellow Christians. We can and must learn from them.

The practical corollary of this observation is that there is no ideal social structure for an American parish. The Synod of Bishops in 1987 and John Paul II have asked for a greater effort in the renewal of parishes.[78] But the local churches must deal with their unique situations. In this country, large city parishes near business and commerical areas have had great success in outreach programs that contact people where they work and shop during the day. In large parishes with the decreasing number of priests, smaller communities of faith within the larger parish can help. Where lay people have been invited into a collaborative model of ministry within a parish or other apostolate, there has usually been a positive response. But there are certain fundamental gospel commitments that authentic liturgy prompts. Fruitful reception of Vatican II is tested by the way in which the local church makes visible the serving Christ. In other words, one test of honest liturgy is its expression in a deepening sense of social justice. The washing of feet on Holy Thursday can promote this sense but cannot substitute for the actual service of a parish community.

Our American sense of time was examined in chapter 4, because it offered any honest reader a chance to concretize all the questions that had been asked in the previous three chapters. Here is where creation and new creation find their testing. We looked at a few cultural examples of American time (out of many such possibilities) to reenforce our argument that the final test of ongoing conversion and authentic liturgy is the use of time. Liturgy constantly refers to God's future, so that we will transform our present. The paschal mystery of Christ's dying and rising is made present in our time so that the conversion of the world might continue. On the other hand, an affluent society tends to be politely unenthusiastic about God's future when it is too content with the present time. Here may be one of the tests of the American church's witness within its culture: to proclaim God's future so that it does have some impact on the way Americans live the present moment. A sense of mission, constantly renewed in worship and sacrament, transforms our present use of time for the sake of God's future.

Chapters 5 and 6 looked once again at the gathered and praying community in the United States. As anyone involved in ministry knows, catechetical and liturgical programs do not assure a process of conversion. On the other hand, when there is a vision of what God has called a local church or a particular parish community to be and to do, it says much about the honest worship of that community. Among Andrew Greeley's notable contributions to our assessment as a local church, his emphasis on the symbolic imagination of American Catholics is particularly important. It is this imagination that links our cultural and religious experience and that can clarify our tasks as American Christians. Liturgy by its very nature calls out of us a response for all that God has done for us. The rhetoric of persuasion begins with the narratives of Christians individually and communally, who once again, like the disciples at Emmaus, "recognize" the Lord at the table of their lives. Such narratives not only invite a liturgical participation that challenges the community's intentions and meanings but also suggest what the local churches gathered at the throne of the Lamb will sing.

# Notes

## Introduction

1. I recognize that the term "American" includes the various and unique cultures of Canada and the United States, as well as those of Central and South America. Throughout this book I refer to the U.S. sociocultural scene with the convenient term "American" without intending any prejudice concerning its equally appropriate reference to other American countries. Similarly, I employ the phrase "American church" as a concise way of referring to the American Roman Catholic communion, realizing that it is equally appropriate in describing other Christian communions.

2. J. Anthony Lukas, *Common Ground: A Turbulent Decade in the Lives of Three American Families* (New York: Alfred A. Knopf, 1985), 353.

3. Vatican II, *The Church's Missionary Activity* (*Ad Gentes*) 15 (830), in *Vatican Council II: The Conciliar and Post Conciliar Documents,* ed. A. Flannery (rev. ed.; Northport, N.Y.: Costello, 1988). The page number of the citation in the Flannery edition will be given in parentheses after the paragraph number. The Latin title of Vatican II's documents will be given only in the initial citation.

4. Richard McBrien, *Catholicism: Completely Revised and Updated* (San Francisco: HarperSan Francisco, 1994), 723.

5. J. Fitzpatrick, "Hispanic Parishes Where Something Seems to Be Going Right," in *Strangers and Aliens No Longer,* Part One, *The Hispanic Presence in the Church of the United States* (Washington, D.C.: United States Catholic Conference, 1993), 24. Fitzpatrick cites John Paul II's praise for Sts. Cyril's and Methodius's accomplishments in translating the scriptures from Greek into the language of the Slav people and what an excellent grasp of the culture this task presumed (ibid., 24–25).

6. Ronald Grimes speaks of liturgy as "one of the hardest cultural forms to evaluate" in his address "Liturgical Renewal and Ritual Criticism," in *The Awakening Church: 25 Years of Liturgical Renewal,* ed. L. J. Madden (Collegeville, Minn.: Liturgical Press, 1992), 12.

7. Monika Hellwig, "Twenty-five Years of a Wakening Church: Liturgy and Ecclesiology," in *The Awakening Church: 25 Years of Liturgical Renewal,* ed. L. J. Madden (Collegeville, Minn.: Liturgical Press, 1992), 67.

8. See, e.g., John Paul II, "The Vocation and the Mission of the Lay Faithful in

the Church and in the World" (*Christifideles Laici*), Dec. 30, 1988 (Washington, D.C.: United States Catholic Conference, n.d.), 130-33.

9. Paul VI, *On Evangelization* (*Evangelii Nuntiandi*) 4.4 (208). The translation is found in *Proclaiming Justice and Peace: Documents from John XXIII-John Paul II*, ed. M. Walsh and B. Davies (Mystic, Conn.: Twenty-Third Publications, 1984). When citing Paul VI's letter, I give the paragraph number followed in parentheses by the page number in Walsh and Davies.

10. "Catholicism in the United States is divided into a white, suburban, middle-class church and an urban, lower class church made up of people of color. These two churches go their own way, seldom interacting, and this serves to widen the chasm that divides Hispanic Catholicism from Euro-American Catholicism" (Jay Dolan, "Conclusion," in *Hispanic Catholic Culture in the U.S.*, ed. J. P. Dolan and A. F. Deck [Notre Dame: University of Notre Dame Press, 1994], 453).

11. John Paul II, "The Vocation and the Mission of the Lay Faithful," 91.

12. David Power, *Unsearchable Riches: The Symbolic Nature of Liturgy* (New York: Pueblo, 1984), 146.

13. Cf., e.g., F. Schupp, *Glaube, Kultur, Symbol: Versuch einer kritischen Theorie sakramentaler Praxis* (Düsseldorf: Patmos, 1974); P. Tillich, *Theology of Culture* (London: Oxford University Press, 1959).

14. Anscar J. Chupungco, O.S.B., *Cultural Adaptation of the Liturgy* (New York: Paulist, 1982); idem, *Liturgies of the Future: The Process and Methods of Inculturation* (New York: Paulist, 1989); idem, *Liturgical Inculturation: Sacramentals, Religiosity, and Catechesis* (Collegeville, Minn.: Liturgical Press, 1992); F. Senn, *Liturgy in Its Cultural Setting* (Philadelphia: Fortress, 1983); C. F. Starkloff, "Inculturation and Cultural Systems," *Theological Studies* 55 (1994): 66-81, 274-94; G. Wainwright, "Christian Worship and Western Culture," *Studia Liturgica* 12 (1977): 20-33; G. Martinez, "Cult and Culture: The Structure of the Evolution of Worship," *Worship* 64 (1990): 406-33; R. Schaeffler, "Kultur und Kult," *Liturgisches Jahrbuch* 41 (1991): 73-87. The works cited give extensive bibliographies of earlier works.

15. Michael B. Aune, "Worship in an Age of Subjectivism Revisited," *Worship* 65 (1991): 224-38. His article is a response to two articles by M. Francis Mannion, "Worship in an Age of Subjectivism," *Liturgy* 80 (July 1989); "Liturgy and the Present Crisis of Culture," *Worship* 62 (1988): 98-123.

16. I am aware that the Greek word *ekklēsia* means a "gathering, assembly." At the risk of tautology, I employ the phrase "gathered church" because in English usage "church" for many connotes "institutional church," a more limited understanding of the term.

17. For the current discussion of the connections between liturgy and theology, see K. W. Irwin, *Context and Text: Method in Liturgical Theology* (Collegeville, Minn.: Liturgical Press, 1994), 44-62.

18. Grimes, "Liturgical Renewal and Ritual Criticism," in *The Awakening Church*, ed. Madden, 12.

## Chapter 1: The Times and Places of the New Creation

1. See Secretariat for the Liturgy and Secretariat for Black Catholics, *Plenty Good Room: The Spirit and Truth of African American Catholic Worship* (Washington, D.C.: United States Catholic Conference, 1990) §61, 35-36.

2. Clifford Geertz, *The Interpretation of Cultures* (New York: Basic Books, 1973), 89.

3. Ibid., 12.

4. Paul Tillich, *Theology of Culture* (London: Oxford University Press, 1959), 47.

5. Ibid., 41.

6. Vatican II, *The Church in the Modern World* (*Gaudium et spes*) 44 (946); Paul VI, *On Evangelization* 20 (213). In citing the documents of Vatican II, I will give both the Latin and the English title in the first entry, followed by the paragraph number.

7. National Conference of Catholic Bishops, *The Hispanic Presence: Challenge and Commitment* (Washington, D.C.: United States Catholic Conference, 1984) #1,5 (4), citing Vatican II's *Church in the Modern World* 58, and Paul VI's *On Evangelization* 20 (213).

8. For an extended discussion of these stages, see *One Faith, One Lord, One Baptism: The Hopes and Experiences of the Black Community in the Archdiocese of New York*, 2 vols. (New York: Archdiocese of New York) 2:74–81.

9. Geertz, *Interpretation of Cultures*, 90.

10. Stephen Hart, "Privatization in American Religion and Society," *Sociological Analysis* 47 (1987): 320–21.

11. Robert Bellah, *Habits of the Heart: Individualism and Commitment in American Life* (Berkeley: University of California Press, 1985), 226.

12. Andrew Greeley, *The Catholic Myth: The Behavior and Beliefs of American Catholics* (New York: Charles Scribner's Sons, 1991), 159.

13. For a discussion of this development, see T. Talley, "From Berakah to Eucharistia: A Reopening Question," in *Living Bread, Saving Cup,* ed. K. Seasoltz (Collegeville, Minn.: Liturgical Press, 1982), 80–101.

14. An important example is found in a first-century Christian manual, the *Didache.* See chapters 9 and 10 in R. C. D. Jasper and G. J. Cuming, *Prayers of the Eucharist* (New York: Pueblo, 1980), 23–24.

15. Karl Rahner, "On the Theology of Worship," in *Theological Investigations XIX* (New York: Crossroad, 1983), 141–49.

16. M. Skelley sums up this Rahnerian theme: "In every experience of our graced transcendence we are given an experience of God who is eternally open to us and eternally hidden from us" (*The Liturgy of the World: Karl Rahner's Theology of Worship* [Collegeville, Minn.: Liturgical Press, 1991] 70).

17. *Church in the Modern World* 34 (934).

18. See Skelley, *Liturgy of the World,* 98–99.

19. *Church in the Modern World* 39 (938).

20. Rahner, "Theology of Worship," 147.

21. Skelley, *Liturgy of the World,* 31–32.

22. *Church in the Modern World* 43 (944).

23. Secretariat for the Liturgy and Secretariat for Black Catholics, *Plenty Good Room,* §§101, 102 (55).

24. *Church in the Modern World* 31 (931).

25. Ibid., 11 (912).

26. Skelley, *Liturgy of the World,* 94.

27. For a sketch of this history, see Aylward Shorter, *Toward a Theology of Inculturation* (Maryknoll, N.Y.: Orbis, 1988), 137–76.

28. Ibid., 143–45.

29. For an evocative description of Ricci's cultural attitudes, see J. D. Spence, *The Memory Palace of Matteo Ricci* (New York: Viking, 1984).

30. *Decree on the Church's Missionary Activity* (*Ad Gentes*) 9 (823-24); *Dogmatic Constitution on the Church* (*Lumen Gentium*) 17 (368-69).

31. *On the Church's Missionary Activity* 11 (825).

32. *On the Church in the Modern World* 53 (958). Chapter 2 of this decree is devoted to the question of culture.

33. Ibid., 5-6 (906-7).

34. Ibid., 26 (927).

35. Ibid., 58 (963); also 44 (946).

36. *On the Church's Missionary Activity* 22.

37. National Conference of Catholic Bishops, *Hispanic Presence,* II, 9 (9).

38. See Shorter, *Toward a Theology,* 206-11.

39. *On Evangelization* 15.3 (211).

40. Ibid., 18 (212).

41. See J. Ysebaert, *Greek Baptismal Terminology: Its Origins and Early Development* (Nijmegen: Dekker & Van De Vegt, 1962), 131-61.

42. *Rite of Christian Initiation of Adults* §51, prepared by ICEL and the Bishops' Committee on the Liturgy (Chicago: Liturgy Training Publications, 1988), 22-23.

43. *On Evangelization* 20 (213).

44. John Paul II, "The Vocation and the Mission of the Lay Faithful in the Church and in the World," Dec. 30, 1988 (Washington, D.C.: United States Catholic Conference, n.d.), 96 (my emphasis).

45. Wayne A. Meeks, *The First Urban Christians: The Social World of the Apostle Paul* (New Haven: Yale University Press, 1983), 8.

46. Robert Schreiter, *Constructing Local Theologies* (Maryknoll, N.Y.: Orbis, 1985), 2-3.

47. For Schreiter's discussion of these points, see *Constructing Local Theologies,* 4-5.

48. For a careful discussion of these complex "histories," see, e.g., David O'Brien, *Public Catholicism* (New York: Macmillan, 1989), 158-85, 236-52.

49. *On Evangelization* 20.1 (213).

50. John Ciardi, *Good Words to You* (New York: Harper & Row, 1987), 342 (my emphasis).

51. *On Evangelization* 21 (213).

52. In a letter of Cardinal Villot to Bishop R. Alberti on the occasion of the second Latin American meeting on liturgy in 1977 this same idea is stressed: "The liturgy is neither authentic nor really effective if it does not bring about a continuous conversion that causes it to be translated into reality, into a new way of living . . ." (*Notitae* 13 [1977]: 459-67) as given in *Documents on the Liturgy* (Collegeville, Minn.: Liturgical Press, 1982), 222-23.

53. Shorter, *Toward a Theology,* 222-23.

54. *L'Osservatore Romano,* 28 June 1982, pp. 1-8, as cited in Shorter, *Toward a Theology,* 231. Shorter, however, points out that this papal support is always conditioned by a cautious fear of culturalism and what might appear as a negative attitude toward non-Christian cultures (ibid., 236).

55. John Paul II, "One Church, Many Cultures," Annual Address to the College of Cardinals, 1984, as given in *The Church and Culture Since Vatican II,* ed. J. Gremillion (Notre Dame: University of Notre Dame Press, 1985), 215. This collection also gives the texts of five addresses of John Paul II on culture (pp. 162-222).

56. R.-E. Prell-Foldes, "The reinvention of reflexivity in Jewish prayer: The self and community in modernity," *Semiotica* 30 (1980): 73.

57. Notre Dame Study of Catholic Parish Life, Reports #10 and 15 (henceforth cited as NDS with report number).

58. See Andrew Greeley, *American Catholics since the Council: An Unauthorized Report* (Chicago: Thomas More Press, 1985), 27–29.

59. NDS #5.

60. Jay Dolan, "Conclusion," in *Hispanic Catholic Culture in the U.S.*, ed. J. P. Dolan and A. F. Deck (Notre Dame: University of Notre Dame Press, 1994).

61. G. Gallup, Jr., and J. Castelli, *The American Catholic People: Their Beliefs, Practices, and Values* (Garden City, N.Y.: Doubleday, 1987).

62. NDS #4, 10.

63. See Patrick H. McNamara, *Conscience First, Tradition Second* (Albany: State University of New York Press, 1992), 39.

64. Greeley, *Catholic Myth,* 4.

65. Andrew Greeley and Mary Durkin, *How To Save the Catholic Church* (New York: Viking, 1984), 16–17.

66. Ibid., 167.

67. Ibid., 171–73.

68. Ibid, 89.

69. Greeley, *American Catholics,* 72. Peter Steinfels recently cited a presumably more limited *New York Times*/CBS poll (April 1994) where only 37 percent of those polled said they participated in Sunday mass as well as the avowal of Cardinal Law of Boston that only 25 to 30 percent in his diocese did so ("Ancient Rock in Crosscurrents of Today: Searching its Soul," *New York Times Sunday,* May 29, 1994).

70. Greeley and Durkin, *How to Save the Catholic Church,* 184–93.

71. Greeley, *American Catholics,* 71, 60; idem, *Catholic Myth,* 133–37.

72. David Tracy, *The Analogical Imagination: Christian Theology and the Culture of Pluralism* (New York: Crossroad, 1981), 12.

73. See Andrew Greeley, *Religious Change in America* (Cambridge, Mass.: Harvard University Press, 1989) 42–56.

74. Greeley, *Catholic Myth,* 24–33.

75. Ibid., 136.

76. Ibid., 30.

77. McNamara, *Conscience First,* 115–16.

78. Bernard Lonergan, *Method in Theology* (New York: Herder & Herder, 1972), 79.

79. For an insightful treatment, see M. J. Himes and K. R. Himes, *Fullness of Faith: The Public Significance of Theology* (New York: Paulist, 1993), 104–24.

80. Vatican II, *Declaration on Religious Liberty* (*Dignitatis Humanae*), Dec. 7, 1965.

81. J. P. Fitzpatrick, *One Church Many Cultures: The Challenge of Diversity* (Kansas City: Sheed & Ward, 1987), 115–17.

82. David N. Power, *Culture and Theology* (Washington, D.C.: Pastoral Press, 1990), 4.

### Chapter 2: The Postconciliar Liturgy in the American Church

1. Bishops' Committee on the Liturgy, *Music in Catholic Worship* (Washington, D.C.: United States Catholic Conference, 1972), 1.

2. See M. Sandoval, *On the Move: A History of the Hispanic Church in the United States* (Maryknoll, N.Y.: Orbis, 1990), 7–22.

3. David O'Brien gives his description of the term in *Public Catholicism* (New York: Macmillan, 1989), 9.

4. O'Brien, *Public Catholicism*, 33.

5. But the subsequent appointment of bishops was made by Rome; see O'Brien, *Public Catholicism*, 19–20.

6. But even in this period Catholics enjoyed equal citizenship in only five of the thirteen states; see J. T. Ellis, *American Catholicism* (Chicago: University of Chicago Press, 1955), 42–43.

7. By 1810, this direction of vernacular liturgy had been reversed; see J. Dolan, *American Catholic Experience* (Garden City, N.Y.: Doubleday, 1985), 113–21; and J. T. Ellis, "Archbishop Carroll and the Liturgy of the Vernacular," *Worship* 26 (1952): 545–52; J. Gurrieri, "John Carroll and the Shape of the American Catholic Liturgy," in *Perspectives on the American Catholic Church 1789–1989*, ed. S. Vicchio and V. Geiger (Westminster, Md.: Christian Classics, 1989), 183–96, esp. 190–93 on the vernacular question. A further sign of disavowing these specific American contributions was the adoption by the first American synods of laws originally issued by European synods regulating liturgical life; see Dolan, *American Catholic Experience*, 112. Nathan Mitchell has reminded me that, throughout the nineteenth century, Catholic hymnals that included vernacular material continued to appear.

8. The woman in question was a South American female missionary, and Carroll did show some interest in finding out more about her. See M. A. O'Ryan, "John Carroll, First Bishop of Baltimore, and His Views on Women," Working Paper Series 23, No.1, Spring, 1991, Cushwa Center for the Study of American Catholicism, University of Notre Dame, 21. For a discussion of his relation to teaching orders of sisters, see pp. 14–24. In his zeal for education, however, he tried to turn contemplative orders such as the Carmelites and Poor Clares into active congregations.

9. The initial problem of episcopal oversight of priests was later complicated by the insistence of Rome on irremovable pastors. See G. Fogarty, "The Parish and Community in American Catholic History," in *Building the American Catholic City: Parishes and Institutions*, ed. B. C. Mitchell (New York: Garland, 1988), 1–25.

10. Cited by W. Carey, "People, Priests, and Prelates: Ecclesiastical Democracy and the Tension of Trusteeism" (Ph.D. dissertation, University of Notre Dame, 1987), 52 (my emphasis).

11. See O'Brien, *Public Catholicism*, 14–15.

12. Joseph Chinnici, *Living Stones: The History and Structure of Catholic Spiritual Life in the United States* (New York: Macmillan, 1989), 57.

13. Ibid., 63.

14. See Jay Dolan's description in *Immigrant Church: New York's Irish and German Catholics* (Baltimore: Johns Hopkins University Press, 1975), 149–58; also his *Catholic Revivalism: The American Experience* (Notre Dame: University of Notre Dame Press, 1978).

15. Mary Douglas has paid particular attention to the ways in which an unchanging liturgy assures the religious and cultural identity of its users; see *Natural Symbols* (New York: Pantheon, 1970), 1–53..

16. See A. Taves, *The Household of Faith: Roman Catholic Devotions in Mid-*

*Nineeenth Century America* (Notre Dame: University of Notre Dame Press, 1986); Joseph Chinnici, "Organization of the Spiritual Life: American Devotional Catholic Works, 1791–1866," *Theological Studies* 40 (1979): 229–55.

17. Chinnici, *Living Stones,* 85.

18. Timothy L. Smith, "Religion and Ethnicity in America," *American Historical Review* 83 (1978): 1161, 1167–68.

19. Ibid., 1175.

20. Ibid., 1179.

21. Andrew Greeley has made this point a number of times, most recently in *The Catholic Myth: The Behavior and Beliefs of American Catholics* (New York: Charles Scribner's Sons, 1991), 154ff.

22. See Sandoval, *On the Move,* 25–40; and M. Witchger, "Recent History of Hispanic Ministry in the United States," in *Prophetic Vision: National Pastoral Plan for Hispanic Ministry,* ed. S. Galeron, R. Icaza, R. Urrababo (Kansas City: Sheed & Ward, 1992), 183–99; for more extensive background, see *Fronteras: A History of the Latin American Church in the USA Since 1513,* ed. M. Sandoval (San Antonio: Mexican American Cultural Center, 1983). See also R. Gonzales and M. LaVelle, *The Hispanic Catholic in the United States* (New York: Northeast Catholic Pastoral Center for Hispanics, 1985).

23. *Prophetic Voices: The Document on the Process of the III Encuentro Nacional Hispano de Pastoral* (Washington, D.C.: Secretariat for Hispanic Affairs, United States Catholic Conference, 1986), 7.

24. *The Hispanic Presence: Challenge and Commitment,* A Pastoral Letter on Hispanic Ministry (Washington, D.C.: United States Catholic Conference, 1984), #1, 4, 9 (3, 4, 9).

25. Witchger, "Recent History of Hispanic Ministry," 184.

26. J. Fitzpatrick, "A Survey of Literature on Hispanic Ministry," in *Strangers and Aliens No Longer,* Part One, *The Hispanic Presence in the Church of the United States* (Washington, D.C.: United States Catholic Conference, 1993), 65.

27. Sandoval, *On the Move,* 61–66.

28. Ibid., 96–101.

29. See B. Glos and E. Hemrick, "Survey of Hispanic Priests, Seminarians and Candidates," in *Strangers and Aliens No Longer,* Part One, *The Hispanic Presence in the Church of the United States* (Washington, D.C.: United States Catholic Conference, 1993), 101–23.

30. See Joseph Fitzpatrick, *One Church Many Cultures: The Challenge of Diversity* (Kansas City: Sheed & Ward, 1987), 153.

31. See M. Sandoval, *Hispanic Challenges to the Church* (Croton, N.Y.: n.p., 1978).

32. Fitzpatrick, *One Church Many Cultures,* 126–27.

33. National Conference of Catholic Bishops, *The Hispanic Presence,* 12, a (14).

34. Virgil Elizondo, *The Christian Identity and Mission of the Catholic Hispanic in the U.S.* (San Antonio: Mexican American Cultural Center, 1980), 5. Elizondo is citing Paul VI's Radio Message to the Hispanic People, August 18, 1977.

35. Greeley, *Catholic Myth,* 120–25; Fitzpatrick ("A Survey of Literature," 77) also cites a more recent study by L. Young using somewhat different data from that employed by Greeley.

36. "Vatican Report on Sects, Cults, and New Religious Movements,"*Origins* 16 (1986): 7–8, as cited in Fitzpatrick, "Survey of Literature," 77–78.

37. See A. Pérez, "The History of Hispanic Liturgy Since 1965," in *Hispanic Culture in the U.S.*, ed. J. Dolan and A. F. Deck (Notre Dame: University of Notre Dame Press, 1994), 360–408.

38. *Documents of American History*, ed. J. T. Ellis (Milwaukee: Bruce, 1961), 132–33. J. Chinnici offers another excellent example in "American Catholics and Religious Pluralism 1775–1820," *Journal of Ecumenical Studies* 16 (1977): 727–41.

39. For a fine discussion of this phenomenon in connection with the growth of other parishes, see Fogarty, "Parish and Community."

40. See Fitzpatrick, "Survey of Literature," 65–66.

41. This was acknowledged by the bishops; see *The Hispanic Presence*, 12, e (17).

42. See Fitzpatrick, *One Church Many Cultures*, 142–52.

43. National Conference of Catholic Bishops, *The Hispanic Presence*, #16, (30–31).

44. Smith, "Religion and Ethnicity," 1161.

45. See, e.g., Dolan, *Immigrant Church*; and C. J. Barry, *The Catholic Church and the German-Americans* (Milwaukee: Bruce, 1953).

46. J. McGreevy, "'Race' and Twentieth Century American Catholic Culture," Working Paper Series 24, No.4, Spring 1993, Cushwa Center for the Study of American Catholicism Series, University of Notre Dame, 9 (my emphasis).

47. When various speeches had been given at a diocesan celebration in 1906, Archbishop Messmer noted that no speech had been given in a foreign language "but all in the tongue of this great nation, to which we are so intimately attached," as cited by J. Grummer, "The Parish Life of German-Speaking Roman Catholics in Milwaukee, Wisconsin, 1840–1920" (Ph.D. dissertation, University of Notre Dame, 1988), 238.

48. E. M. McMahon, "What Parish Are You From? A Study of the Chicago Irish Parish Community and Race Relations 1916–1970" (Ph.D. dissertation, Loyola University, 1989), 97–98, 178–84.

49. See Grummer, "Parish Life of German-Speaking Roman Catholics," 119–30.

50. Ibid., 133.

51. For a history, see C. Davis, *The History of Black Catholics in the United States* (New York: Crossroad, 1993).

52. See McGreevy, "'Race,'" 7.

53. See, e.g., D. Clark, "A Pattern of Urban Growth: Residential Development and Church Location in Philadelphia," 76–87; and E. Kantowicz, "Church and Neighborhood," in *Building the American Catholic City: Parishes and Institutions*, ed. B. C. Mitchell (New York: Garland, 1988), 58–75.

54. Ibid., with supporting bibliography.

55. Ibid., 10.

56. See, e.g., McMahon, "What Parish," 292–305.

57. McGreevy, "'Race,'" 18–28.

58. For one example, see ibid., 20–21.

59. Ibid., 15–18.

60. See S. J. Ochs, "Desegregating the Altar: The Struggle for Black Catholic Priests 1854–1960," Working Paper Series 19, No.3, 1988, Cushwa Center for the Study of American Catholicism, University of Notre Dame, 6–10.

61. Ibid., 10–35.

62. Robert Hovda gives a more recent example of Father Aubry Osborn in *This*

*Far By Faith: American Black Worship and Its African Roots* (Washington, D.C.: National Office for Black Catholics, 1977), 3–5.

63. See, e.g., C. Davis, "God's Image in Black: The Black Community in Slavery and Freedom," in *Perspectives on the American Catholic Church 1789-1989*, ed. S. Vicchio and V. Geiger (Westminster, Md.: Christian Classics, 1989), 105–22; for the ownership of slaves by religious, see ibid., 110–11; for the "explanation" of Gregory XVI's categorical condemnation of the slave trade (1839) by Bishop John England of Charleston, see ibid., 111–12.

64. William Stang, *Pastoral Theology* (Dublin: M. H. Gill, 1897), 177–78, as cited in Leslie W. Tentler, "Catholic Women and Their Church: A View from Detroit," Working Paper Series 16, No.2, 1985, Cushwa Center for the Study of American Catholicism, 12.

65. See, e.g., James Kenneally, *The History of American Catholic Women* (New York: Crossroad, 1990), 43–59.

66. Tentler, "Catholic Women," 17. See also Kenneally, *History of American Catholic Women*, 1–22.

67. Ibid., 19.

68. Anne Carr, *Transforming Grace* (San Francisco: Harper & Row, 1988), 139.

69. See n. 65.

70. Andrew Greeley's remarks on the connections between the image of church and the image of woman are very challenging; see Andrew Greeley and Mary Durkin, *Angry Catholic Women: A Sociological Investigation* (Chicago: Thomas More, 1984), 39, 41–42.

71. For a table of these letters from 1974 to 1987, see Maureen Aggeler, *Mind Your Metaphors: A Critique of Language in the Bishops' Pastoral Letters on the Role of Women* (New York: Paulist, 1991 ), 127. For the ensuing events, see also J. Deedy, *American Catholicism: And Now Where?* (New York: Plenum Press, 1987), 204–10.

72. Ibid., 108–18.

73. John Paul II, *Familiaris Consortio;* see also Mary Durkin's references to this theology in the pope's letter (Greeley and Durkin, *Angry Women*, 121–23).

74. See, in particular, for the analysis of the text and its modifications in 1 Corinthians, Elisabeth Schüssler Fiorenza, *In Memory of Her: A Feminist Theological Reconstruction of Christian Origins* (New York: Crossroad, 1987), 205–41.

75. Ibid., 124.

76. See Ellis, *American Catholicism* , 89–90, 99–100.

77. William Halsey, *The Survival of American Innocence: Catholicism in an Era of Disillusionment 1920-40* (Notre Dame: University of Notre Dame Press, 1980), 2–3.

78. Ibid., 4.

79. For historical overviews of the American liturgical movement, see E. A. Diederich, "Gerald Ellis, S.J. (1894-1963)," *The Yearbook of Liturgical Studies* 4 (1963): 3–21; G. Diekmann, "Is There a Distinctive American Contribution to the Liturgical Renewal?" *Worship* 45 (1971 ): 578–87; W. J. Leonard, "The Liturgical Movement in the United States," in *The Liturgy of Vatican II,* ed. W. Barauna (Chicago: Franciscan Herald Press, 1966), 294–321; Gerald Ellard, "The Liturgical Movement: In and For America," *Thought* 7 (1932): 474–92.

80. See N. H. Barrett, "The Contribution of Martin B. Hellriegel to the American Catholic Liturgical Movement" (Ph.D. dissertation, St. Louis University, 1976), 106ff. For the social dimension of Michel's work, see John Coleman, *An American Strategic Theology* (New York: Paulist, 1982), 134–35.

81. See P. Marx, *Virgil Michel and the Liturgical Movement* (Collegeville, Minn.: Liturgical Press, 1957); J. Hall, *The Full Stature of Christ: The Ecclesiology of Dom Virgil Michel* (Collegeville, Minn.: Liturgical Press, 1976); and Mark Searle, "The Liturgy and Catholic Social Doctrine," in *The Future of the Catholic Church in America: Major Papers of the Virgil Michel Symposium* (Collegeville, Minn.: Liturgical Press, 1991), 43-73.

82. See Marx, *Virgil Michel,* 367-69; for the contexts, see R. S. Appleby, "Present to the People of God: Transformation of the Roman Catholic Parish and Priesthood," in *Transforming Parish Ministry: The Changing Roles of Catholic Clergy and Women Religious,* ed. J. Dolan et al. (New York: Crossroad, 1989), esp. 26-34.

83. Cited in J. Garner, "The Vision of a Liturgical Reformer: Hans Ansgar Reinhold, American Catholic Educator" (Ph.D. dissertation, Teachers College, Columbia University, 1972), 7.

84. Virgil Michel, "The Liturgy, the Basis of Social Regeneration," *Orate Fratres* 9 (1935): 544.

85. Ibid., 545.

86. Virgil Michel, "Frequent Communion and Social Regeneration," *Orate Fratres* 10 (1935): 198-205.

87. Virgil Michel, "The Scope of the Liturgical Movement," *Orate Fratres* 10 (1936): 489.

88. Searle, "Liturgy and Catholic Social Doctrine," 54.

89. Several commentators have made this comparison between Michel's ecclesiology and that of Pius XII; see K. Himes, "Eucharist and Justice: Assessing the Legacy of Virgil Michel," *Worship* 62 (1988): 201-24; Hall, *Full Stature of Christ;* and Searle, "Liturgy and Catholic Social Doctrine," 39-40.

90. See Barrett, "Contributions of Martin B. Hellriegel," 107ff.; Marx, *Virgil Michel,* 187-89; Hall, *Full Stature of Christ,* 52-54.

91. Hall, *Full Stature of Christ,* 124-26, 140-44.

92. See J. L. Klein, "The Role of Gerald Ellard (1894-1963) in the Development of the Contemporary American Liturgical Movement" (Ph.D. dissertation, Fordham University, 1971).

93. *Gaudium et spes* 55.

94. Mary Collins, "Participation: Liturgical Renewal and the Cultural Question," in *The Future of the Catholic Church in America: Major Papers of the Virgil Michel Symposium* (Collegeville, Minn.: Liturgical Press, 1991), 20-42.

95. Marx, *Virgil Michel,* 219-54.

96. Gerald Ellard, *Christian Life and Worship* (Milwaukee: Bruce, 1933); idem, *Men at Work and Worship* (New York: Longmans, Green 1940).

97. See Barrett, "Contribution of Martin B. Hellriegel." If I may be permitted a personal recollection, as a young seminarian I heard Monsignor Hellriegel lecture at Pius X School of Music, Manhattanville College (New York) in the summer of 1949. I can still recall my initial reactions of shock and wonder that the riches of the liturgical tradition that Hellriegel had pastorally implemented were still mostly unknown and unappreciated in most seminaries, much less parishes in this country.

98. Cited in Garner, "Vision of a Liturgical Reformer," 248.

99. L. Madden, "The Liturgical Conference of the U.S.A.: Its Origin and Development (1940-68)" (Ph.D. dissertation, Trier Theological Faculty, 1960), 61; see also Barrett, "Contribution of Martin B. Hellriegel," 248.

100. Madden, "Liturgical Conference," 221.

101. Ibid., 221–39.

102. Andrew Greeley and Mary G. Durkin, *How To Save the Catholic Church* (New York: Viking, 1984), 171–78.

103. Ibid., 165.

104. NDS #4:4.

105. NDS #4:5.

106. NDS #5:8.

107. J. Gremillion and J. Castelli, *The Emerging Parish: The Notre Dame Study of Catholic Life Since Vatican II* (San Francisco: Harper & Row, 1987), 71.

108. NDS #8:4.

109. NDS #8:9. Philip Murnion's study of 350 parishes in the archdiocese of New York seems to reflect similar results: the theopolitan parish (29 percent of the sample) offers a careful balance between community building and outreach to the larger community, while the public action parish (17 percent) concentrates on its mission to the world. The sectarian type of parish (25 percent) is active but inward looking, while the sacramental service parish (28 percent) provides sacramental participation but not a sense of mission; see his *Forming the Parish Community* (Washington, D.C.: United States Catholic Conference, 1978), 20–22.

110. G. Gallup, Jr., and J. Castelli, *The American Catholic People: Their Beliefs, Practices, and Values* (Garden City, N.Y.: Doubleday, 1987), 52. The Gallup surveys tend to ask more general questions of Catholics than the Notre Dame Study.

111. Ibid., 53.

112. Greeley, *Catholic Myth*, 148; he summarizes a few of the results from the study commissioned by the Knights of Columbus.

113. Gallup and Castelli, *American Catholic People*, 49.

114. Ibid., 48.

115. Greeley, *Catholic Myth*, 4–5; idem, "Why do Catholics Stay in the Church? Because of the Stories," *New York Times Magazine*, July 10, 1994, 38–41. Greeley's latest book, which will presumably enlarge on this thesis, is *Religion as Poetry* (New York: Transaction Publishers, forthcoming).

116. Andrew Greeley, *Religious Imagination* (New York: W. H. Sadlier, 1981), 10.

117. Ibid., 16. Obviously these summaries do not do justice to the systematic way in which Greeley and William McCready have worked out these seminal ideas. The reader is urged to read their exposition.

118. Greeley, *Religious Imagination*, 18.

119. Ibid., 27–28.

120. Ibid., 38.

121. Greeley and Durkin, *How to Save the Catholic Church*, 186–87. Greeley and Durkin list other factors that contribute to these poor liturgical celebrations: poor preaching, boring vernacular reenactments, the poor quality of liturgical music, and too few devotional reminders of this correlation (ibid., 188–94).

122. Greeley, *Catholic Myth*, 45. Greeley uses this last insight to postulate the fundamental differences between the Catholic and Protestant worldviews.

123. Ibid., 15–25; see also Andrew Greeley, *Religious Change in America* (Cambridge, Mass.: Harvard University Press, 1989), 42–56. Gallup cites a 1977 study in which 73 percent of Catholics, of whom eight out of ten were under fifty years of

age, supported birth control as an option (Gallup and Castelli, *American Catholic People*, 50).

124. Gallup and Castelli, *American Catholic People*, 49. Gallup also cites Dean R. Hoge's study that shows 67 percent of American Catholics thought it might help the church to allow the occasional celebration of the Latin mass (Gallup and Castelli, *American Catholic People*, 50).

125. Gallup and Castelli, *American Catholic People*, 26–30.

126. Ibid., 30. This is true even of young Catholics between the ages of eighteen and twenty-nine (ibid., 32). These increases are predictably higher in regions considered more progressive (e.g., the Midwest ranks highest and the East lowest).

127. NDS #4:4; #6:6. The Notre Dame Study tested a thousand parishes in this country and usually dealt with "core," or practicing, Catholics. Thirty-six parishes were then studied in some depth by visiting teams. Greeley has questioned the value of the study because it did not work with probability samples (see *Catholic Myth*, 148n).

128. NDS #4:5.

129. Ibid., #4:4–8. For a contrasting view, see Greeley, *Catholic Myth*, 158–60.

130. NDS #6:5.

131. Ibid., #5:4, 6.

132. Ibid., #5:5.

133. Ibid., 5:7.

134. Ibid., #6:4, #10:9. These remarks do not rule out possible misperceptions by pastors or people about priorities and commitments (cf. NDS #7:12–13).

135. NDS #6:5.

136. Ibid.

137. For such assessments, see R. Bellah et al., *The Good Society* (New York: Alfred A. Knopf, 1991), 206–11.

138. Smith, "Religion and Ethnicity in America," 1183.

### Chapter 3: A Test of Liturgy: The Gathered American Community

1. R. Bellah, R. Madsen, W. Sullivan, A. Swidler, S. Tipton, *Habits of the Heart: Individualism and Commitment in American Life* (Berkeley: University of California Press, 1985), 71–75.

2. Monika Hellwig, "Twenty-five Years of a Wakening Church: Liturgy and Ecclesiology," in *The Awakening Church: 25 Years of Liturgical Renewal*, ed. L. Madden (Collegeville, Minn.: Liturgical Press, 1992), 55. For a more negative reading of these changes, see C. Fracchia, *Second Spring* (San Francisco: Harper & Row, 1980), 83–84.

3. *On the Sacred Liturgy* 5 (3).

4. *On the Church* I:1 (350); VII:48 (408). Similar descriptions can be found in *On the Sacred Liturgy* 26 (10), *On the Church's Missionary Activity* (*Ad Gentes*) 1 (813), 5 (817); *On the Church in the World* 42 (942), 45 (947).

5. *On the Sacred Liturgy* 7 (5).

6. The eucharistic prayer was regularly referred to as *actio* ("the action") even up to Vatican II.

7. See J. Ratzinger, *Volk und Haus Gottes in Augustins Lehre von der Kirche* (Munich: K. Zink, 1954), 242–45; this remains one of the most insightful discus-

sions of these connections. But Ratzinger's thought should be balanced by the work of W. Simonis, *Ecclesia Visibilis et invisibilis: Untersuchungen zur Ekklesiologie und Sakramentenlehre in der afrikanischen Tradition von Cyprian bis Augustinus* (Frankfurt am Main: J. Knecht, 1970), 91–100.

8. Yves Congar, "Introduction Générale: La Théologie Augustinienne," in *Oeuvres de Saint Augustin,* vol. 28, *Traités Anti-Donatistes,* vol. 1 (Paris: Desclée de Brouwer, 1963), 115.

9. The notions of "action" and of "praxis" are central to the work of Jürgen Habermas and his critical theory. His thought has had a great deal of influence on theologians; see J. Habermas, *Theory and Practice* (Boston: Beacon, 1974).

10. For an introduction to Habermas's thought, see T. McCarthy, *The Critical Theory of Jürgen Habermas* (Cambridge, Mass.: MIT Press, 1978). My intention here is not to apply Habermas's thought to sacrament but rather to insist on the communicative mission of the church and how sacrament and liturgy form a part of that mission.

11. This is a highly condensed summary of some of the salient points of Habermas's system. For an excellent and less condensed summary and critique, see F. D. Dallmayr, *Polis and Praxis* (Cambridge, Mass.: MIT Press, 1984), 224–53. While agreeing with Dallmayr's major points, the model is still useful because it raises some of the essential questions about communication and culture.

12. Paul Lakeland, *Theology and Critical Theory: The Discourse of the Church* (Nashville: Abingdon, 1990), 104.

13. Ibid., 121–22.

14. See again the analysis of Maureen Aggeler, *Mind Your Metaphors: A Critique of Language in the Bishops' Pastoral Letters on the Role of Women* (New York: Paulist, 1991).

15. See S. J. Ochs, "Desegregating the Altar: The Struggle for Black Catholic Priests 1854–1960," Working Paper Series 19, No. 3, Spring, 1988, Cushwa Center for the Study of American Catholicism, University of Notre Dame.

16. For a thorough discussion of the theological background of this description, see J. M. zu Schlochtern, *Sakrament Kirche: Wirken Gottes im Handeln der Menschen* (Freiburg: Herder, 1992), 19–67, esp. 46–60.

17. Zu Schlochtern summarizes this line of argument (which is that of P. Hünermann); see *Sakrament Kirche,* 318–24, and 328–29 for his observations on the limitations of the model.

18. Ibid, 331.

19. Jean-Marie Tillard, *Church of Churches: The Ecclesiology of Communion* (Collegeville, Minn.: Liturgical Press, 1992), 156 (author's emphasis).

20. Michael Warren, "The Local Church and its Practice of the Gospel: The Materiality of Discipleship in a Catechesis of Liberation," *Worship* 67 (1993): 433–60.

21. Clarence Rivers, address given at the conference on Worship and Spirituality in the Black Community, 1977, Washington, D.C.; printed in *This Far by Faith: American Black Worship and Its African Roots* (Washington, D.C.: National Office for Black Catholics, 1977), 39–57.

22. Ibid., 40; see also J. Francis, "Keeping the Bread Fresh," *Origins* 18 (1988): 301–7.

23. *Plenty Good Room: The Spirit and Truth of African American Catholic Worship* (Washington, D.C.: United States Catholic Conference, 1990), 35.

24. Ibid., 44.

25. Augustine, Sermon 229E, in *The Works of Saint Augustine: Sermons III/6*, trans. by E. Hill (New Rochelle, N.Y.: New City Press, 1993), 283 (my emphasis); see also Cardinal M. Pellegrino, "General Introduction," in *The Works of Saint Augustine: Sermons I* (Brooklyn, N.Y.: New City Press, 1990), 88–93.

26. Gallup gives some interesting comparisons between American Catholics and Protestants on the question of allowing more immigration: "American Catholics are still better disposed than Protestants toward new immigrants" (G. Gallup, Jr., and J. Castelli, *American Catholic People: Their Beliefs, Practices, and Values* (Garden City, N.Y.: Doubleday, 1987), 114.

27. NDS #1:3. The same could be said for black Catholics.

28. As cited in Joseph Fitzpatrick, *One Church Many Cultures: The Challenge of Diversity* (Kansas City: Sheed & Ward, 1987), 128–30.

29. Andrew Greeley, *American Catholics since the Council: An Authorized Report* (Chicago: Thomas More Press, 1985), 31. In the preceding pages of the same book, Greeley gives specifics: Catholics of the 1980s are "half-again as likely to attend college" compared with white Protestants in the same age cohort (ibid., 27); they are half-again as likely to select managerial and professional careers as white Protestants (ibid., 28); Catholics make up a fifth of the professorate of academic institutions in this country (ibid., 32). See also Greeley, *The Catholic Myth: The Behavior and Beliefs of American Catholics* (New York: Charles Scribner's Sons, 1991), 72–76.

30. NDS #4:7–8. This terminology is derived from the important study of P. L. Benson and D. L. Williams, *Religion on Capitol Hill: Myths and Realities* (San Francisco: Harper & Row, 1982), 107–12. They also recognize six religious types (legalistic, self-concerned, integrated, people-concerned, nontraditional, and nominal) in interviewing and assessing members of Congress. They point out "membership in a particular denomination obviously does not accurately predict the type of religionist one is. Among Roman Catholics in our sample, at least one fell into each of the six categories" (ibid., 137).

31. Philip Murnion, *Forming the Parish Community* (Washington, D.C.: United States Catholic Conference, 1978), 20–22.

32. Robert Wuthnow, *The Restructuring of American Religion* (Princeton: Princeton University Press, 1988), 55.

33. Ibid., 56–57.

34. American bishops, "Statement on Secularism," as cited in Wuthnow, *Restructuring*, 58–59 (my emphasis).

35. Wuthnow, *Restructuring*, 63.

36. John Coleman, *An American Strategic Theology* (New York: Paulist, 1982), 157.

37. Ibid. Coleman adds, however, that more recent historical criticism would nuance this judgment.

38. In the early use of the term by Alexis de Tocqueville, individualism meant both separation with one's family and friends from the larger society and unmitigated selfishness; see N. Glazer, "Individualism and Equality in the United States," in *On the Making of Americans: Essays in honor of David Riesman*, ed. H. Gans et al. (Philadelphia: University of Pennsylvania Press, 1979), 127–28. But Tocqueville also believed that individualism would make people more dependent on each other, if only out of self-interest.

39. Habermas associates bourgeois culture with a "possessive individualism" in which basic needs are dysfunctionally understood; see McCarthy, *Critical Theory of Jürgen Habermas*, 372–74.

40. Mary Douglas, *Natural Symbols: Explorations in Cosmology* (New York: Pantheon, 1970), 19–36.

41. Bellah et al., *Habits of the Heart*, 334.

42. S. Tipton, "Moral Languages and the Good Society," *Soundings* 69 (1986): 167. See also the clarifying discussion of C. Jencks, "The Social Basis of Unselfishness," in *On the Making of Americans: Essays in honor of David Riesman*, ed. H. Gans et al. (Philadelphia: University of Pennsylvania Press, 1979), 63–86, especially his distinction of "communitarian unselfishness" (pp. 64–65).

43. See W. Sullivan, "Religious Communities of Memory and Hope," *Origins* 17 (1988): 229, 231–34.

44. See Robert Wuthnow, *Acts of Compassion: Caring for Others and Helping Ourselves* (Princeton: Princeton University Press, 1991), 112–14.

45. In addition to Greeley's figures, see also Wuthnow, *Restructuring*, 85–86.

46. See C.-F. Lee and R. Potvin, "A Demographic Profile of U.S. Hispanics," in *Strangers and Aliens No Longer*, Part One, *The Hispanic Presence in the Church of the United States* (Washington, D.C.: United States Catholic Conference, 1993), 31–61, esp. 47–55.

47. See Christopher Lasch, "The Communitarian Critique," in *Community in America* (Berkeley: University of California Press, 1988), 177.

48. J. P. Diggins, *The Lost Soul of American Politics: Virtue, Self-interest and the Foundations of Liberalism* (Chicago: University of Chicago Press, 1984), 150–51.

49. See John Coleman, "Values and Virtues in Advanced Modern Society," in *Changing Values and Virtues*, ed. D. Mieth and J. Pohier, Concilium 191 (Edinburgh: T. & T. Clark, 1987), 3–13.

50. See J. Gremillion and J. Castelli, *The Emerging Parish: The Notre Dame Study of Catholic Life Since Vatican II* (San Francisco: Harper & Row, 1987), 58–60.

51. For their discussion of the "public church," see R. Bellah et al., *The Good Society* (New York: Alfred A. Knopf, 1991), 179–219.

52. D. Hollenbach has caught the dilemma of the churches in this matter: "If the meaning of justice has been fractured into incompatible fragments, each being advocated by a particular ideological camp, then the nice synthesis of faith and culture suggested in church-type ecclesiologies is an illusion. . . . We would face what George Lindbeck (1971), with a good Lutheran sense of irony, has called the 'sectarian future of the church'" (D. Hollenbach, "Justice as Participation," in *Community in America* [Berkeley: University of California Press, 1988], 221).

53. Ibid., 223.

54. Greeley, *Catholic Myth*, 148–53. P. M. Forster and T. P. Sweetser cite their parish evaluations on preaching: 65 percent of American Catholics said they liked most of the homilies they heard at Sunday mass (*Transforming the Parish: Models for the Future* [Kansas City: Sheed & Ward, 1993], 17). But in comments from the evaluation, they mention a number of complaints: irrelevant and boring homilies, the need for more positive and inspiring homilies, a sense of the problems of contemporary Christians, etc. (pp. 17–18).

55. "It is the story of the speaking subject, immersed in the density of the life of praxis, embedded within a sociohistorical formation process in which the subject

already understands himself, albeit prereflectively, as the one who is speaking" (C. Schrag, *Communicative Praxis and the Space of Subjectivity* [Bloomington: Indiana University Press, 1986], 123).

56. This is a paraphrase of Michael Polanyi's axiom, "We know more than we can tell."

57. One example is the way in which television viewers interact socially with media figures whom they do not know personally or ever meet face-to-face. The research of J. Caughey and others has shown, for example, that in relating to a television or movie character the spectator employs the same culturally encoded cues that are operative in any social relation. The apparently passive viewer has become a performer in what is unfolding before her. See J. L. Caughey, *Imaginary Social Worlds: A Cultural Approach* (Lincoln: University of Nebraska Press, 1984), 35–38.

58. See W. F. Fore, *Television and Religion: The Shaping of Faith, Values and Culture* (Minneapolis: Augsburg, 1987), 5–68.

59. N. Postman, *Amusing Ourselves to Death: Public Discourse in the Age of Show Business* (New York: Penguin, 1985), 92.

60. R. Merelman gives an extended analysis of television as an example of "loosely bounded culture" which is similar to Bellah's charge of individualism. See R. Merelman, *Making Something of Ourselves: On Culture and Politics in the United States* (Berkeley: University of California Press, 1984), 70–115.

61. R. Wuthnow, *Meaning and Moral Order: Explorations in Cultural Analysis* (Berkeley: University of California Press, 1987), 125.

62. Ibid., 14.

63. Ibid., 140.

64. Karl Rahner, "The Word and the Eucharist," in *Theological Investigations IV* (Baltimore: Helicon, 1966), 264–65.

65. Lakeland (*Theology and Critical Theory*, 127) points out that Habermas would recognize the process as quite similar to his own concerns.

66. For a detailed description, see J. Fitzpatrick, "Hispanic Parishes Where Something Seems to Be Going Right," in *Strangers and Aliens No Longer*, Part One, *The Hispanic Presence in the Church of the United States* (Washington, D.C.: United States Catholic Conference, 1993), 12–16. Fitzpatrick, however, also gives an example of another parish in the Bronx where the initial attempts at basic communities failed because of the lack of dialogue between the several ethnic groups of the parish (ibid., 20). The *Encuentro* process, which brought together bishops, priests, and laity for prayer, reflection, and implementation of a Hispanic pastoral plan, began on a grass-roots level, then diocesan and national levels. At the III Encuentro, it was urged that the basic Christian communities be established for the implementation of the commitments of the gathering (see *Prophetic Voices: The Document on the Process of the III Encuentro Nacional Hispano de Pastoral* [Washington, D.C.: United States Catholic Conference, 1986], 15; see also M. S. Galeron, "Some Key Aspects to the *Pastoral Plan*," in *Prophetic Vision: National Pastoral Plan for Hispanic Ministry*, ed. S. Galeron et al. [Kansas City: Sheed & Ward, 1992], 229–38).

67. See T. Rausch, "Reception," in *The New Dictionary of Theology*, ed. J. Komonchak et al. (Wilmington, Del.: Michael Glazier, 1987), 829.

68. The better-known form of "reception" is ecumenical. The World Council of Churches, for example, asked the churches in 1982 to review the Lima document, *Baptism, Eucharist, and Ministry*, and to ascertain whether its results resonated with their own awareness of the "faith of the church though the ages."

69. See E. Kilmartin, "Reception in History: An Ecclesiological Phenomenon and its Significance," *Journal of Ecumenical Studies* 21 (1984): 36–37.

70. See the articles of A. Houtepen and U. Kühn in *Ecumenical Perspectives on Baptism, Eucharist and Ministry*, ed. M. Thurian, Faith and Order Paper No. 116 (Geneva: World Council of Churches, 1983), esp. 149–50 and 165–66.

71. The problem of reception becomes more complicated in viewing the history of the councils of the church. There is a shift in the early Middle Ages from reception as a form of intercommunion among local churches to a more juridical understanding of reception in which the universal church legislates and local churches implement (e.g., Trent and Vatican I). See Kilmartin, "Reception in History," 37–38; and M. Garijo, "Der Begriff 'Rezeption' und sein Ort im Kern der katholischen Ekklesiologie," in *Theologischer Konsens und Kirchenspaltung*, ed. P. Lengsfeld, H.-G. Stobbe (Stuttgart: Kohlhammer, 1981), 100–105.

72. E. Kilmartin cites the important example of how the calling down of the Holy Spirit in liturgical celebrations [*epiclesis*] was received by different communities in the fourth century ("Reception in History," 41).

73. See, e.g., Rausch, "Reception," 828.

74. Kilmartin, "Reception in History," 43.

75. Ibid.

76. Both the origin and the authorship of the Apostolic Tradition continue to be disputed. See P. Bradshaw, *The Search for the Origins of Christian Worship* (New York: Oxford University Press, 1992), 90–92.

77. Ibid., 37.

78. NDS #4:4.

79. Wuthnow, *Meaning and Moral Order*, 66.

80. Ibid., 76.

81. Again, Wuthnow's observation is pertinent: "Two symbols are discursively connected but one is emphasized rather than the other" (ibid., 72).

82. Greeley, *The American Catholic, A Social Portrait* (New York: Basic Books, 1977), 273.

83. This is also the positive evaluation of R. Schreiter, "Who are American Catholics and What Do They Believe?" *New Theology Review* 2 (1989): 34–47.

84. NDS #15:8; Murnion, *Parish Life in the United States*, 33.

85. See P. Murnion's eloquent statement, "A Sacramental Church in the Modern World," *Origins* 14 (1984): 81–90; see also M. Francis Mannion, "Liturgy and the Present Crisis of Culture," *Worship* 62 (1988): 98–123.

86. Roger Kessing's warning on culture also applies to a theology of church: "Cultures must generate viable patterns-of-life ecosystems. . . . It is how humans live, not how they conceptualize the game of life, that is directly shaped by selective pressures" ("Theories of Culture," *Annual Review of Anthropology* 3 [1974]: 91).

87. "Vatican Report on Sects, Cults and New Religious Movements," *Origins* 16 (1986): 1–8.

88. "Vatican Report," quoted by Fitzpatrick, "A Survey of Literature on Hispanic Ministry," in *Strangers and Aliens No Longer*, Part One, *The Hispanic Presence in the Church of the United States* (Washington, D.C.: United States Catholic Conference, 1993), 78.

89. See U.S. Bishops, "Guidelines for Lay Preaching," *Origins* 18 (1988): 402–4.

90. The Notre Dame Study noted two basic profiles that emerge from their study of parishioners' religious practices: (1) a "mystical communion/postconcil-

iar" type that favors expressive religiosity and post-Vatican II private devotional-ism, and (2) an institutional type that prefers pre-Vatican II prayer and devotions and basic public practices (mass and communion) (NDS #4:6).

91. An interesting point of comparison is the ecclesiology and liturgical praxis of the nineteenth-century German Catholic church; see R. W. Franklin, "Johann Adam Moehler and Worship in a Totalitarian Society," *Worship* 67 (1993): 2–17.

92. Coleman, "Values and Virtues in Advanced Modern Societies," 12.

93. For a summary of this research and comparisons with young Protestants, see Patrick H. McNamara, *Conscience First, Tradition Second: A Study of Young American Catholics* (Albany: State University of New York Press, 1992), esp. 36–41.

94. Ibid., 39.

95. Ibid., 133.

96. American bishops, *Economic Justice for All: Catholic Social Teaching and the American Economy* (Washington, D.C.: United States Catholic Conference, 1986), §325.

97. Ibid., §331.

## Chapter 4: American Time and God's Time

1. *On Evangelization* 26–27.

2. "People in organized religious congregations participate, in larger numbers and with greater generosity in time and money, than any other groups in the United States, in communities that transcend the family and its informal circle of friends" (R. Bellah et al., *The Good Society* [New York: Alfred A. Knopf, 1991], 217.

3. For a different sociocultural context and the questions of time/feast, see A. Aubrey, "The Feast of Peoples and the Explosion of Society—Popular Practice and Liturgical Practice," in *The Times of Celebration,* ed. D. Power, Concilium 142 (New York: Seabury, 1981), 55–64.

4. Stephen Jay Gould, *Time's Arrow, Time's Cycle: Myth and Metaphor in the Discovery of Geological Time* (Cambridge, Mass.: Harvard University Press, 1987), 2. See also S. W. Hawkins, *A Brief History of Time* (Toronto: Bantam Books, 1988), 152.

5. See R. Haegerstrand, "Time and Culture," in *The Formulation of Time Preferences in a Multidisciplinary Perspective,* ed. G. Kirsch et al. (Hant, England: Gower, 1988), 33–42, especially 35.

6. See S. Kern, *The Culture of Time and Space 1880–1918* (Cambridge, Mass.: Harvard University Press, 1983), 11–16.

7. Ibid., 33–35, 313–14.

8. J. Rifkin, *Time Wars: The Primary Conflict in Human History* (New York: H. Holt, 1987), 48; see also T. Shibutani, *Social Processes* (Berkeley: University of California Press, 1986), 70; Clifford Geertz, *The Interpretation of Culture* (New York: Basic Books, 1973), 389–98, for a famous example in another culture.

9. See A. Giddens, *The Constitution of Society* (Berkeley: University of California, 1984), 110ff.

10. Ibid., 132; also 119–22.

11. See J. P. Robinson, *How Americans Use Time* (New York: Praeger, 1977), 27–31; see also M. Jahoda, "Time: A Social Psychological Perspective," in *The Rhythms of Society,* ed. M. Young and T. Schuller (London: Routledge, 1988), 157.

12. See J. Nowotny, "From the Future to the Extended Present," in *The Formulation of Time Preferences in a Multidisciplinary Perspective,* ed. G. Kirsch et al. (Hant, England: Gower, 1988), 17–31.

13. It is certainly not by chance that the French regularly use our expression in saying "le weekend" rather than "fin de semaine," as the French Academy has often lamented.

14. C. Velez-I, "Ourselves Through the Eyes of an Anthropologist," in *The Chicanos As We See Ourselves,* ed. A. D. Trejo (Tucson, Ariz.: University of Arizona Press, 1980), 45.

15. Hugh Daziel Duncan, *Symbols in Society* (London: Oxford University Press, 1968), 26.

16. See D. Yankelovitch, *New Rules* (New York: Basic Books, 1982), 71–76.

17. Christopher Lasch, *The Culture of Narcissism: American Life in an Age of Diminishing Expectations* (New York: Warner, 1979), 107.

18. Even the use of tenses in American English to mark time suggests this point; see R. Merelman, *Making Something of Ourselves: On Culture and Politics in the United States* (Berkeley: University of California Press, 1984), 60–61.

19. Daniel Bell, *The Cultural Contradictions of Capitalism* (New York: Basic Books, 1978), 90–91.

20. N. Postman, *Amusing Ourselves to Death: Public Discourse in the Age of Show Business* (New York: Penguin, 1986), 100.

21. Merelman, *Making Something of Ourselves,* 90–92.

22. Rifkin, *Time Wars,* 164ff.

23. Ibid., 167.

24. Robert Wuthnow, *Acts of Compassion: Caring for Others and Helping Ourselves* (Princeton: Princeton University Press, 1991), 5–6.

25. Ibid., 14.

26. Ibid., 322 n. 11. Wuthnow points out that in his survey "Catholics are about equally likely to place high value on the importance of helping the needy (77 percent and 71 percent, respectively, said this was very important) and of giving time to help other people (66 percent and 62 percent, respectively)" (ibid., 130).

27. *Economic Justice for All: Catholic Social Teaching and the U.S. Economy* (Washington, D.C.: National Conference of Catholic Bishops, 1986), §338.

28. See the papers on liturgical time presented at the Societas Liturgica meeting in Paris in 1982, *Studia Liturgica* 14 nos. 2, 3, 4 (1982).

29. As cited by Robert Taft, *The Liturgy of the Hours in the East and West* (Collegeville, Minn.: Liturgical Press, 1986), 14.

30. Ibid., 167.

31. Robert Taft, "Toward a Theology of the Christian Feast," in *Beyond East and West: Problems in Liturgical Understanding* (Washington, D.C.: Pastoral Press, 1984), 3.

32. See J. Jungmann's remarks, *Missa Solemnia* (New York: Benziger, 1950), 1:383 n. 39; see also M. P. Ellebracht, *Remarks on the Vocabulary of the Ancient Orations in the Missale Romanum* (Nijmegen: Dekker & Van De Vegt, 1966), 55.

33. Ellebracht, *Remarks,* 10.

34. See, e.g., A. Adam, *The Liturgical Year: Its History and its Meaning after the Reform of the Liturgy* (New York: Pueblo, 1981), 26–27.

35. See A. J. MacGregor, *Fire and Light in the Western Triduum: Their Use at Tenebrae and at the Paschal Vigil* (Collegeville, Minn.: Liturgical Press, 1992), 366–68.

36. Easter Sunday, the Easter Vigil in *The Sacramentary* (New York: Catholic Book Company, 1985), no.10 (p. 172).

37. For a summary of basic literature and bibliographies, see. B. Van Iersel, "Some Biblical Roots of the Christian Sacrament," in *Sacraments in General,* ed. E. Schillebeeckx and B. Willems, Concilium 31 (New York: Paulist, 1968), 5–20; G. Wainwright, *Eucharist and Eschatology* (1969; reprint, New York: Oxford University Press, 1981), 127 n. 204; idem, "Sacramental Time," in *The Ecumenical Moment* (Grand Rapids: Eerdmans, 1983), 120–33.

38. Brevard S. Childs, *Memory and Tradition in Israel* (London: SCM Press, 1962), 53–54 (my emphasis).

39. Leo the Great, Sermon 26, "On the Feast of the Nativity, VI" in *Nicene and Post-Nicene Fathers* (New York: Scribner, 1895), 12:137.

40. Cf. B. de Soos's remarks in *Le Mystère Liturgique d'après Saint Léon le Grand* (Münster: Aschendorff, 1958), 24–25.

41. "*Hodie* enim non solum paradisi possessores firmati sumus, sed etiam coelorum in Christo superna penetravimus" (Sermon 44, as cited by de Soos, *Le Mystère,* 26 [my emphasis]).

42. This same notion of "today" is seen in Hebrews 3:7–4:13, in which the writer repeatedly cites the refrain of Psalm 9:7–11: "*Today,* if you should hear his voice." "Today," as the moment of salvation for the Jews in the desert, has now become such a moment for the New Testament community, in danger of apostasy, to whom the writer of Hebrews addresses himself. See A. T. Lincoln, "Sabbath, Rest and Eschatology in the New Testament," in *From Sabbath to Lord's Day: A Biblical, Historical and Theological Investigation,* ed. D. A. Carson (Grand Rapids: Zondervan, 1982), 205ff.; also Harold W. Attridge, *The Epistle to the Hebrews* (Philadelphia: Fortress, 1989), 128.

43. T. Talley, "A Christian Heortology," in *The Times of Celebration,* ed. D. Power, Concilium 142 (New York: Seabury, 1981), 15.

44. The *New American Bible* of 1970 translates Greek *hosakis* as "every time," whereas typical lexicons translate "as often as"; see J. H. Thayer, *A Greek-English Lexicon of the New Testament* (Grand Rapids: Zondervan, [1885]), 465; F. W. Gingrich, *A Shorter Lexicon of the Greek New Testament* (Chicago: University of Chicago Press, 1965), 153. Both phrases are correct as a translation into current English usage but are not synonymous from a philosophical or theological point of view unless "every time" is reduced to meaning "with every repetition." My argument is not with a particular translation but is intended to underscore how popular conceptions of time may not reflect the larger biblical or liturgical meaning of time.

45. Augustine, *St. Augustine's Confessions* 11.14, trans. W. Watts (Cambridge, Mass.: Harvard University Press, 1979), 2:237–39.

46. Karl Rahner, "Experiencing Easter," in *Theological Investigations VII* (New York: Herder & Herder, 1971), 161–62.

47. See Karl Rahner, *Foundations of Christian Faith* (New York: Seabury, 1978), 337ff.

48. Rahner, "Experiencing Easter," 162.

49. This is so central to Rahner's thought that he finally argues that someone who is faithful to his/her conscience and does not explicitly believe in Christ's resurrection is still oriented toward this mystery ("Experiencing Easter," 164, 168).

50. Karl Rahner, "The Person in the Sacramental Event," in *Theological Investigations XIV* (New York: Seabury, 1976), 171–72.

51. Ibid., 172–73.

52. Simon de Vries seems to be making a similar point in his distinction between a "sacerdotal" Christianity's quantitative time (in which past and future are frozen into a timeless present) and the "nonsacerdotal" approach with its urgent biblical awareness of qualitative time ("Time in the Bible," in *The Times of Celebration,* ed. D. Power, Concilium 42 (New York: Seabury, 1981), 12. See also Johannes B. Metz's warning about a theology caught in the "grip of timelessness" in his *Faith in History and Society: Toward a Practical Fundamental Theology* (New York: Seabury, 1981), 171–75.

53. Rahner, *Foundations,* 94–95.

54. For a contrasting view to Rahner's thought on time, see W. Pannenberg, "Constructive and Critical Functions of Christian Eschatology," *Harvard Theological Review* 77 (1984): 119–39.

55. Paul Ricoeur, *Time and Narration,* 3 vols. (Chicago: University of Chicago Press, 1984–88), 1:52.

56. Ibid., 2:23.

57. Ibid.

58. D. Carr, "Narrative and the Real Word: An Argument for Continuity," *Harvard Theological Review* 25 (1986): 128.

59. "Because communicative praxis involves not only the texts of spoken and written discourse but also the concrete actions of individuals and the historically effective life of institutions, its texture encompasses a wider metaphorical range than that of textuality per se. It includes also the texture of human projects, of motivations, and decisions, of embodiment, and of wider processes of social formation" (Calvin Schrag, *Communicative Praxis and the Space of Subjectivity* [Bloomington: Indiana University Press, 1986], 24).

60. Ibid., 146.

61. No. 411 in P. Bruylants, *Les oraisons du Missel Romain* (Louvain: Mont César, 1952), 2:115.

62. No. 997, *Sacramentum Veronense,* ed. L. C. Mohlberg (Rome: Herder, 1966), 127.

63. Aidan Kavanagh, "Reflections on the Study from the Viewpoint of Liturgical History," in *The Awakening Church: 25 Years of Liturgical Renewal* (Collegeville, Minn.: Liturgical Press, 1992), 88. His citation is from K. Flanagan, "Resacralizing the Liturgy," *Blackfriars* 68 (1987): 65.

64. See D. R. Hoge, "Interpreting Change in American Catholicism: The River and the Floodgate," *Review of Religious Research* 27 (1986): 289–99.

65. Hoge would argue that Greeley's assertion that the temporary drop in attendance at mass in the 1970s was principally due to Paul VI's position on contraception should be nuanced by the inclusion of these other factors. See Hoge, "Interpreting Change," 292.

66. Ibid., 296–97.

67. See Herbert J. Gans, "Symbolic Ethnicity: The Future of Ethnic Groups and Cultures in America," in *On the Making of Americans: Essays in honor of David Riesman,* ed. H. Gans et al. (Philadelphia: University of Pennsylvania Press, 1979), 193–220.

68. Ibid., 205 (my emphasis). Gans gives a Catholic example on p. 213.

69. Yankelovich, *New Rules,* 71.

70. Ibid., 56–57.

71. One indication, though certainly no proof, of this statement might be one of the questions asked in the NCR/Gallup poll (*National Catholic Reporter*, September 11, 1987), "Do you think a person can be a good Catholic without . . ." followed by a number of specific examples (mass attendance every Sunday, obeying the church's teaching on birth control, etc.). In response to the specific question "without donating time or money to help the poor," the percentage of people ages eighteen to twenty-nine who answered affirmatively was only 45 percent (p. 7), while most other answers got much higher percentages. (For an analysis of this poll, see W. D'Antonio, J. Davidson, D. Hoge, and R. Wallace, *American Catholic Laity in a Changing Church* [Kansas City: Sheed & Ward, 1989]). Once again, the importance of personal contact with sympathetic priests and the hearing of good homilies were rated as having considerable influence on young Catholics.

72. See C. Dooley, "Liturgical Catechesis: Mystagogy, Marriage or Misnomer?" *Worship* 66 (1992): 386–97.

## Chapter 5: In the New Wilderness

1. Jean-Marie Tillard, *Church of Churches: The Ecclesiology of Communion* (Collegeville, Minn.: Liturgical Press, 1992), 145.

2. Thus, the much-used term "public Catholicism" refers to the church's role in influencing directly or indirectly public policy "in accord with its self-understanding within democratic pluralism" (C. Kauffman, in his foreword to David O'Brien, *Public Catholicism* [New York: Macmillan, 1989], xvii–xviii).

3. NDS #13, esp. 12.

4. David Roozen, W. McKinney, J. Carroll, *Varieties of Religious Presence: Mission in Public Life* (New York: Pilgrim Press, 1984).

5. Ibid., 32–36.

6. Ibid., 175.

7. NDS #4:7–8. As cited in chapter 3, Philip Murnion's study of 350 parishes in the archdiocese of New York seems to parallel these results: the theopolitan parish (29 percent of the sample) offered a careful balance between community building and outreach to the larger community; the public action parish (17 percent) concentrated on its mission to the world. The sectarian type of parish (25 percent) was active but inward-looking, while the sacramental service parish (28 percent) provided sacramental participation but not a sense of mission (see P. Murnion, *Forming the Parish Community* [Washington, D.C.: United States Catholic Conference, 1978], 20–22).

8. See NDS #4:8: "Perhaps one of the reasons foundational beliefs do not predict well to parish purpose is that age and sex differences along the agentic/communal dimension are minimal; young Catholics and women are *not* more likely to be communal, as one might have suspected."

9. NDS #4:4.

10. See NDS #7:10: ". . . sophisticated analyses that compare Catholics within demographic categories—e.g., age, sex, education—still miss the embeddedness of Catholics in their local parish. Parishioners soak up the ideas they hear around them. . . . While there is a certain amount of parochialism in any parish, the parish

is also a crossroads for transcending generational, educational, age, and income differences."

11. See, e.g., C. Fracchia, *Second Spring* (San Francisco: Harper & Row, 1980), 83–84.

12. Andrew Greeley, *The American Catholic: A Social Portrait* (New York: Basic Books, 1977), 272.

13. Andrew Greeley, *The Catholic Myth: The Behavior and Beliefs of American Catholics* (New York: Charles Scribner's Sons, 1991), 158.

14. W. L. Miller, *The First Liberty* (New York: Alfred A. Knopf, 1986), 288, as cited in J. Coleman, "American Catholicism," in *World Catholicism in Transition,* ed. T. M. Gannon (New York: Macmillan, 1988), 24.

15. Robert Wuthnow, *Acts of Compassion: Caring for Others and Helping Ourselves* (Princeton: Princeton University Press, 1991), 11–14.

16. Frederick Jackson Turner, *The Frontier in American History* (New York: H. Holt, 1920). Later T. McAvoy proposed that there were connections between Turner's thesis and the Americanism that Rome condemned, such as an individualism that did not need external authority and liturgical and devotional changes that might foster ecumenism ("Americanism and Frontier Catholicism," *Review of Politics* 5 [1943]: 275–301).

17. See T. W. Spalding, "Frontier Catholicism," *Church History Review* 91 (1977): 470–84, esp. 475–77. This thesis acknowledges that there were immigrants in the west, but to the extent that they lived on the frontier, they changed from their eastern counterparts. The American novelist Willa Cather has given a classic description of this in her books, for example, *O Pioneers* and *My Antonia.*

18. Spalding, "Frontier Catholicism," 477.

19. For example, Greeley, *Catholic Myth,* 44–48; for the charge of individualism, see NDS #4:8.

20. Herbert J. Gans, *Middle American Individualism: The Future of Liberal Democracy* (New York: Free Press, 1988), x.

21. R. Bellah, R. Madsen, W. Sullivan, A. Swidler, S. Tipton, *The Good Society* (New York: Alfred A. Knopf, 1991), 87–89.

22. Gans, *Middle American Individualism,* 17.

23. In response to questions about motivations for going to the Eucharist, the Notre Dame Study noted that "only 6% . . . said they attended Mass because the Church requires them to do so, whereas 28% say they go because they enjoy taking part in the liturgy. A further 37% cite the feeling of being in contact with God . . . as compared with 20% who go to receive Holy Communion and 19% who are drawn by the need to hear the Word of God" (NDS #6:5).

24. Wuthnow, *Acts of Compassion,* 10.

25. Ibid., 14.

26. Ibid., 152; Bellah et al., *Habits of the Heart: Individualism and Commitment in American Life* (Berkeley: University of California Press, 1985), 228, based on a 1978 Gallup survey.

27. Wuthnow, *Acts of Compassion,* 125–26.

28. Ibid., 127.

29. Ibid., 130 and 322 nn. 10, 11.

30. See S. Tipton, "The Church as a School for Virtue," *Daedalus* 117 (1988): 166–67; R. Bellah et al., *Habits of the Heart,* 72–73. Catherine Bell, from a ritual

point of view, sees this individualism and its "expressive language" somewhat differently: "Catholic identity now lies in dynamics of self-expression instituted and nourished in a liturgical medium by which a group of individuals is empowered to experience themselves as a particular manifestation of the church" ("Ritual, Change and Changing Rituals," *Worship* 63 [1989] 40–41). Comparing the postconciliar liturgy with previous ritual forms, she adds: "In each case the particular ritual schemes of the Mass functioned in their specific sociohistorical milieu to make strategic distinctions that defined both community and personal identity in effective ways." Whether this evokes or symbolizes an authentic ecclesial presence is another question.

31. Bellah et al., *Habits of the Heart,* 246–48.

32. Gans, *Middle American Individualism,* 113.

33. Greeley, *Catholic Myth,* 159.

34. Timothy Smith, "Religion and Ethnicity in America," *American Historical Review* 83 (1978): 1155–85.

35. Ibid., 1179 (my emphasis).

36. Robert Orsi, *The Madonna of 115th Street: Faith and Community in Italian Harlem 1880–1950* (New Haven: Yale University Press, 1985).

37. Ibid., 44–45.

38. Ibid., 75–106.

39. Ibid., 169.

40. Ibid., 171.

41. The Fordham University study of this question is particularly important; see *The Future of Catholic Institutional Ministries* (New York: Third Age Center, Fordham University, 1992).

42. Calvin O. Schrag, *Communicative Praxis and the Space of Subjectivity* (Bloomington: Indiana University Press, 1986), 182.

43. Ibid., 37–39, 45.

44. P. Hünermann, "Figur des Lebens," as cited by J. M. zu Schlochtern, *Sakrament Kirche: Wirken Gottes im Handeln der Menschen* (Freiburg: Herder, 1992), 321.

45. Ibid.

46. Catherine de Hueck, *Friendship House* (New York: Sheed & Ward, 1947), 65, as cited in *One Faith, One Lord, One Baptism: The Hopes and Experiences of the Black Community in the Archdiocese of New York,* 2 vols. (New York: Archdiocese of New York, 1988), 2:1978.

47. An example of the lack of this kind of leadership on the local level might be that, as reported in the NCR/Gallup poll (1987), of the people who go to weekly mass, only a third have ever heard of the peace pastoral (see *National Catholic Reporter,* September 11, 1987, p. 13).

48. "Communcation has both a linguistic and an actional dimension. There is a rhetoric of speech and there is a rhetoric of action" (ibid., 22).

49. "[N]arration, as the unity of story, storyteller, audience, and protagonist, is what constitutes the community, its activities, and its coherence in the first place. . . . To sum up: *a community exists where a narrative account exists of a we which persists through its experiences and actions*" (D. Carr, "Narrative and the Real World: An Argument for Continuity," *History and Theory* 25 [1986]: 128, 130 [my emphasis]).

50. Paul VI, *On Evangelization* 21.

51. See Brevard S. Childs, *Memory and Tradition in Israel* (London: SCM Press, 1962), 53–56.

52. Johannes B. Metz, "A Short Apology for Narrative," *Concilium* 85 (1973): 84–96.

53. See B. Mahaney, "The Affective Narrative: A Grammar of Praxis," *Irish Theological Quarterly* 54 (1988): 50–58.

54. "Our data leave no doubt about the historical trends behind the decline. Between 1966 and 1984 the U.S. Catholic church witnessed a 20 percent loss in the number of active diocesan priests. . . . The projections to 2005 forecast continued losses, leading to a total decline of 40 percent of the 1966 number of active diocesan priests. . . . Thus while the Catholic lay population will probably grow more than 65 percent between 1966 and 2005, the priesthood population will decline 40 percent in the same period. . . . This knowledge is eminently practical as church leaders face the growing dilemma of full pews and empty altars" (R. A. Schoenherr and L. A. Young, *Full Pews and Empty Altars: Demographics of the Priest Shortage in the United States Catholic Dioceses* (Madison: University of Wisconsin Press, 1993), 309–10. One figure given is that more than three hundred parishes across the country are currently led by sisters or laity owing to lack of priests (P. Steinfels, "Ancient Rock in Crosscurrents of Today," *New York Times,* Sunday, May 29, 1994, p. 10).

55. The translation of the Vatican document is the *Directory for Sunday Celebrations in the Absence of a Presbyter* and can be found in *Origins* 18 (1988): 301–7. The statement of the American bishops' Committee on the Liturgy is *Gathered in Steadfast Faith* (Washington, D.C.: United States Catholic Conference, 1991).

56. John M. Huels, "Chronicle: Sunday Liturgies Without a Priest," *Worship* 64 (1990): 451–60; for an extensive bibliography on mostly critical reactions to Sunday liturgies without priests, see p. 454 n. 4.

57. Ibid., 460.

58. Augustine of Hippo, Sermon 272, *The Works of Saint Augustine: Sermons III/7*, translated by E. Hill (New Rochelle, N.Y.: New City Press, 1993), 300.

59. Rosemary Radford Ruether, *Woman-Church: Theology and Practice of Feminist Liturgical Communities* (San Francisco: Harper & Row, 1985), 92.

60. See NDS #10:8–9.

61. NDS #1:6. This is averaged on the one thousand parishes studied.

62. NDS #9:12.

63. Maria Pilar Aquino, "Women," in *Prophetic Vision: National Pastoral Plan for Hispanic Ministry,* ed. S. Galeron et al. (Kansas City: Sheed & Ward, 1992), 327. See also A. M. Isai-Diaz and Y. Tarango, *Hispanic Women: Prophetic Voice in the Church* (San Francisco: Harper & Row, 1988); also J. Redmont, *Generous Lives: Catholic Women Today* (New York: W. Morrow, 1992), 305–21.

64. Andrew Greeley and Mary G. Durkin, *Angry Catholic Women: A Sociological Investigation* (Chicago: Thomas More, 1984), 41.

65. For a particularly balanced and eloquent statement of this, see M. Collins, O.S.B., "Women in Relation to the Institutional Church," an address given at the Leadership Conference of Women Religious (LCWR) 1991 National Assembly, Albuquerque, New Mexico, August 26, 1991: "In the North American expression of neo-clerical praxis, the cultural model for women's ministries, liturgical and pastoral, is 'Rosie the Riveter.' Women workers supply: wherever there is a dearth

of churchmen to fill available positions, women are being invited to step in. In the neo-clerical doctrine that articulates this praxis, God did not make women inferior, but neither did God make them equal" (p. 8). In a similar vein, see Redmont, *Generous Lives,* 229–53.

66. No longer able to accept male-dominated liturgies, small groups of women, as early as the 1980s, apparently began to celebrate their own liturgies. See M. S. Thompson, "Women and American Catholicism, 1789–1989," in *Perspectives on the American Catholic Church 1789–1989,* ed. S. J. Vicchio and V. Geiger (Kansas City: Sheed & Ward, 1989), 140; Ruether, *Woman-Church,* 67–68; Redmont, *Generous Lives,* 92–94, 278–82; M. Collins, "Women in Relation to the Institutional Church."

67. This situation has been discussed extensively; see, e.g., J. Deedy, *American Catholicism: And Now Where?* (New York: Plenum, 1987), 175–210; Ruether, *Woman-Church; Women in the Church I,* ed. M. Kolbenschlag (Washington, D.C.: Pastoral Press, 1989); Greeley and Durkin, *Angry Catholic Women.*

68. See, e.g., G. I. Loya, "The Hispanic Woman: Pasionaria and Pastora of the Hispanic Community," in *Frontiers of Hispanic Theology in the United States,* ed. A. F. Deck (Maryknoll, N.Y.: Orbis, 1992), 124–33.

69. Greeley and Durkin, *Angry Catholic Women,* 136–37.

70. Again, some of the women interviewed by Jane Redmont are particularly eloquent on these themes; see *Generous Lives,* 320–24.

### Chapter 6: American Sacramental Praxis

1. Clifford Geertz, *The Interpretation of Cultures* (New York: Basic Books, 1973), 113–14 (author's emphasis); see also C. Bell, *Ritual Theory, Ritual Practice* (New York: Oxford University Press, 1992), 28–29.

2. See the perceptive article of Riv-Ellen Prell-Foldes, "The reinvention of reflexivity in Jewish prayer: The self and community in modernity," *Semiotica* 30 (1980): 73–96, esp. 90.

3. Augustine of Hippo, Sermon 223, *The Works of Saint Augustine: Sermons III/6,* trans. E. Hill (New Rochelle, N.Y.: New City Press, 1993), 210.

4. See Daniel Bell, *The Cultural Contradictions of Capitalism* (New York: Basic Books, 1976), 148.

5. Herbert Gans, *Middle American Individualism* (New York: Free Press, 1988), 45–46.

6. NDS #4 ("Religious Values and Parish Participation: the Paradox of Individual Needs in a Communitarian Church") deals not only with parishioners' involvement in their parish but also with their operational definitions of why a parish exists. While lay liturgical roles are the second most characteristic form of participation in the parish, the understanding of the parish as "a place offering worship and Sacraments, liturgies," ranks in the fourth place (ibid, 4–5).

7. Robert Wuthnow, *Meaning and Moral Order: Explorations in Cultural Analysis* (Berkeley: University of California Press, 1987), 76.

8. See Vatican II, *On the Sacred Liturgy* 11, 14 (6–8).

9. Cited in M. B. de Soos, *Le Mystère Liturgique d'après Saint Léon le Grand* (Münster: Aschendorff, 1958), 94 (my emphasis).

10. Leo underlines this union by attaching the prefix *com/con* to his verbs: *com-*

*mortui, et consepulti, et conresuscitati sumus,* "together we have died, been buried and have risen" (M. Herz, *Sacrum Commercium: Eine Begriffsgeschichtliche Studie zur Theologie der Römischen Liturgiesprache* (Munich: K. Zink, 1958), 257 n. 31d.

11. Another example of this Leonine influence can be seen in the prayer that accompanies the pouring of the water into the wine in the preparation of the eucharistic gifts: "By the mystery of this water and wine may we come to share (*consortes*) in the divinity of Christ who humbled himself to share (*particeps*) in our humanity." This text derives from the Leonine prayer found in the Christmas cycle of the liturgical year. For the underlying theology, see A. Härdelin, *Aquae et Vini Mysterium: Geheimnis der Erlösung und Geheimnis der Kirche im Spiegel der mittelalterlichen Auslegung des gemischten Kelches* (Münster: Aschendorff, 1973).

12. See Wayne A. Meeks, *The First Urban Christians: The Social World of the Apostle Paul* (New Haven: Yale University Press, 1983), 100, 159.

13. See H. Conzelmann, *1 Corinthians: A Commentary on the First Epistle to the Corinthians* (Philadelphia: Fortress, 1975), 171–73; J. Betz, *Die Eucharistie in der Zeit der Griechischen Väter* (Freiburg: Herder, 1964), 2:110–14; P. Neuenzeit, *Das Herrenmahl: Studien auf paulinischen Eucharistieauffassung* (Munich: Kösel, 1960), 178–83.

14. Conzelmann suggests that *metechomen ek* explains the meaning of *koinōnia,* which refers to "communion with the death of Christ" (*1 Corinthians,* 171). X. Léon-Dufour also argues for a "communion of persons"; he says that communion refers to the frequent Pauline phrases of dying and rising. Further, he notes that normally *koinōnia* takes the dative case in the New Testament and secular usage, while Paul uses the dependent genitive with the word to indicate a very close union between the faithful and Christ (*Sharing the Eucharistic Bread: The Witness of the New Testament* [New York: Paulist, 1982], 209–10).

15. See A. Thaler, *Gemeinde und Eucharistie: Grundlegung einer eucharistischen Ekklesiologie* (Freiburg: Universitätsverlag, 1988), 66–68.

16. W. F. Orr and J. A. Walther, *First Corinthians* (Garden City, N.Y.: Doubleday, 1976), 269; also Meeks, *First Urban Christians,* 98–100.

17. Vatican II, *On the Sacred Liturgy* 7 (4).

18. Ibid., 11 (6–7).

19. For Peter Lombard's and Odo of Ourscamp's explanations, see J. Finkenzeller, *Lehre von den Sakramenten im allgemeinen: Von der Schrift bis zur Scholastik* (Freiburg: Herder, 1980), 101–2.

20. See R. Duffy, "The Kiss of Peace: Reach Out and Touch Someone?" *Pastoral Musician* 15 (1991): 38–41.

21. Augustine of Hippo, Sermon 227, *The Works of Saint Augustine: Sermons III/6 (184–229Z) on the Liturgical Seasons,* translated and annotated by E. Hill (New Rochelle, N.Y.: New City Press 1993), 255.

22. *The General Instruction of the Roman Missal* (Washington, D.C.: United States Catholic Conference, 1982), #56b, p. 33.

23. C. Taylor is particularly helpful here: "The meanings and norms implicit in these practices are not just in the minds of the actors but are out there *in the practices themselves,* practices which cannot be conceived as a set of individual actions, but which are essentially modes of social relation, of mutual action" ("Interpretation and the Sciences of Man," in *Interpretive Social Science: A Reader,* ed. P. Rabinow and W. M. Sullivan [Berkeley: University of California Press, 1979], 48 [my emphasis]).

24. "Texture encompasses not only the texture of textuality but also the texture of the tissues of human action and the fibers of institutional life" (C. Schrag, *Communicative Praxis and the Space of Subjectivity* [Bloomington: Indiana University Press, 1986], 92 [my emphasis]).

25. Ibid., 143.

26. Mary Collins, "Obstacles to Liturgical Creativity," in *Liturgy: A Creative Tradition,* ed. M. Collins and D. Power, Concilium 162 (New York: Seabury, 1983), 25.

27. Whether music is a language with fixed connotations is a much debated question. See, e.g., S. Langer, *Philosophy in a New Key: A Study in Symbolism of Reason, Rite and Art,* 3rd ed. (Cambridge, Mass.: Harvard University Press, 1979), 228. For different positions, see J. P. Burkholder, "On Interpreting Music in an Historical Framework," *Soundings* 70 (1987): 199–217; also J.-J. Nattiez, *Music and Discourse: Toward a Semiology of Music* (Princeton: Princeton University Press, 1990), 107–29. A special debt of gratitude is owed to David Tracy's important discussion of a "classic" in theology in *The Analogical Imagination: Christian Theology and the Culture of Pluralism* (New York: Crossroad, 1981), which has become a classic itself.

28. Ricoeur has been criticized for his overly facile movement from text to the discourse of action in which "the display of human actions and institutional processes of sociohistorical formation is glossed and subordinated to textual and linguistic inscriptions" (Schrag, *Communicative Praxis,* 30); see also R. Duffy, "Seminar on Sacramental and Liturgical Theology," *Proceedings of The Catholic Theological Society of America* 40 (1985): 207–9.

29. See Paul Ricoeur, *Interpretation Theory: Discourse and the Surplus of Meaning* (Fort Worth, Tex.: Texas Christian University Press, 1976); also D. Power, *Unsearchable Riches: The Symbolic Nature of Liturgy* (New York: Pueblo, 1984) and J. Van Den Hengel, *The Home of Meaning: The Hermeneutics of the Subject of Paul Ricoeur* (Washington, D.C.: University Press of America, 1982).

30. Ricoeur speaks of the text in almost biblical terms as a "presence" that can be actualized now for the reader. See Van Den Hengel, *Home of Meaning,* 192.

31. Paul Ricoeur, "Phenomenology and Hermeneutics," in *Hermeneutics and the Human Sciences,* ed. John B. Thompson (Cambridge: Cambridge University Press, 1981), 3.

32. Paul Ricoeur, "What is a Text?" in *Hermeneutics and the Human Sciences,* ed. John B. Thompson (Cambridge: Cambridge University Press, 1981), 159.

33. Jerrold Levinson gives nine dimensions of the total historical and sociocultural context of a musical work that must be taken into account in "What a Musical Work is," *Journal of Philosophy* 77 (1980): 5–28. There is also the contemporary concern about "authentic performance" with period instruments and awareness of the performance praxis of Beethoven's time which differs from ours in some important ways.

34. NDS #14:7.

35. Only two of the thirty-six parishes closely studied by the Notre Dame Study had any post baptismal followup (NDS #14:7).

36. The Notre Dame Study found that the parishes with the most sense of "community" have nearly twice as many staff and nearly twice as many lay volunteers in their leadership structures as the nine parishes with the least sense of "community" (NDS #10:12). I have put "community" in quotation marks because I am not using the term in exactly the same sense as the NDS.

37. *Rite of Christian Initiation of Adults* (Chicago: Liturgy Training Publications, 1988), Introduction, par. 4, 3.

38. *On the Church* 7 (356).

39. *On the Sacred Liturgy* 2 (1) (my emphasis).

40. Augustine of Hippo, Sermon 272, *The Works of Saint Augustine: Sermons III/7*, translated and annotated by E. Hill (New Rochelle, N.Y.: New City Press, 1993), 300.

41. P. M. Forster and T. P. Sweetser, *Transforming the Parish: Models for the Future* (Kansas City: Sheed & Ward, 1993), 21.

42. NDS #14:7.

43. Franz Josef van Beeck, *God Encountered*, Volume 1, *Understanding the Christian Faith* (San Francisco: Harper & Row, 1989), 222 (my emphasis).

44. Michael Warren, *Faith, Culture, and the Worshipping Community* (New York: Paulist, 1989), 59.

45. Paul VI, *On Evangelization* 13 (210).

46. Vatican II, *On the Church* 10 (360–61).

47. See, e.g., D. Power, *Gifts That Differ: Lay Ministries Established and Unestablished* (New York: Pueblo, 1980), 129.

48. The Greek word *synergos* literally means "working with" (e.g., Rom. 16:3, 9, 21; Phil. 2:25; 4:3. See J. H. Thayer, *A Greek-English Lexicon of the New Testament* (Grand Rapids: Zondervan, n.d.), 603–4.

49. R. A. Schoenherr and L. A. Young, *Full Pews and Empty Altars: Demographics of the Priest Shortage in United States Catholic Dioceses* (Madison: University of Wisconsin Press, 1993), 343.

50. See G. Arbuckle, *Out of Chaos: The Refounding of Religious Communities* (New York: Paulist, 1988).

51. One expression of this can be found in V. Donovan's "Refounding Church— A Paradigm Shift," in P. M. Forster and T. P. Sweetser, *Transforming the Parish: Models for the Future* (Kansas City: Sheed & Ward, 1993), 140–48. The implementation of the model that I am personally familiar with derives from the Franciscan Friars of Holy Name Province, New York, whose mission statement says: "We foster Christian discipleship by collaborating with those whom we serve, and by standing in solidarity with all people, especially the alienated, the immigrant and the poor" as cited in "Partners in Evangelization: Lay Persons in Ministry and Mission," *Holy Name Province: Toward 2000*, No.15, April 15, 1992. In my personal ministerial experience the experimental parish of St. Séverin in Paris, France, employed a similar model in its concept of team ministry, a model of collaboration that began in the 1940s with the encouragement of Cardinal Suhard.

52. This gathering in 1985 had been preceded by I Encuentro in 1972 and II Encuentro in 1977.

53. U.S. Conference of Catholic Bishops, *The Hispanic Presence: Challenge and Commitment* (Washington, D.C.: United States Catholic Conference, 1984), 32.

54. For the breakdown of the percentages for the various groupings, see D. Blanchard, "The III Encuentro: A Theological Reflection on a Classic Church Event," in *Prophetic Vision: Pastoral Reflections on the National Pastoral Plan for Hispanic Ministry* (Kansas City: Sheed & Ward, 1992), 202–8. According to the introduction to the actual document that issued from III Encuentro, "a total of 1,148 people from

134 dioceses attended the Encuentro. Fifty-six were bishops or major superiors, 168 priests, 125 religious men and women, and 799 laity. Among the participants were 545 women, 153 youth, 47 migrant workers" (Secretariat for Hispanic Affairs, *Prophetic Voices: The Document on the Process of the III Encuentro Nacional Hispano de Pastoral* [Washington, D.C.: United States Catholic Conference, 1986], 5).

55. As D. Blanchard points out (see n. 54 above), the encuentro is a practical realization of canon #212 of the New Code of Canon Law, which says that not only are the faithful free to make their needs known to the pastors of the church but at times are duty bound to do so.

56. *Prophetic Voices,* 20.

57. P. Steinfels gives an account of such a parish, St. Thomas the Apostle in Los Angeles, in "Ancient Rock in Crosscurrents of Today," *New York Times,* Sunday, May 29, 1994, pp. 1, 10. Joseph Fitzpatrick's account of Dolores Mission, Los Angeles, and Gaudalupe Parish, San Jose, might serve as other examples ("Hispanic Parishes Where Something Seems to be Going Right," in *Strangers and Aliens No Longer,* Part One, *The Hispanic Presence in the Church of the United States* [Washington, D.C.: United States Catholic Conference, 1993], 3–9, 12–16).

58. A classic work that I follow in this discussion is that of W. Dürig, *Pietas Liturgica: Studien zum Frömmigkeitsbegriff und zur Gottesvorstellung der abendländischen Liturgie* (Regensburg: Pustet, 1958), esp. 58–97.

59. Ibid., 70–71.

60. Ibid., 75–76.

61. See G. Gallup, Jr., and J. Castelli, *The American Catholic People: The Beliefs, Practices and Values* (Garden City, N.Y.: Doubleday, 1987), 30–31; NDS #6:6–7; NDS #15:8. In the NDS citations, there are interesting indications of how regions of the country affect the choice and strength of these devotions.

62. *On the Sacred Liturgy* 13 (7).

63. *Documents on the Liturgy (1963–1979): Conciliar, Papal and Curial Texts* (Collegeville, Minn.: Liturgical Press, 1982), no. 3934. See also A. Gurevich, *Medieval Popular Culture: Problems of Belief and Perception* (Cambridge: Cambridge University Press, 1988); R. and C. Brooke, *Popular Religion in the Middle Ages: Western Europe 1000–1300* (London: Thames & Hudson, 1984).

64. *Documents on the Liturgy,* 3936. Peter Brown has added notably to this discussion in *The Cult of the Saints: Its Rise and Function in Latin Christianity* (Chicago: University of Chicago Press, 1981).

65. See Jay Dolan, *The American Catholic Experience* (Garden City, N.Y.: Doubleday, 1985), 209–10, 221–40; J. Chinnici, *Living Stones: The History and Structure of Catholic Spiritual Life in the United States* (New York: Macmillan, 1989), 16–17, 26; Jay Dolan, *The Immigrant Church* (Notre Dame: University of Notre Dame Press, 1983), 150–51.

66. See J. A. Gurrieri, "John Carroll and the Shape of the American Catholic Liturgy," in *Perspectives on the American Catholic Church 1789–1989,* ed. S. J. Vicchio and V. Geiger (Westminster, Md.: Christian Classics, 1989), 186–88; see also P. Malloy, "A Manual of Prayers (1583–1850): A Study of Recusant Devotions" (Ph.D. dissertation, Notre Dame University, 1991), 137–53.

67. See A. Taves, *The Household of Faith: Roman Catholic Devotions in Mid-Nineteenth-Century America* (Notre Dame: University of Notre Dame Press, 1986).

68. See Chinnici, *Living Stones,* 63–69.

69. J. Chinnici, O.F.M., ed., *Devotion to the Holy Spirit in American Catholicism* (New York: Paulist, 1985), 14.

70. See R. M. Icaza, "Prayer, Worship, Liturgy," in *Frontiers of Hispanic Theology in the United States,* ed. A. F. Deck (Maryknoll, N.Y.: Orbs, 1992), 134-53, esp. 141-48 for some other examples.

71. The Youth Day in Denver, Colorado, with Pope John Paul II in 1993 might serve as an example as well as the Youth Day at the Religious Education Conference in Los Angeles each year. We might also profit from the long and successful experience of the French church with their youth pilgrimages to the cathedral of Chartres and the Pentecost gatherings of youth with the monks of Taizé. In both cases, young people enter into the process of reevangelization, liturgy, and devotion with an inspiring enthusiasm.

72. David Power, "On Blessing Things," in *Blessing and Power,* ed. D. Power and M. Collins, Concilium 178 (Edinburgh: T. & T. Clark, 1985), 33.

73. *Documents on the Liturgy,* 1716.

74. David Power, *Unsearchable Riches: The Symbolic Nature of Liturgy* (New York: Pueblo, 1984), 73.

75. Power, *Unsearchable Riches.*

76. NCR/Gallup Poll, *The National Catholic Reporter,* September 11, 1987, p. 7.

77. See M. Himes and K. Himes, *Fullness of Faith: The Public Significance of Theology* (New York: Paulist, 1993), 157-83; P. J. Henriot, "Liturgy and Social Concerns," in *The Awakening Church: 25 Years of Liturgical Renewal,* ed. L. J. Madden (Collegeville, Minn.: Liturgical Press, 1992), 115-20.

78. John Paul II, "The Vocation and the Mission of the Lay Faithful in the Church and in the World" (*Christifideles Laici*), Dec. 30, 1988 (Washington, D.C.: United States Catholic Conference, n.d.), 72-73.